# When Small Countries Crash

# When Small Countries Crash

### Scott B. MacDonald
### and Andrew R. Novo

Transaction Publishers
New Brunswick (U.S.A.) and London (U.K.)

Library of Congress Catalog Number: 2010035054
ISBN: 978-1-4128-1483-6
Printed in the United States of America

Library of Congress Cataloging-in-Publication Data

MacDonald, Scott B.
    When small countries crash / Scott B. MacDonald and Andrew Novo.
        p. cm.
    Includes bibliographical references.
    ISBN 978-1-4128-1483-6 (alk. paper)
    1. Financial crises--Europe--Case studies. 2. Financial crises--Caribbean Area--Case studies. 3. States, Small--Economic conditions. 4. Global Financial Crisis, 2008-2009. I. Novo, Andrew R. (Andrew Robert), 1980- II. Title.
    HB3782.M33 2011
    330.9'0511--dc22

                                                2010035054

# Contents

# Foreword

Much has been written about the Great Recession and the 2008 financial crisis, its origins market dislocations and implications. This book brings a different angle to the debate. It centers the discussion on "small" players, countries with populations less than 10 million that pursued the financial excesses of big players with equal stamina. The common thread is their downfall, a "massive, uprooting economic downturn that carries in its wake socio-political upheaval." The book is a lesson in history, finance, and economics.

The book takes an historical turn and looks back at examples such as Scotland in 1690s (Chapter 2), when disastrous self-inflicted speculation ended costing Scotland's autonomy; the Caribbean islands (Chapter 3) in 1910-early 1920s, when outside pressures and agendas combined with domestic incompetence and corruption led to financial and political disaster; and Austria (Chapter 4) in 1931 and the failure of the country's largest bank.

The historical discussion would not be complete had it left out the banking crisis in the Nordic countries in the early 1990s. The book zeroes in on Finland (Chapter 5), which experienced a dramatic financial and economic crisis, the consequence of which was a reduction of per capita GDP of nearly 15 percent. A side trip to Albania (Chapter 6) underscores the difficulties of financial liberalization in yet a different context, one in which a small economy transitions from communism to a market economy, without having put in place a strong institutional framework.

The reader is now ready to review the devastating impact of the 2008-2009 financial crisis, the role played by some small economies, and the ripple effects on larger economies. Following the first round of global de-leveraging, in the US (the sub-prime excess), Iceland (de-leveraging of banks), Ireland, and the UK (de-leveraging of housing), the global economy has embarked on the second phase of de-leveraging, one of reducing sovereign risk. It entails two types of adjustments: For larger countries at the heart of the financial crisis, those that transferred risk from the private to the public sector, the adjustment requires a policy mix which at a minimum stabilizes debt levels; for generally smaller countries that have relied on easy credit to fuel growth over the past decade and are unable (or perceived as such) to service the debt as growth is seen as too sluggish, the adjustment requires aggressive fiscal consolidation and structural change.

The story of Iceland, Ireland, and more recently of Greece is indeed one of de-leveraging at the national scale. It is about poor planning and poor understanding of risk, by default or by design; if the latter, it is about greed and power, and therefore, it is about a "bruising and disorienting blow to the society." Ultimately, the roots of the problem tend to lie in the lack of pursuit of structural changes when the forces of economic union and/or globalization require such changes to take place. Small countries, unlike larger economies, remain more readily under the radar screen of the collective financial consciousness until the inevitable is reached and imbalances are uncovered.

It takes about a decade to recover from these shocks. Astoundingly then, the examples the book lays out so superbly underscore how little policy making draws from past policy mistakes. That is partly because there remains a fundamental misalignment between short-run election-driven political cycles and longer-run economic policies that are put in place. The book's discussion shows that a strong institutional framework that transcends elections is a necessary but not sufficient condition for minimizing policy mishaps.

Kathleen Stephansen
Managing Director, Head of Economic Strategy
AIG Asset Management

# Acknowledgments

This book was created from two influences: a longstanding fascination for the process of economic development and decades of work and study in finance and international affairs. Dr. Scott MacDonald's connection to small economies began with his academic work on Trinidad and Tobago in the 1980s analyzing the challenges of maintaining a democratic form of government with a capitalistic economic model. Trinidad's experience stood in sharp contrast with the number of authoritarian governments then dominating Latin America, Africa, the Middle East, and Asia. Although Trinidad and Tobago had many flaws, it was a fascinating case of a parliamentary system surviving despite massive economic challenges, some domestic, but many external in nature.

Dr. MacDonald's career in finance, beginning in the early 1980s, has provided an up front seat to some of the major developments in the global economy including: the Latin American debt crisis of the 1980s, the Mexican devaluation of 1994-95, the Asian contagion in 1997-98, 9/11, the 2002 US corporate meltdown, the Financial Panic of 2007-08 and the ensuing global recession and round of sovereign debt crises. Working at the Office of the Comptroller of the Currency, investment banks Credit Suisse and Donaldson, Lufkin & Jenrette, and Aladdin Capital Holdings has given Dr. MacDonald an opportunity to be involved in things well beyond his own small world.

Dr. Andrew Novo comes to the subject with a different set of experiences. An Oxford-trained historian and expert on the Mediterranean world, both ancient and modern, he has also worked in finance as a credit analyst at Aladdin Capital and in investor relations on Wall Street. Before pursuing his D.Phil, he worked for Harvard Business School's department on Business, Government, and International Economy and at Harvard University for Professor Niall Ferguson.

While both authors assume responsibility for the contents and views expressed in this book, they wish to extend their appreciation for the assistance of others who helped in providing constructive criticism, editorial suggestions, and access to documents. Research for this book was conducted in a number of locations, using both interviews and archival materials. We would like to thank Chief Economist Kathleen Stephansen at AIG, Jonathan Lemco at Vanguard, and Bruce Zagaris of Berliner, Corcoran & Rowe. In Ireland, the authors wish to thank Ali Ugur and Mike Percival from the Irish Banking Federation, Dermont O'Leary and Deirdre Ryan at Goodbody, Dara Doyle at Bloomberg, Alan McQuaid at Bloxham, and Quentin Fottrell at Dow Jones. Special thanks are also due to Mr. Theodore Pepanides and Mr. George Polychronopoulos for their insights into Greece's financial troubles. Our appreciation is also extended to Mary Speck whose work on Cuba in the early twentieth century was insightful and highly useful. Rafael Perl at the Organization for Security and Co-operation (OSCE) in Vienna, Austria was a major help in tracking down people who helped with the Albanian chapter. Martin Nance, an old friend at Quadrant Structured Investment Advisors, was a real gentleman in wading through the entire book and providing important feedback.

Andrew Novo would like to give particular thanks to his wife, Natalie, for all her love and support.

Scott MacDonald would like to express his gratitude for the help provided by Elizabeth MacDonald at the Scottish National Library and Seonaid McDonald, assistant archivist, at the Bank of Scotland, and Grant MacDonald at James Thin booksellers in Edinburgh. Their help in tracking down books and other publications was most helpful. This book is also testament to the lasting inspiration provided by the late Professor Albert L. Gastmann, Trinity College. Final thanks are given to his wife, Kateri, and his two children, Alistair and Estelle, for their patience in allowing him the time to finish this book. MacDonald's family, including his mother Anita and Aunt Beverly, remains an inspiration and a source of comfort to him.

Although many hands helped stir the intellectual pot, the authors take full responsibility for their work and any errors in this text.

Scott B. MacDonald
Andrew R. Novo

# 1

# When Small Countries Crash

With a population of slightly more than 11 million people and an economy accounting for around two percent of the Euro-zone's gross domestic product (GDP), Greece is one of the world's small economies. In late 2009, it was revealed that the country's debt to GDP ratio for the year was in the region of 115 percent. This massive borrowing was done to sustain a standard of living well beyond the country's means, reflecting a societal inclination to live off of external borrowing and was complicated by a disinclination to pay taxes. It was also sustained by northern European banks, pension funds, and other investors (like insurance companies) that benefited from the higher yield provided by Greek bonds, which considering the country's European Union membership, were regarded as largely "risk free." The result was the development of a society constructed around external borrowing through loans where painful decisions pertaining to badly needed structural changes in the economy were postponed year after year.

Living on borrowed money (and borrowed time) Greece, enjoyed the good life. This was most obvious in an Organization for Economic Cooperation and Development (OECD) report on pensions. In the UK, the typical retired person received a public pension equal to 28.9 percent of average earnings. In Germany, the figure was 40.5 percent; in Greece it was 93.6 percent.[1] Moreover, the average age for retirement in Greece in 2010 was around 61 years of age, with the deeply fragmented system providing for early retirement—as early as 55 for men and 50 for women—in a number of professions classified as "arduous and unhealthy."[2]

Since the Greek economy was not wealthy enough to generate the money needed to fund such government spending, including the extraordinarily generous pension programs, the needed capital was borrowed. While times were good and Greece could count on continued economic growth and relatively cheap access to capital, the model was sustainable. In the aftermath of the tightening in global capital markets in 2008-2009, it became more difficult to borrow. Moreover, international investors, looking more closely at budget deficits, were rocked by the news in late 2009 that Greece's numbers had been fudged and were actually far worse than initially portrayed. Those numbers would be revised again in early 2010 from 12.7 percent of GDP to close to 14 percent. Those same investors panicked when confronted with the size of the short-term repayment schedule and the meagerness of the Greek treasury.

The Greek situation was not helped by massive public demonstrations and riots against austerity measures that were perceived as an attack by Germany and the International Monetary Fund against the government largesse to which many Greeks felt entitled. This soon set investors to examining countries with similar profiles, resulting in contagion. The same concerns were soon articulated about Spain and Portugal, both of which had large fiscal deficits, rising debt levels, and onerous repayment schedules. But contagion was not limited to Spain and Portugal; concerns were also raised over the United Kingdom heading into a coalition government in May 2010 with its own large deficits and rising public sector debt. Additionally, nervous investors looked to the largest northern European banks with substantial exposures to Greece, Spain, and Portugal. On top of that, many pension funds and insurance companies in the Nordic and Benelux countries, France and Germany suddenly found their portfolios looking at potentially large losses if Greece defaulted. The long-running experiment of creating a peaceful and prosperous integrated Europe, bolstered by a generous social welfare system, was unexpectedly running aground in the streets of Athens.

What commenced as the problems of a small country, Greece, eventually percolated into a full-blow crisis about the future of the joint currency, the euro, and, with it, the 27-member European Union (E.U.). In response to the crisis, the E.U. cobbled together a combined set of rescue packages worth roughly €860 billion ($1.1 trillion) of which €110 billion was earmarked for Greece alone. Amid angry demonstrations and riots by Greeks protesting austerity measures in March, April, and May of 2010, the future of the euro, the European Union, and the global economic recovery itself became obscured by clouds of tear gas.

## The Purpose of This Book

There has always been a morbid fascination with financial crashes. The creation and bursting of financial bubbles has a certain tragic flare, especially when the damage includes the collapse of economies, the fall of governments, and even the end of nations. A country's finances are intimately connected not only with the finances of other countries, but also with the health of its own political system. One of the major causes for the French Revolution was the poor state of the French economy. As the nation tumbled into bankruptcy, the monarchy was unable to maintain its grip on power. As a direct result of France's financial crisis, King Louis XVI was marched to the guillotine in 1793. Financial decline and political disorder often go hand in hand. There was a distant but real connection between the storming of the Bastille in 1789 and the black clad anarchists in ski masks, torching automobiles and throwing rocks at Athenian police in 2010, crying for dramatic political change in their society.

Large systemic financial crises are interesting history. The following pages seek to capture some of the drama of financial collapses and their impact on small countries. Small countries are often overlooked, but they hold a unique place in the history of financial and economic crises. Although the small size of the countries involved does not always translate into a full-blown global crisis, the risk of contagion, especially within a globalized economy, cannot be understated. The countries in this book were selected for a number of reasons—the devastating impact of a financial crisis on the national economy; the potential ripple effects of a crisis coming out of a small country into larger countries (transfer or contagion risk); the colorful nature of some of the key actors; and the access to reliable data. There was also an effort to provide a rough historical timeline, commencing with the Scots in the 1690s to the ripples of the Financial Panic of 2007-2008 and the ensuing global Great Recession, and the Greek-driven European Union sovereign debt crisis that began in 2009.

The trials and travails of small countries are particularly worth examining in light of the role that Iceland, Ireland, Dubai, and Greece had in the end of the easy money period that marked the first decade of the twenty-first century. The easy money period (roughly 2002-2007) had a distinct lack of major sovereign debt defaults (a historical aberration). This was supported by the cheap money policies from the major global central banks, the most prominent being the US Federal Reserve, the

European Central Bank, and the Bank of England. Such policies were largely the result growth-focused policies of low interest rates and de-regulation designed, in theory, to help the global economy grow after the 2001-2002 recession.

The risk from too much easy money galvanized sub-prime lending in the United States, which was aided and abetted by what some have called the "shadow banking" system of American mortgage lenders, hedge funds, and investment banks. This came to an end in 2007 as interest rates rose and squeezed markets revealing substantial structural problems. The result was the worst financial and economic crisis since the 1930s. While the last minute rescue of Bear Stearns by J.P. Morgan Chase in March 2008 and the September failures of Lehman Brothers and Washington Mutual, as well as the multi-billion dollar rescues of Merrill Lynch and Wachovia Bank caught the world's attention, the same financial tsunami waves swept through European nations where leverage—this time of consumers and governments—proved to be daunting.

The financial crises that hit the global economy between 2007 and 2010 are well documented. The US mortgage mess is well covered by such titles as Charles R. Morris' *The Two Trillion Dollar Meltdown: Easy Money, High Rollers, and the Great Credit Crash*, Paul Muolo's *Chain of Blame: How Wall Street Caused the Mortgage and Credit Crisis*, and Michael Lewis' *The Big Short: Inside the Doomsday Machine*. A more systemic approach is provided by Roger Lownstein's *The End of Wall Street*, Charles Gasparino's *The Sellout: How Three Decades of Wall Street Greed and Government Mismanagement Destroyed the Global Financial System*, and Andrew Ross Sorkin's *Too Big to Fail: The Inside Story of How Wall Street and Washington Fought to Save the Financial System—and Themselves*.

There has also been coverage of individual companies: Christine Richard's excellent *Confidence Game: How a Hedge Fund Manager Called Wall Street's Bluff* (about short seller Bill Ackman and MBIA), Vicky Wards' *The Devil's Casino: Friendship, Betrayal, and the High Stakes Games Played Inside Lehman Brothers*, and Larry McDonald's *A Colossal Failure of Common Sense: The Incredible Inside Story of the Collapse of Lehman Brothers*. There is even coverage of the government role as written by David Wessels' *In Fed We Trust: Ben Bernanke's War on the Great Panic* and former Treasury Secretary Henry M. Paulson's "insider" account *On the Brink: Inside the Race to Stop the Collapse of the Global Financial System*. To this should be added the excellently researched and more academic *This Time Is Different: Eight Centuries of Financial Folly* by economists Carmen M. Reinhart and Kenneth Rogoff.

Considering all of this (and there is more), no one has written specifically of the experience of small countries in financial crises. Nevertheless, in recent times the financial crises of small countries have played a role in rocking the global financial system.

The role of small countries in the recent global financial turmoil is readily evident. In the late 2000s, Latvia, a small Baltic country, was savagely hit after a long build-up in debt (most notably mortgages from Swedish banks), while Ireland, sometimes referred to as the "Celtic Tiger," witnessed the near-crash of its banking system, including a scandal at one of the country's more respected institutions, Anglo-Irish Bank. In November 2009, one of the crisis's waves caught up with a horribly overleveraged Dubai, one of the seven units that constitute the United Arab Emirates. Known for its flashy skyscrapers, luxury resorts, and man-made islands, Dubai had racked up $107 billion in debt, much of it owed to European banks.[3] The exposure of Greece's grotesque balance sheet soon followed. Significantly, the trouble of a number of small economies threatened to create a daisy-chain reaction of sovereign debt problems that had the possibility of rippling into some of the world's largest and most heavily leveraged economies: the United States, Japan, the United Kingdom, and Italy.

As the following pages demonstrate, the story of small countries suffering from financial missteps is a long and painful one. The experiences of Iceland, Ireland, and Greece are just the most recent in a long line of crises in small economies. In addition to modern examples, we have dusted off the cobwebs on a few of history's small-country crises beginning with the Scots in the late seventeenth century and ending with the crises of today. Between those historical bookends four other chapters are dedicated to Caribbean follies, the most significant being Cuba's "Dance of the Millions," a spectacular sugar-related run of greed in the late 1910s and early 1920s (in what historian Hugh Thomas has called "a dream-like atmosphere more reminiscent of a film comedy than real life"), Austria's contribution to the Great Depression, the ill-fated failure of one of its largest banks, Credit-Anstalt (referred to as the "first thunderclap of the present crisis" by *Time* magazine in 1931), the massive wave of bank failures that hit Finland, (as well as Norway and Sweden) in the early 1990s, and the Albanian pyramid schemes in 1996-97 that toppled the government and almost caused a civil war. The size and scope of the last event was captured by an IMF economist, Christopher Jarvis: "The pyramid scheme phenomenon in Albania is important because its scale relative to the size of the economy was unprecedented, and because the political and social consequences of the collapse of the pyramid schemes were profound."[4]

But of all the stories told, perhaps Scotland's Darien Scheme is the most compelling as the consequences were the most profound for the respective country. The Darien Scheme is a tragic story of a small economically backward country in northern Europe in the 1690s to early 1700s struggling to deal with new ideas about finance, trade, and risk-taking as well as Scotland's place in the world. Simply stated, this was a poor country, with a history of political turmoil and awash with new ideas. What occurred was an attempt to create a Scottish colony based on trade in tropical Darien, now part of Panama. To finance such a venture—which was horribly planned—it is estimated that roughly a fifth of the wealth of Scotland was used and lost. The expedition was an unmitigated failure with a large number of settlers dying and the survivors trickling back to Scotland, where the economy struggled and the political landscape shifted toward outright union with England. By 1707 Scotland lost its sovereignty.

## Operationalizing Our Terms

Before advancing further, it is important to define our terms. By "small countries," we mean nations with a population of 10 million or less. This accounts for over 100 of the world's countries, over half of the total number, including numerous countries in the Caribbean and the South Pacific.[5] Europe and the Middle East also have their fair share of small countries. Small countries are a heterogeneous group. There are considerable differences between the wealthiest of these small countries like Kuwait, Abu Dhabi, Singapore, Brunei, and Luxembourg on one hand, and others—Haiti and Liberia, for example—that define the nature of poverty and political instability in today's world.

We would clarify that the word "crash" is used in relation to a massive, uprooting economic downturn that carries in its wake socio-political upheaval. It does not necessarily mean blood in the streets although in a few cases like Albania in the 1990s this was the case. In most instances it has led to demonstrations and acute public discontent, ultimately resulting in the ouster through constitutional means of incumbent governments. In some cases, it has resulted in the government turning to outside assistance such as the International Monetary Fund, an institution that is often at the center of the debate of how much sovereignty should be surrendered to external actors. Nonetheless, the end result is a bruising and disorienting blow to the respective society, which can take years to recover. Small countries tend to be far more sensitive about external actors being involved in their economies. Simply stated, the United States can usually ignore the IMF (at least for a while), Greece does not have the same latitude.

The cases selected in this book share similar characteristics in that they are as a group, small economies, buffeted by financial shocks, both external and local. Those financial shocks come in different forms, ranging from bank failures, financial panics, bursting of bubbles, and unsustainable build-ups in external debt. While we regard each country's experience as unique, we ultimately share the views of the economist Charles Kindleberger: "For historians each event is unique. Economics, however, maintains that forces in society and nature behave in repetitive ways."[6] That repetitive way in the case of this book is the build up of excessive leverage, ultimately resulting in an inability to repay the debt. This involves everything from bad lending practices on the part of banks, government assumption of too much debt, and financial fraud. Throughout the following pages it will be demonstrated that humans have an amazing ability to fall into the same traps repeatedly; old wine continually finds its way into new bottles.

### Overarching Themes

While this work does not intend to be a major thesis on economic theory, there are a few overarching themes.

1. Smaller economies tend to be more vulnerable to economic shocks, many of which are externally generated. Small economies confront particular challenges in terms of economies of scale, diversification, and depth of expertise and workforce. The smaller the country the more limited the resources, or at least, the more limited the depth of those resources.

Bonham C. Richardson took note of small-country vulnerability in his study *The Caribbean in the Wider World, 1492-1992*. Richardson attributed the Caribbean's vulnerability to its history of domination "by external power holders who have transformed landscapes and local populations to meet outside market needs."[7] Although many Icelanders, Greeks, and Irish were involved in the early twenty-first century financial upheaval and made their own share of blunders, no doubt many of their fellow citizens felt they were victims of powerful external actors. Indeed, the accelerated globalization in the late twentieth and early twenty-first century clearly created many new partners in unexpected ways, especially in international finance. Moreover, the ability of international investors to short—that is to bet against countries and their companies by using such derivative instruments as credit default swaps—enhanced Icelandic and Irish sensitivity to being a target of unseen and malicious international forces, (usually in the form of hedge funds). At the same time, we are keenly aware that within this context of vulnerability there is a considerable distance in terms of economic and financial sophistication, starkly emphasized by any comparison between Haiti and Honduras on one hand and Iceland and Ireland on the other.

2. Whether dealing with large economies or small economies, there is a certain point where any rationality in the market is sucked out and replaced by irrationality. As market conditions shift and caution is overcome by greed, common sense departs. Scott Adams, the cartoonist best known for "Dilbert," wrote: "Nothing defines humans better than their willingness to do irrational things in the pursuit of phenomenally unlikely payoffs. This is the principle behind lotteries, dating and religion." We adhere to the behavioralist school of economics and do not agree with the rational market thesis. When financial panic sets in, investors have a tendency to stampede. The sad truth is that when young traders have bug-eyed bosses tapping them on the shoulder ordering them to sell at almost any price as markets fall, the finely tuned math of quantitative models becomes irrelevant.[8]

3. Financial innovation usually brings substantial gains, but if misapplied, or applied with little or no oversight and regulation, the consequences can be damaging. This seems to be the case in particular when leverage is used—in excess. There is a lengthy track record on this front, but derivatives have blazed a trail since the 1980s with one crisis after another. This covers such ground as Orange County and Long-Term Capital Management to Bear Stearns, Lehman Brothers, and Dubai World. While it is important to recognize that financial innovations have helped construct a path to greater economic advances, there is a human tendency to exploit them as well.

4. A lack of financial transparency and disclosure obscures problems related to the size and duration of the debt load, the structure of the transaction and, in some cases, outright fraud. The issue of transparency and disclosure becomes all the more important in that when financial crashes occur, whether in large or small economies, there is often a whiff of scandal. While Darien was a national tragedy that cost many Scots their life-savings if no their lives, a handful of individuals made fortunes. Two centuries later, Albania's pyramid schemers lined their

pockets with $2 billion worth of saver's money. The same could be said for the Caribbean strongmen who happily pilfered the national accounts and bilked millions from reckless foreign investors. Along these lines, transparency is defined as "openness, honesty, and accountability in public and private transactions."[9] It is a critical component of what creates confidence in financial systems and reinforces the idea that basic rules and regulations will be upheld in everything from financial transactions to property rights.

5. Each of the cases examined in the following chapters has a group of core participants driving events. These individuals were financially motivated and often politically connected. There are no political vacuums. Management teams at banks and other financial institutions are articulate in the right arenas in advancing their interests. They can also overlap in politics, seeking to influence policy outcomes. Small countries with small economies are particularly vulnerable to the cronyism and nepotism that often accompanies highly interconnected societies. A handful of policymakers can move the entire system, work behind closed doors with each other, and influence compliant politicians, through their membership in common directorships, leadership boards, and government councils.

Such a group becomes a major force that can determine the rules of the game. This can translate into less regulation on the way up and increased resistance in dealing with some of the consequences (like absorbing the losses) on the way down. It can also lead to personal differences influencing policy-making. In small countries these conditions could be further aggravated by a certain level of clannishness that layer societies, as was the case in Scotland, Albania and, to a certain extent, in Iceland.[10]

6. Big countries need to be aware of problems in small countries. While small countries are often overwhelmed by developments coming from larger economies, the converse can be true. This was certainly the cases of Austria and Greece. Austria's problems in the early 1930s were rooted in events outsides the country, but the failure of Credit-Anstalt in 1931 was a tipping point for the eventual default of the world's third largest economy, Germany. Greece in 2010 was hurt by the drying up of liquidity in capital markets, but its threatened default rocked global markets and called the economic basis of the enlarged European Union and the euro into question.

7. Financial crashes can have massive political and social consequences, which usually take years to repair. The capacity to bounce

back can be a long process—as demonstrated by the cases of Scotland, Cuba, Austria, Albania. In all likelihood, Iceland, Ireland, and Greece face similarly long roads to recovery. Economists Carmen M. Reinhart and Kenneth Rogoff in their study of eight centuries of financial crises observed: "This view of the way into a crisis is sobering; we show that the way out can be quite perilous as well. The aftermath of systemic banking crises involves a protracted and pronounced contraction in economic activity and puts significant strains on government resources."[11] The more limited the resources, the more difficult it is to find an exit strategy. This also puts pressure on countries to seek alliances with larger countries or as part of larger regional blocs, like the European Union. This could have been a significant difference in Ireland's ability to stave off a total collapse and bounce back at a faster pace than Iceland, which found itself largely friendless (except for Norway) in the world as it sank into a major economic collapse. And it was certainly the case for Greece in 2010 when the European Union cobbled together a €110 billion rescue facility to keep Athens from heading down the road to a sovereign default.

One last point should be made. For all the devastating impact financial miscalculations can have on small economies, they have had their share of successes. Some of the world's most successful economies have been and continue to be small economies closely linked to financial services. The Grand Duchy of Luxemburg, the Bahamas, Mauritius, the Cayman Islands, Bermuda, Singapore, and Hong Kong are notable examples. As a group these economies are fully integrated into the global economy, often have what are regarded as successful tourist and/or financial sectors, and boast relatively high standards of living. At the same time, it should be remembered that in spite of the troubles confronting the financial sectors in Iceland, Ireland, and Latvia in the twenty-first century, they have previously been relatively successful economies. Time will tell whether they fully recover. An intriguing question remains why countries like Luxembourg and Singapore, very globalized economies and tightly linked to international finance, have not blown up and Iceland and Ireland have?

For those who lived through the crash of small countries' economies caused by financial disasters, the words of Genghis Khan, one of the world's greatest conquerors, have an echo: "I am the punishment of God.... If you had not committed great sins, God would not have sent a punishment like me upon you." Certainly when the world turned upside down in Scotland, Cuba, Austria, Albania, Latvia, Ireland, Iceland, and

Greece, there was more than just a little bit of the feeling that the wrath of God had come to visit. That was certainly part of the sentiment in Scotland in the late seventeenth and early eighteenth century, the subject of our next chapter.

## Notes

1.  Michael Skapinker, "The Sad End of Greece's Better Tomorrow," *Financial Times*, May 18, 2010, p. 9.
2.  Derek Gatopoulous, et al. "Europe Bristles At Paying for Greek Retirement," CBS News, May 17, 2010. http://www.cbsnews.com/stories/2010/05/17/ap/world/main6491990.shtml.
3.  Chip Cummins, "Emirates" Capital Feels the Heat from Dubai," *Wall Street Journal*, November 28-29, 2009. A10.
4.  Christopher Jarvis, "The Rise and Fall of Albania's Pyramid Schemes," *Finance and Development*, March 2000, http://www.imf.org/external/pubs/ft/andd/2000/03/jarvis.htm.
5.  The number of 5 million people was the cut-off to define a small country point for B. Jalan in: *Problems and Policies in Small Economies*, (New York: St. Martin's Press, 1982).
6.  Charles P. Kindleberger, *Manias, Panics, and Crashes: A History of Financial Crises,* (New York: John Wiley & Sons, Inc. 1978, 1996). p. 11.
7.  Bonham C. Richardson, *The Caribbean in the Wider World, 1492-1992*, (New York: Cambridge University Press, 1992). p. 3. Also see Anne Sibert, "Undersized: Could Greenland Be the New Iceland? Should It Be?; *VOX*, August 10, 2009, http://www.voxeu.org/index.php?q=node/3857 and William Easterly and Aart Kray, "Small States, Small Problems?" Policy Research Paper 2139, The World Bank, 1999.
8.  This is not to argue that quantitative models have no value; they play an important role in finance. There is often too much reliance or blind faith given to numbers. More than once we have heard that numbers do not lie.
9.  The definition for transparency comes from the International Monetary Fund. Check the IMF website. http://www.imf.org/external/nplexr/glossary/showTerm.asp#19.
10. Charles Farrugla has noted that: "Many necessary decisions and actions can be modified, adjusted, and sometimes totally neutralized by personal interventions and community pressures. In extreme cases, close personal and family connections lead to nepotism and corruption." Charles Farrugla, "The Special Working Environment of Senior Administrators in Small States," *World Development* 21, 1993; 417-457.
11. Carmen M. Reinhart and Kenneth Rogoff, *The Time Is Different: Eight Centuries of Financial Folly*, (Princeton: Princeton University Press, 2009), p. xxix. Richard A. Posner, in *A Failure of Capitalism: The Crisis of '08 and the Descent Into Depression*, noted: "The Great Depression of the 1930's inflicted horrendous costs, quite apart from the suffering inflicted on tens of millions of Americas, not to mention—since it was a global depression—more tens of millions abroad…. And without the depression there might have been no Nazi Germany and World War II." Posner goes on to describe what the impact of the 2007-08 crisis could have on the United States. "The costs of the present depression may include a swing to excessive regulation, a politically as well as economically unhealthy dependence of business on government largesse…, a huge loss of economic output, an immense

increase in the national debt, a high inflation rate, a decline in US world economic power, a weakening of the nation's geopolitical power as the country turns toward to address its economic problems and increased political instability in many parts of the world."

# 2

# Sinking Scotland

During the last decade of the seventeenth century many Scots ardently believed that a Scottish settlement at Darien, on the Isthmus of Panama, would be able to take advantage of its strategic location and enrich itself through trade with both the Atlantic and Pacific. A handful of Scottish entrepreneurs dreamed that the trading entrepôt would sit astride the flow of Spanish gold and silver from South America and allow Scotland to share in the riches of the New World. The Darien venture ultimately became a national gamble, a speculative bet to win power and fortune. It proceeded haphazardly, on a wave of public enthusiasm, with little accurate information, and less disclosure to the great majority of investors. Decision-making was confined in the hands of a few influential financiers and merchants who dreamed of making it big.

As a small and backward economy, Scotland was not prepared for the enormous financial cost of the venture. The nation was even less able to cope with the consequences of its disastrous failure. In the end, the Darien scheme produced phenomenally dramatic results. Not only was the colony itself destroyed, with the colonists killed or infected by disease, thousands of investors were ruined and the country itself bankrupted. As a result of the catastrophe, the government of Scotland did not simply fall—it ceased to exist as a sovereign entity—signing a treaty of union with England in 1707.

## A Poor Country on Europe's Periphery

The Kingdom of Scotland in the 1690s was part of a political arrangement that had one crown shared by the Stuarts presiding over England and Scotland. It was an unwieldy arrangement with a single king reigning over two different nations with two parliaments and two different national identities. This situation was also complicated by two different levels of economic development. England was moving toward industrialization and was increasingly engaged in international trade. After a series of successful wars against Spain and Holland, it had secured its position as Europe's dominant maritime power. Prosperous colonies had been established in the Caribbean, producing cash crops, particularly sugar. Settlements such as Boston, New York, and Jamestown were growing the seeds of colonies in North America. The British East India Company had established trading posts and built factories on the Indian subcontinent. New products like sugar, tobacco, and tea came to England from these various colonies as London developed into a financial and political capital.

While England pushed into a brave new future, Scotland was mired in the past. For the most part, the million Scots scratched a meager existence off a fragile and primitive agricultural economy dependent on a narrow base of exports. The export of agricultural produce left many Scottish farmers on the brink of starvation, barely able to meet basic human needs. Four out of five Scots made their living from the soil or the sea. For want of effective drainage systems, much of the best land lay waterlogged and unused. Subsistence farms consisted of cabins of turf or unmortared stone, often without windows or a chimney. The door, and a hole cut in the roof, above the hearth, often provided the only light and ventilation. Cuisine was equally rudimentary, often consisting of a diet of oatmeal and beer. In this environment, sanitation was poor and disease was a constant worry. Conditions were practically medieval and poverty was widespread.[1]

Industry, commerce, and finance—such as they were—orbited the cities of Edinburgh and Glasgow, which were a home to a small middle class of merchants, lawyers, and other professionals. The industrial revolution that was taking root in England was but a dull echo. At the same time, Scotland was slowly moving in the direction of commerce and trade. Moreover, Scotland's small, yet influential merchant community, with outposts in both London and Amsterdam, was increasingly exposed to new ideas of risk taking and its relationship to finance.

Politically, Scotland was evolving past the turmoil that plagued Britain during the seventeenth century. It had been very much involved in the English Civil War, the rule of Oliver Cromwell, the Stuart Restoration of Charles II and the Glorious Revolution of 1688, which deposed James II and put the Protestant monarchs William III and Mary II jointly on the English throne.

By the closing decade of the seventeenth century, Scotland enjoyed relative political calm, with an active Scots Parliament deciding policy and with the authority of the king far away in London. Following the Glorious Revolution, parliament evolved a greater role in the political and economic life of Scotland. The Scottish Parliament took a more pro-active role in economic policy, experimenting with the hearth tax and poll tax as alternatives to land taxes. Furthermore, the Scottish Parliament provided legislation to establish the Bank of Scotland in 1695 as well as the Company of Scotland. Yet, political tensions lay close to the surface in a nation still seeking to consolidate its identity as distinctly Scottish and Presbyterian, while remaining part of a broader Atlantic world. Historian George S. Pryde noted that though the Scottish Parliament "exercised its new powers with vigor, good sense and responsibility," he also recognized that "there was no room in the one island for two parliaments, [Scottish and English] pursuing, under one King, conflicting aims in foreign and commercial affairs."[2]

As Scotland looked out into the world in the 1690s, it was confronted by an Atlantic-European trade area that was dominated by the English, Dutch, and French. Spain and Portugal, the dominant of from the sixteenth century remained powerful. The concept of the nation-state, originating around 1648 with the Treaty of Westphalia, was still evolving. Europe's competing nations pursued the policy of mercantilism in their approach to maritime and colonial expansion and therefore took a dim view of any rival to their colonial and financial interests. In spite of the obvious obstacles, many in Scotland believed that trade was the key to riches. There was a growing belief that political power followed economic power. To achieve this, the newly forming Atlantic world beckoned.

Ambitious Scottish financiers and entrepreneurs like William Paterson and Andrew Fletcher thought of the Company of Scotland as an instrument by which the Scots would acquire their fair share of wealth through trade. The general public in the Lowlands agreed. To Scottish nationalists, the creation of a global trading company, and the wealth it would generate, would help maintain Scottish control over local affairs and keep the English at arm's length despite the union of crowns. Indeed, the English parliament's action to disallow any English investors from being involved with the Company of Scotland was emblematic of Scottish nationalism. The prohibition raised the stakes for the new venture, transforming the Company of Scotland from a trading company under the guidance of London's community of sophisticated traders into a colonial pioneer. All of the company's hopes for success rested on the wild gamble that a trading colony in the Caribbean would be the key to Scotland's riches.

To understand the thinking of Scotland's elite at this time, it is important to fully convey the attractiveness of maritime trade at the close of the 1600s. During the late fifteenth century, Spanish and Portuguese ships had penetrated the Indian Ocean and the Atlantic. Portugal had established nautical trade routes to the riches of India and the Far East. Spain, following the voyages of Columbus, had conquered and colonized much of the Caribbean along with Central and South America. Spain mined the silver and gold in these new territories sending tons of treasure back to Europe each year.

On the heels of exploration and expansion came the development of innovative organizations capable of conducting large-scale, long-distance trading activities, the most important of which was the joint-stock company. Despite the considerable dangers of shipwreck, hostile locals, pirates, and tropical diseases, many were willing to take the necessary risks in the hopes of realizing massive profits from acquiring (through trade or force) exotic goods like: pepper, nutmeg, spices, gold, silver, and sugar. For example, the voyage to India of Portuguese explorer Vasco da Gama's—the first successful European venture around the Cape of Good Hope—lost two of its three ships. The lone survivor's cargo of pepper paid for the entire expedition and still gave da Gama a hefty profit. The trade that was to follow soon brought considerable wealth to one of Europe's smallest and poorest nations.

Trade and joint-stock trading companies combined nicely with the new doctrine of the age—mercantilism. The mercantilists arrived upon the historical stage in a meaningful fashion in the seventeenth century. As a group they were concerned with the issue of unity—the creation of a national system of weights and measures, a national system of taxes and tariffs, and a unified monetary system and coinage, along with the elimination of internal tolls on roads and rivers, . This put the monarchs of the time on the same side as the rising commercial classes, who desired peace, stability and the development of a national market economy. As economist Daniel Fusfeld wrote: "Out of the political and economic alliances between crowns, merchants, rural gentry, and professional people emerged economic policies designed to unify the nation under a single strong ruler, develop its military and naval strength, and increase its wealth through both domestic production and foreign trade."

Although there were to be national variations, the basic themes of mercantilism remained nationalism, self-sufficiency, and national power.

The first major English venture into the world of trading companies was the Muscovy Company, founded in 1553. In 1581, it was followed by the Levant Company. In 1600, the East India Company (EIC) was formed. It was based in London and chartered by Queen Elizabeth I. The EIC's charter granted it a monopoly of English East India commerce, which gave it a prominent role in promoting and developing European-Asian trade during the early modern period. Other trading companies followed: the Royal African Company (1672), the Hudson's Bay Company (1670), the Levant Company and the Russian Company.[3]

Not to be left out of these new developments, the Dutch began to pioneer their own institutions. Having come of age as a nation at the close of the sixteenth century, gaining independence after a bitter struggle against Spain, the Dutch prospered as a result of an extensive merchant fleet and a powerful navy. Over time, they assumed a dominant position in international trade establishing colonies in the Americas (including New Amsterdam, later re-named New York), trading posts in Africa and colonies in Asia. In their rise to prominence in trade, the United Provinces of the Netherlands have been regarded as one of the world's first modern states. Unlike Spain or Portugal, and much of the rest of the continental Europe, the Netherlands was a republic, dominated by middle-class burghers who endowed the state with a strong entrepreneurial streak. Proudly Protestant and rigidly egalitarian, the Dutch entrepreneurial streak took them out into the Atlantic, around Africa, eventually into the Indian Ocean and beyond. Dutch settlements and trading posts sprang up throughout the world: in North America, the Caribbean, the northern coast of South America, in Africa, India, and Indonesia.

The idea of trading companies was not, however, limited to the English and Dutch. The French too established a number of such ventures—the Compagnie Senegal, Compagnie des Iles d'Amerique, and Compagnie des Indes Occidentales. Other countries, such as Denmark, Sweden, Prussia-Brandenburg, and the Duchy of Courland were also involved in the creation of similar institutions in an attempt to expand the power of their merchants beyond their shores.

The lure of such foreign adventures did not pass Scotland by. As one historian observed:

> The acquisition of a little money naturally stimulated a desire for more, and it had become apparent that Scotland could only grow rich by increasing trade. Now trade seemed more important than the subsistence agriculture with which the greater part of the country had hitherto been content, and in particular there was a great interest in the possibility of colonial trade.[4]

Yet nothing was to come easily for Scotland. Although Scottish merchants were initially allowed to partake in England's opening of Atlantic opportunities and in developing trade with its colonies, there eventually arose a growing sense of resentment toward Scottish competition. Consequently, the Westminster Parliament, ever ruthless in defense of England's commercial interest, was active in protecting domestic traders from Scottish competition as reflected by traders and marketing restriction imposed upon Scottish imports of cattle and linen.[5]

Yet, for all  the protectionist efforts to promote local industry there is evidence that trade occurred between Scotland and the Americas. At least five Scottish owned ships were cleared for the colonies in 1681. Others followed. The South Carolina Company's attempt to establish a colony in 1683 involved more ships crossing the Atlantic. The fundamental idea behind the South Carolina venture was to found a colony to which Scottish vessels carrying Scottish goods could directly trade for mainland plantation tobacco, then a hot commodity in Europe. Although the Spanish destroyed this settlement in 1686—demonstrating just how precarious such ventures could be—the Scots were increasingly lured to trade in the Americas.

While Scottish merchants in Scotland were attracted to the idea of expanding overseas trade, the real stimulus for an overseas trading company was to come from the community of Scots merchants in London. Well-established in international trade and with considerable experience, the London community fully understood the usefulness of a trading company. They were also keenly aware of the highly competitive nature of the East India Company, which was making it increasingly difficult to carry out private trade with the Indies. With the understanding that their countrymen in Scotland were anxious to secure foreign trade on a broader scale, a number of the London Scottish community came to believe that they needed to secure a legal basis for their operations. Consequently, in early May 1695, a London merchant named James Chiesly turned to his friend, William Paterson, and asked about the possibility of founding an East India Company in Scotland.[6]

Paterson was about thirty-five years old, married, and relatively prosperous. Born in Dumfries-shire, Scotland in the year 1658, much of his earlier life is unknown. It is believed he was of "lowly birth" and left Scotland as a young man for England where he worked as a peddler. At some point, he decided to try his luck in the West Indies, then a place of pirates, traders, sugar planters, and colonial wars against the Spanish. From his experiences in this high-stakes world, ideas about Darien were hatched. He made his fortune in the West Indies and was to vastly increase it in London's budding financial markets after his return to the city in 1687. By 1694, Paterson was a major force in establishing the Bank of England, an institution that was to become England's central bank. Equally at home in London and in the newly emerging Atlantic trade world, Paterson emerged as an entrepreneur of consequence. He was certainly a talented and industrious individual.

David Sinclair, author of *The Pound: A Biography*, describes Paterson as "a controversial figure, the sort of man we would now dignify with the title of entrepreneur but seen by many in his own day and later as a ruthless buccaneer and even something of a confidence trickster."[7] The same author also notes that Paterson was "one of the luminaries of the developing financial market." Historian John Prebble, who studied his character in some depth, described Paterson as "imaginative, energetic, compassionate and naïve" as well as "humorless, tiresome, and depressingly serious about all things."[8]

Like many men of his day, Paterson was convinced of the importance of trade for the health of the national economy. Widely traveled and having spent time both among the entrepreneurial Dutch and in the city of London, he was convinced that Scotland should also develop its trade as a path to national greatness. Paterson fixated on Darien, on the Isthmus of Panama. He was convinced that this slim neck of land that joined North and South America while dividing the Atlantic from the Pacific was where Scotland's destiny lay. The instrument was to be a great emporium, strategically situated to engage, free from tariffs, the trade of the entire world.[9] What Paterson glossed over, but must have had some idea about, was Darien's tropical climate. He also paid little attention to the fact that Darien, indeed all of Panama, already had a colonial master—Spain.

In May 1695, Paterson produced a draft of an act intended for the Scottish Parliament, providing for privileges and concession to launch a trading company. The draft for the act was approved by the Scots London merchants and was then sent to their friends in Edinburgh, who then presented it to the Scottish Parliament on June 12, 1695 and referred to the Committee of Trade.[10]

It is important to clarify that Paterson envisioned a Scottish East India Company as a joint venture with Englishmen, many of whom resented the heavy-handed East India Company. The East India Company had jealously guarded its monopoly of trade with the East, buying influence, co-opting some competitors, and ruthlessly excluding others. Considering the growing attraction of trade in England, the East India Company naturally incurred resistance, which over time would undo it. Consequently, Paterson was not wrong in assuming that the creation of a rival company would attract supporters, especially among frustrated English merchants with deep pockets.

Momentum had already gathered for the passage of a trade bill. A pamphlet appeared on the streets and in the coffee-houses on Edinburgh, entitled "Proposals for a Fund to Carry on a Plantation," which was a "concise, orderly plan for the creation of a joint-stock company with powers to trade, to establish colonies in America, Asia, or Africa, and to hold them in the name of the Crown of Scotland, to purchase ships, and to open a bank in Edinburgh."[11] Thought to be the work of Paterson, the pamphlet helped stir enthusiasm and public interest in such a scheme.

On June 15, 1695, the bill for what was known as "the Act in Favor of the Scots Company Trading in Africa and the Indies" was read and considered by the Committee of Trade. To push through the Act, the Scottish merchants were forced to take the initiative. King William was exerting pressure on the Parliament to end its session, due to the embarrassment arising from the enquiry into the Massacre of the Mac-Donald's at Glencoe by the pro-government Campbells. While this was significant scandal to the Scottish public and certainly damaging to the King's government in Scotland, Edinburgh's merchants regarded it as potentially disastrous. With considerable force, they managed to push the Act through the Committee, pass it in parliament , and on June 26, 1695 the aging Lord Tweeddale, head of government for his Majesty, gave it royal assent by touching the Act with his scepter.

If the company's conception had been relatively easy, its birth was not. Complications arose almost immediately between the merchants of London and Scotland. It was decided in late October that the capital of the Company was to be 600,000 pounds with half raised in England and the rest in Scotland and the Continent. It is important to underscore that the launching of the company coincided with the financial boom of the 1690s. Economic growth had been stimulated in London's stock market as idle trading capital was diverted to domestic use, which included a great number of new joint-stock companies. Along these lines, a new trading company seemingly with royal support was attractive. By October 29, 1695 the Company had the 300,000 pounds assigned in England. Moreover, the issue had been over-subscribed, indicating considerable interest. At the time, few people realized that the Darien

Company, as it came to be called, was to be the last great bond-float of the 1690s boom.

In spite of its auspicious beginnings, the Darien Company's success would not last. A vengeful East India Company mobilized and put pressure on the English Parliament to put the Scottish upstarts in their place. In December 1695, the Lords and Commons went to King William III, presenting an address of protest against the Scots Company. King William declared himself "ill served in Scotland." In January 1696, by Parliamentary decree, all English investors in the scheme were ordered to withdraw their money under pain of impeachment—and these suddenly had to be repaid to the tune of 300,000 pounds. The English part of the venture had collapsed. Subscriptions would have to be raised elsewhere. Paterson left London for Scotland and the Scots turned to the continent.

### Selling Scotland by the Pound

Fuelled by nationalist sentiments, the Scottish public showed great enthusiasm for the 300,000 pounds subscription that opened in late February 1696. This was an offering made largely to private individuals, namely wealthy merchants and the well connected. Subscriptions also came from the burghs of Edinburgh and Glasgow (3,000 pounds each), Perth (2,000 pounds), and Dunbar (700 pounds).[12] The main drivers were trading corporations and leading citizens. By the beginning of August some 400,000 pounds had been pledged, and the Scots Company held over 34,000 pounds in coin, rather more than six times the amount held by the Bank of Scotland.[13]

While Paterson was one of the key intellectual forces behind the Darien scheme, the Company pulled together other more influential figures representing the Scottish "establishment," giving the new commercial enterprise a stamp of respectability. Key supporters included Archibald Campbell, Duke of Argyll, who was also chief of Clan Campbell; James Hamilton, Baron of Belhaven, and John Hay, Marquis Tweeddale. Argyll was a large shareholder in the Company, while Hamilton was a director of the Company and a supporter in the Scottish Parliament. Tweeddale was a member of the Council-General of the Company and served as Paterson's patron within the Company's higher councils. He was also the son of the Second Earl of Tweeddale, who had approved the Act, allowing for the creation of trading company and colony.[14]

English hostility did not stop at the border. English ambassadors were instructed to convince foreign subscribers in Hamburg and

Amsterdam, where Paterson had connections, to withdraw. Thwarted in England, Paterson and a small group of Scots left Edinburgh for the continent in October 1696. In January, they sought and failed to interest the Dutch and in February Paterson and Henry Erksine, Baron of Cardross arrived in Hamburg. The English, however, were dead set against any Scottish gains. As a key trading partner and maritime power, London could be very persuasive. Sir Paul Rycaunt, an English resident in Hamburg described as a "dry dull man," took delight in thwarting the Scots.[15] After all, from the English viewpoint critical national interests were at risk. So it did not matter if a few German and Dutch arms were twisted to avert the upstart Scots from launching an overseas empire.

The actual selling of shares was done from a subscription book. Unlike Amsterdam or London, Scotland lacked a stock market that centralized its financial activities. Instead, members of the Company conducted their business in the coffeehouse of Mrs. Purdie on the north side of the High Street, in Edinburgh. The minimum amount that could be subscribed, by individuals or by associates was £100 sterling. According to the Secretary of State in Scotland, Sir John Dalrymple, "the frenzy of the Scots nation to sign the Solemn League and Covenant never exceeded the rapidity with which they ran to subscribe to the Darien Company.... Young women threw their little fortunes into the stock, widows sold their jointures to command money for the same purpose."[16] This was an emotional response, not a cold-blooded calculation of the potential value gains to be had through a commercial venture and its business environment. The wave of euphoria and patriotism also ignored the genuine and substantial obstacles confronting the undertaking. Since few Scots had heard of Panama, much less Darien, it was hardly a surprise. The great majority had no idea of what they were getting into.

Those who subscribed to the Darien scheme in Scotland were largely from the Lowlands and urban areas. In a sense this was the part of the population most integrated or at least more aware of the emerging Atlantic world based on trade and commerce. With some knowledge of the bull markets hitting England France, they were more open to speculation. In contrast, the Highland population was not attracted to the Darien scheme. Generally speaking, this segment of the population was less wealthy and less economically integrated. In the Highlands, the idea of putting scarce capital into a speculative venture halfway around the world simply had no appeal.

## Why Darien?

As the Company of Scotland went through its creation, financing and political intrigues, the idea of establishing a trading colony at Darien took center stage. It ultimately became the *raison d'être* for the Company as well as its historical legacy. In July 1696, Paterson was appointed to be on the Committee for Foreign Trade and was invited to give a presentation to the Company's directors as to any ideas he might have about where to place a Scots colony. Only July 23, Paterson arrived at Milne Square with his documents accumulated over the years pertaining to the suitability of Darien. Paterson had long favored Darien and had raised the idea of a colony there (unsuccessfully) in German principalities and Holland.

Although he had no takers on the continent, Paterson had amassed maps, charts, soundings and comments of shipmasters and buccaneers as well as drawings of local Indians and strange plants.[17] His documentation was impressive (though not necessarily correct) and clearly had an impact on the directors, who had little other information. Within a week of Paterson's presentation and allowing them to keep his collection, the directors apparently decided that Darien was Scotland's "promised land." For his efforts, Paterson was given 7,500 pounds of the Company's stock, a substantial though not lavish award.

Although it appeared Paterson had made a most persuasive case, doubts remained. Among the documents accumulated by Paterson and now retained by the directors was a copy of a journal of a young sailor-surgeon and buccaneer, Lionel Wafer. Wafer was decidedly a creature of the newly emerging Atlantic world. Having lived in the Highlands, he grew up to be a ship's surgeon and sailed with buccaneers, a relatively common occupational development on the lawless high seas. Wafer eventually ended up in the Caribbean, participating in a raid on the Spanish town of Santa Maria. Unfortunately for young Wafer, he fell victim to a gunpowder accident that in his own words, burned his knee such "that the Bone was left bare, the Flesh being torn away, and my thigh burnt for a great way above it."[18]

Considering the rudimentary nature of health care in the seventeenth century, especially in the jungles of Central America, Wafer's injury was life threatening. Moreover, his fellow raiders did not have the luxury of carrying him as he would have slowed them down. Wafer, therefore, was left behind. He was lucky enough to be taken in by local Indians who helped him recover for a period of two months. One offshoot of this experience was his account of the Caribbean side of Panama. With a sharp eye for detail, Wafer brought the Darien region vividly to life, making it appear to be a tropical paradise. Wafer adapted to the land remarkably well for a white man. Unlike many Europeans, the young surgeon weathered the rigors of the tropics without succumbing to some exotic disease. In all fairness, his account did mention the harshness of life in Panama and never suggested establishing a colony. None of this adversely affected the directors.

The upshot of Wafer's journal, *A New Voyage and Description of the Isthmus of America,* was that the directors smuggled the young surgeon from London to Edinburgh. Wafer was questioned more intensively and sent in secret back across the border. He was clearly an influence in the selection of Darien, though Paterson remained the main force behind the venture and was instrumental in moving the directors along that fateful track.

### Complications for the Fledging Scottish Financial System

One offshoot of the issuance of the shares was that it put the Company in competition with the newly established Bank of Scotland. Up until the mid-1690s, Scotland's coinage was known for its unreliability. It was believed by a large number of the merchant community that a bank was needed to help develop the country's trade. Considering the growing clout of the merchant community in Scotland, with its links to the London Scots merchant community, this idea soon gained critical mass.

Consequently, the Bank of Scotland was created by an act of the Scottish Parliament on July 17, 1695. The founding act "for the Carrying and Managing of a Public Bank" allowed the bank's directors to raise a nominal capital of 1,200,000 Scottish pounds (100,000 pounds sterling) and granted a monopoly in banking in Scotland for 21 years. Moreover, its proprietors (shareholders) were given limited liability. The last clause of the Act reflected the sense of nationalism at the time in that "all Forraigners, who shall join as Partners of this Bank, shall thereby be and become Naturalized Scotsmen, to all Intents and Purposes whatsoever."[19] For two months following November 1, 1695 a subscription book for the new bank was opened at Patrick Steill's Cross Keys Tavern in Edinburgh.

The newly established Bank of Scotland came into competition in three ways with the Company of Scotland. First, it competed for scarce capital; second, it competed for talent among Scotland's political and merchant elite; finally, it competed in terms of currency. The Bank of

Scotland initially had 172 "Adventureers" of whom 136 lived in Scotland and 36 in London. A detailed examination reveals that in Scotland the leadership of the new bank included 24 nobles, 39 landed proprietors, 41 merchants, 14 lawyers and judges, with seven women subscribing in their own right.[20] It is important to clarify that the Bank, unlike the Company of Scotland, was well connected in London. Among the London subscribers were the Scottish Secretary of State, James Johnson, a number of Government office-holders and four officials of the East India Company, with the rest consisting mainly of merchants, mostly with strong Edinburgh links. Consequently, the Bank of Scotland was not attacked in the same fashion as the Company of Scotland and, in a limited sense, enjoyed an additional pool of funds.

The Bank of Scotland's London connection was further reinforced by the selection of an Englishman, John Holland, as governor. As Alan Cameron, a historian on the Bank of Scotland, noted: "It now seems clear that John Holland's election as Governor was an attempt to deflect the hostility of the English Parliament to all matters Scots. The activities of the Darien Company, to which many of the Bank's Adventurers also subscribed, were the main source of this hostility, and a number of London-Scots merchants narrowly escaped prosecution for treason."[21]

As the Company took shape, the rivalry with the Bank of Scotland intensified. According to Cameron in his history of the Bank of Scotland, it was clear that the directors and Paterson intended to establish the Company as a bank in all but name, hence destroying the Bank of Scotland's legal monopoly. Along these lines, the Company made loans, printed notes and sums of money were sent to London to enter the discount market for exchequer bills. At the end of the day, many of Paterson's supporters regarded the Bank of Scotland as little better than a front for the hated East Indian Company.

This struggle between the two institutions became particularly acute during the summer of 1696 when bank notes of the Darien Company were placed in all the main burgs and the Bank of Scotland's notes were brought so they could be returned. The Bank of Scotland was only to escape failure narrowly, as it was forced to raise more capital and make substantial reduction in expenses—even closing down its branch network. The Bank of Scotland was helped by the growing awareness of Scotland's political elite that such an event would be bad for the economy. Moreover, the survival of the bank was going to be decidedly easier than that of the Company vis-à-vis the English.

### A Tropical Hell Hole

In July 1698, the Scottish Company launched its first expedition to Darien. The fleet numbered five ships; *Unicorn*, *Dolphin*, *St. Andrew*, *Caledonia*, and *Endeavour*. Bearing as they did the aspirations of the Scottish nation, the ships were appropriately named. Nevertheless, as a reflection of Scotland's limited resources, the proudly named ships were all built or chartered in Holland and Hamburg. The commanding officer of the fleet, Captain Pennyquick, was an experienced sailor but a poor leader. Entrusted to Pennyquick's care were 1,200 men and a small number of women and children who were to establish the new colony. Seven councilors were appointed to provide the colony with leadership and make the venture profitable. Selected by a special committee of the Company, the council members consisted of: Major James Cunningham, Daniel Mackay, James Montgomerie, William Vetch, Robert Jolly, Robert Pincarton, and Captain Pennyquick. Cunningham, Montgomerie, and Vetch were military men, while Mackay was a lawyer from the High-lands. Jolly, Pincarton, and Pennyquick were sailors.

Although the councilors were appointed with good intentions, the personal chemistry between the men was poor. The soldiers and sailors were particularly suspicious of each other. The fledging Scottish community was almost immediately divided into factions—a small wonder considering the descriptions of each man. Cunningham was "stiff-necked, egocentric and insolently proud"; Mackay was "hot-tempered but conscientious ... and a hard man to like for he intrigued as busily as he worked"; and Jolly "was a sad and ineffectual man"; and of course, Captain Pennyquick, who was "pig-headed and domineering, suspicious of all but other seamen, and of those too if they challenged his judg-ment."[22] While Vetch and Pincarton held some promise, the flaws of the others would clearly overshadow Scotland's great Atlantic gamble. As it was, Vetch was unable to make the first expedition due to ill health. Although he had fallen from favor with the director of the Company, Paterson also joined the expedition, eventually assuming a place on the council. His stature had declined considerable and it was only after the intervention of some supporters that he was allowed on the expedition with his wife accompanying him.

The fleet carried cargo typical for the day: brandy, pitch, flour, bis-cuits, guns, and ammunition. It also had uniquely Scottish items such as bagpipes, blue bonnets, clay pipes, and packages of leek and cabbage seed.[23] It was believed that those Scottish-made goods would somehow find ready markets in the Caribbean. Other stores included salt from Stockholm, vinegar and wine from La Rochelle in France, and raisins, spices, and soap from Amsterdam. There were even wigs, a farce for the tropical climate and of even less use than bagpipes for trade with the local population.

On July 4, 1698, Captain Pennyquick's small fleet set sail from Leith. The weather was favorable and Atlantic crossing was largely uneventful. After a brief stop in Madiera, the fleet reached the Caribbean in late September with only seventy colonists dying along the way—an acceptable figure for such a voyage at that time. Once in the tropics, however, the weather turned stormy and conditions for the settlers below decks became horrid. The sick were often left to lay in their own filth, with little water to quench their thirst.

In November, the five ships put into Puerto Esconces in modern-day Panama. Captain Pennyquick wrote enthusiastically: "This harbor is capable of containing a thousand sail of the best ships in the world. And without great trouble, wharfs may be run out, to which ships of the greatest burden may lay their sides and unload."[24] The new colony was to be called New Caledonia and the town (which never really developed beyond a well-developed camp) New Edinburgh. Fort St. Andrew was constructed to protect the new settlement. It was fervently hoped that New Caledonia would quickly put down the same roots as the English colonies in New England and the French in New France.

First impressions were deceiving. Darien was to prove anything but hospitable to Scotland's settlers. In fact, it was going to be lethal. As Central American historian Ralph Lee Woodward Jr. described the region:

> It is true, of course, that the great fertility of the soil and a year-round temperature climate bless much of the Isthmus. But steaming rain forests, jagged mountains, and scorched arid zones, have been greater geographical determinants in the development of the country than have the regions to which the designation of 'paradise' might upon first impression be applied.[25]

Another issue of the new environment confronting the Scottish colony was the nature of local politics. Although Spain was in decline, it still claimed the Darien region. The Spanish had, after all, arrived in Panama in the early 1500s and shortly thereafter conquered local Indian populations. The Spanish created a string of colonies from Puerto Rico, to Cuba, Mexico, Panama, and across the north coast of South America. In 1535, the Audencia de Panama was established, with weak authority over the Darien coastline. The Spanish inland city of Panama developed into one of the richest along the entire Spanish Main. Every year it was the final stop of the famous silver train, loaded with treasure from the mines of Peru, before its departure for Spain.

In 1671, Henry Morgan and his buccaneers crossed the isthmus and sacked Panama City. This was a hard blow to Spain, which was forced to move the city to a new site a few miles up the coast. Other buccaneer attacks hit an irreparably weakened Panama throughout the 1680s, while parts of Costa Rica almost slipped into English hands. During roughly the same period, the English also came to dominate the Mosquito Coast (the Caribbean coast of modern-day Nicaragua). The ships and colonists of the Scottish Company were hardly welcome. Considering the chipping away of Spain's control in the area, the Scots were regarded as part of bigger, more systemic threat.

Behind the hostile environment, Scotland's colony came up against a number of other problems. England's colonies in North America and the Caribbean, possessions such as Barbados and Jamaica, were forbidden to trade with the Scottish colony. The English attitude was clear—Darien must fail and the Scots' streak of independence be beaten down. Consequently, the English fleet, which might have been a significant help in protecting the fledging Scottish colony, did nothing to shield it from the Spanish. Meanwhile, trading with the Scots was officially frowned upon. This left the colony at the mercy of a few independent minded traders willing to smuggle goods. The only problem with this was that the colony had to find tradable goods—something that proved impossible.

A long distance from Scotland and re-supply, the Darien colony was in poor shape within a matter of months. In April 1699, torrential rains brought malaria and yellow fever. By June, close to half of the colonists had died or were ill. An expedition to gather fresh supplies from Jamaica returned with the distressing news that King William still forbade any English ship or colony to assist Darien. Equally disastrous, the small colony's leadership was frequently locked in conflict, as strong personalities and pettiness overrode any change of unified leadership rising to the challenge. Liberal supplies of rum, wine, and Madeira also sapped the ability of key individuals to rise above factional disputes. Morale plummeted.

Conditions only got worse when the Scottish colony learned that the Spanish were planning to attack them. A half-hearted Spanish effort to oust the Scots had failed in February 1696. Now, a larger and better organized attack was being planned. Around the same time, the colony finally learnt of the English proclamations against it, and the Council prepared to abandon the settlement. Unable to rely upon English assistance, the leaders of the small and isolated colony felt lost, betrayed, and bitter. Morale was already exceedingly low, and a decision was made to abandon the tropical hell hole. The last settlers were gone by June 22.

Of the five ships that originally set sail for Darien only the *Caledonia* made it back to Scotland. The others were sold or lost at sea. 700 survivors fled to Jamaica and only around 200 made it back to Scotland, including Paterson. Paterson, who had lost his wife to fever, was so ill that he was carried aboard ship and made a slow recovery during the voyage. Pennyquick died at sea of fever. Regarded as a bully and poor leader, he was not mourned.

## The Second Expedition

Back in Scotland, little was known as to the condition of the colony. The belief was that things were going well. Two relief ships, the *Olive Branch* and the *Hopeful Binney* were sent with 300 men and women and provisions. A second major expedition was also planned and provisioned. In 1699, four ships full of supplies and new settlers—some 1,302—set sail for glorious Darien, unsuspecting of the looming tragedy. These ships, *Rising Sun, Duke of Hamilton, Hope of Bo'ness,* and *Hope*, were commanded by Capitan James Gibson. After making it to Madeira and crossing the Atlantic, the new settlers arrived in Darien to find disaster. As the Reverend Francis Borland wrote in his diary: "We found nothing but a vast howling wilderness, the Colony deserted and gone, their huts all burnt, their fort most part ruined, the ground which they had cleared adjoining to the fort all overgrown with weeds; and we looked for peace but no good came, and for a time of health and comfort, but beheld trouble."[26]

Incredibly, despite the gloomy situation, the Scots settlers decided to make a renewed effort to make the Darien adventure work. Fort St. Andrew was repaired, the land was cleared, and some sense of mission was recaptured. Conditions, however, remained poor.

While fever and horrid tropical conditions wrecked havoc upon the ill-prepared northerners, the Spanish were not pleased by the return of the Scottish menace.

The beginning of the end of the Darien scheme came on February 13, 1700. A Spanish military expedition sought to oust the Scots from their forward base at Toubagonti. Captain Campbell of Fonab, one of the colony's more capable leaders and an experienced solider, led a force of Scots and local Indians against the uninspired and poorly-led Spaniards. After a short fight, Spanish forces retreated. Although the Scots treated this as a great victory, the Spanish were hardly put off of ridding themselves of the pesky Scots.

The Spanish soon indicated that they were serious about expelling the Scottish interlopers. A large force was assembled under General Pimiento, who planned a two-pronged assault on the colony. A sizeable fleet of warships sailed from Cartegena in what is present-day Colombia, while an army approached from Panama. By March 1700, the Spanish put Fort St. Andrew under siege. The military action was short-lived as the Scots were vastly outnumbered and cut off from their primary source of drinking water. With casualties mounting and no hope of a rescue mission (let alone any help from local British forces), the Scots capitulated. Scotland's Darien colony came to an end on April 12, 1700.

## Aftermath

The fate awaiting the survivors at Darien was not good. Although the Scots were allowed to sail from Darien in their own ships, conditions were appalling. Most of the remaining ships were hardly seaworthy. Moreover, both the majority of the remaining crew and settlers were ill with fever, which was to kill many during the retreat from Darien. As Reverend Borland noted, they were crowded "like so many hogs in a sty or sheep in a fold, so that their breath and noisome smell infected and poisoned one another.... Malignant fevers and fluxes were the most common diseases, which swept away great numbers of us. From aboard one ship, the *Rising Sun*, they would sometimes bury in the sea eight in one morning."[27] The remaining Scottish ships were filled with the colonists. *Hope of Bo'ness* sailed to Cartegena, in modern Colombia, where her master surrendered his ship to the local authorities. *Rising Sun, Duke of Hamilton*, and *Hope* sailed to Jamaica to re-supply.

The tale of the survivors is tragic. The small fleet left Jamaica in July. The ships had been in bad shape when they left Darien; those conditions had only worsened with the further passage of time. *Hope* sank off the coast of Cuba. *Rising Sun* was damaged in a storm in the Gulf of Florida, but managed to limp into Charleston, Carolina with *Duke of Hamilton*. A few weeks later both ships were sunk in a hurricane.

While the survivors of the two expeditions were seeking to return home, tension rose between the Scottish Parliament and King William. In October 1699, news finally arrived in Scotland that the first expedition had ended in disaster. The Scots asked King William for help, but the request was refused. The mood in Scotland became one of anger toward England. On May 27, 1700, the Scottish Parliament, in an act of defiance declared that the settlement of Darien was legal and that the "government" would provide support. This, of course, begged the question which government—that of King William and Queen Mary or that of the Scottish Parliament, representing one part of the United Kingdom. In this environment of anti-English sentiment, riots against the king broke out in Edinburgh and a Convention of the Estates was called to defy his government.

King William's position softened once he learned that the Darien adventure was over. He asked Spain to release the Scots captured during the first expedition. However, Scotland remained a thorn in his side. The Scots Parliament sought to deny the English monarch his taxes. Although that effort was nullified and ambitious nobles were bought off, King William had little fondness for his northern kingdom.

The Darien tragedy was a severe blow to Scotland. First and foremost it was a crippling blow to the country's finances, wiping away at least a quarter of national wealth. Secondly, it was psychological blow. It demonstrated the acute difficulty any small nation had in attempting to establish colonies in the Atlantic when competing against the superpowers of the time. Faced with such opposition, the Scottish adventure did not stand a chance. Thirdly, the Darien tragedy fatally wounded the myth of Scottish independence. Although Scottish foreign policy had traveled south with King James in 1603 and Scottish national interests were increasingly suborned to English ones, there were many in the northern kingdom who continued to nurture hopes of Scottish separatism. There was an ongoing movement among stubborn Scottish nationalists who refused to surrender entirely to the idea of union. The failure at Darien badly undermined the  idea that Scotland could handle its own affairs, and contributed to the union of 1707.

## Conclusion

Relations between Scotland and England were not good in the aftermath of the Darien disaster. When William died in 1702, his 32-year-old sister-in-law, Anne, became queen of England, with the full support of the English Parliament. Support from the Scottish Parliament, however, was forthcoming only after a considerable amount of politicking, which only further darkened relations between the Scots and English.

Relations between Scotland and England continued to deteriorate, especially in August 1704 when an English ship, the *Worcester*, was seized in the Firth of Forth and her crew arrested. The *Worcester*, commanded by Captain Thomas Green, had pulled into the Firth of Forth for repairs. The welcome they received was totally unexpected. It was believed by Scottish authorities that the *Worcester* belonged to the English East India Company, an institution deeply loathed by the Scots. In retaliation for the English seizing a ship of the Company of Scotland, the *Annadale*, in the Indian Ocean and the rumored death of two Scottish sailors, the secretary of the Scottish Company demanded that the *Worcester* be seized and its crew arrested. Roderick Mackenzie, the company secretary, boarded the *Worcester* and had the ship's captain and some crewmembers put in prison.[28]

The sad tale did not end there. Captain Green and fourteen of his crew were tried in March 1705 by the Scottish Court of the Admiralty. They had been charged with the destruction of a Company of Scotland ship, the *Speedy Return* and the murder of the Drummound brothers. What had made the entire matter so explosive was that the Drummounds were survivors of the Darien disaster. Their alleged murder by the English indeed struck a raw nerve among the population.

Although the basis of the charge was an untrue rumor, Capitan Green and his crew were found guilty. More level-headed parties in Scotland recognized the dangerous nature of the situation vis-à-vis their more powerful neighbor to the south. Gossip circulated in Edinburgh that Capitan Green and his crew were to be reprieved. An angry anti-English mob attacked the Earl of Seafield's carriage and threatened to break into Tolbooth prison and execute the Englishmen themselves.[29] Although Scottish troops were very much in evidence, there was apprehension that a reprieve would result in a breakdown in order. On April 11, 1705 Captain Green, and Englishman, his mate John Madder (a Scotsman) and gunner James Simpson (also English) were hung on the sands of Leith. The remaining crewmembers were reprieved. As Prebble noted of the linkage between Darien and the Worcester incident: "There was scarcely a family in Scotland below the Highland Line that had not lost a son, or a father, a cousin, nephew or friend in that disaster. This was why Scotland hanged Thomas Green, Madder and Simpson, and this was why there could be no forgiveness."[30]

While the chill effect of the Darien scheme was a jolt to Scottish pretensions, the English Parliament's passage of the Alien Act of 1705 was a body blow to any remaining aspirations that Scotland could go it alone. In essence, the English set on reigning in the Scots. By 1705,

English patience with Scotland had worn thin. The *Worcester* incident was the last straw and demanded a hard-nosed response. The northern kingdom was troublesome, constantly threatening to open up as a base for England's Catholic enemies, in particular France, which had given the Stuarts a place of exile and supported their claim to Scotland. Moreover, Scotland's political elite was fractious and exceedingly difficult to deal with. Finally, Scottish merchants were constantly seeking to penetrate English home and overseas markets. Consequently, the English used the one weapon that they could use adeptly without firing a shot or causing the loss of a drop of blood—trade. The English were rapidly developing a global trade regime. Scotland could be part of it or she could languish outside of it. There were to be no half measures. The cost of entry was political union. Scotland would have to surrender all pretenses of independence. In return, Scotland could become part and parcel of one of the world's first global trade regimes.

The Alien Act of 1705 was blatantly anti-Scots and a clear retaliation to the *Worcester* incident. In essence, it meant that estates owned by Scotsmen in England were to be confiscated and exports of linen, cattle, and coal to England were forbidden. According to the Act, after Christmas Day 1705, all Scots who were not resident in England, Ireland, and the English colonies, or serving in Queen's Anne's army and navy, were to be declared aliens.[31]

The Scottish merchant class looked upon the Act with considerable trepidation. Many of the wealthiest and most influential merchants owned property in England or, at the very least, maintained offices and commercial holdings in London. Being cut off from English trade would be a severe blow. Moreover, it would cut Scotland off from London, now emerging as the world's major center for credit, something usually short in supply in the north.

The decision to consummate the Union with England occurred only after an intense and emotionally draining national debate. And the Darien gamble hung over this landscape like a dark cloud. Those favoring union did so with the conviction that Scotland could only benefit from a more complete union. Clearly, the failure of the Darien adventure demonstrated the difficulty a small country like Scotland had in competing for trade. If, it was reasoned, that Scottish merchants had the weight of England behind them they would be able to prosper and certainly better compete with other European traders. Union also meant access to English colonies in the Americas and India, two lucrative markets.

The Darien Scheme began as a daring national gamble; it ended in disastrous failure. Speculation on a vast scale  ruined the Scottish economy and ultimately ended Scotland's independence. As in any mass speculation gone awry, there was a degree of human suffering and ruin. At the same time, the closer binding of the Scottish economy to the larger and more globalized English one ironically opened the door to greater prosperity for the Scots as a people. Recovery, however, proved to be a long road and one over which the shadow of the Darien tragedy remained for many years.

## Notes

1.  Tom Steel, *Scotland's Story* (London: Fontana/Collins, 1989), p.135.
2.  George S. Pryde, *Scotland from 1603 to Present Day* (London: Thomas Nelson and Sons, Lt., 1969), p. 49 and p. 51.
3.  See K.G. Davies, See K.G. Davies, *The Royal Africa Company* (London: Longmans, Green, 1957); M. Epstein, *The English Levant Company: Its Foundation and Its History to 1640* reprinting ed. (New York: Franklin, 1908, 1969); T.S. Willion, *The Early History of the Russian Company, 1553-1603* (Manchester, UK: University of Manchester Press, 1956) and Alfred C. Wood, *A History of the Levant Company* (Oxford: Oxford University Press, 1935).
4.  Eric Link later, *The Survival of Scotland* (Garden City, New Jersey: Doubleday + Company, Inc. 1968), p. 307.
5.  Craig Rose, *England in the 1690s: Revolution, Religion and War* (London: Black-well Publishers, 1999), p. 233.
6.  Hiram Bingham, "The Early History of the Scots Darien Company," *The Scottish Historical Review*, Vol. III (1996), p. 212.
7.  David Sinclair, *The Pound: A Biography* (London: Century: 2000), p. 186.
8.  John *Prebble, Darien: The Scottish Dream of Empire*, (Birlinn Ltd, 2000), p. 14.
9.  Linklater, *The Survival of Scotland,* p. 308.
10. Bingham, "The Early History of the Scots Darien Company," *The Scottish Historical Review*, p. 214.
11. *Prebble*, Darien, p. 22.
12. Shaw, *The Political History of Eighteenth-Century Scotland*, p. 6.
13. Cameron, *Bank of Scotland*, p. 25.
14. Other significant players were the merchant James Balfour (a founding member), James Maule, 4th Earl of Panmure (member of the Council Genera of the Company), and Andrew Fletcher of Saltoun, one of Scotland's greatest patriots.
15. Prebble, *Darien*, p. 88.
16. Cited by W.R. Scott, *The Constitution and Finance of English, Scottish and Irish Joint-Stock Companies to 1720*. Vol. II (Cambridge: Cambridge University Press, 1912), p. 216.
17. Prebble, *Darien*, p. 63.
18. From Lionel Wafter, A Description of the Isthumus of Dairen, http://webprinceton. edu.sites.english.eng321/WAFER.HTM.
19. Website of the Bank of Scotland, "http://www.bankforfscotland.co.uk/info/history/history-info.html.

20. Alan Cameron, *Bank of Scotland, 1695-1995: A Very Singular Institution* (Edinburgh: Mainstream Publishing Company, 1995), p. 21.
21. Ibid.
22. Prebble, *Darien*, pp. 109-112.
23. Steel, *Scotland's Story*, p. 144.
24. Quoted from Steel, p. 145.
25. Ralph Lee Woodward, Jr. *Central America: A Nation Divided* (New York: Oxford University Press, 1976), p. 4.
26. Quoted from Steel, *Scotland's Story*, p. 146.
27. Ibid., p. 147.
28. Ibid., p. 155.
29. Ibid.
30. Prebble, *Darien*, p. 9.
31. Steel, p. 155.

# 3

# Caribbean Follies

Scotland's failure in Darien, as described in chapter 2, had been largely self-induced. Ignorance, greed, and a series of poor choices created the Darien mess. Outside powers like Spain and Britain were all too eager to heap misery on the hapless Scots, but their tragedy was largely one of their own making. This chapter will focus on a slightly different problem confronting small economies, namely their vulnerability to financial and political pressure from larger, more powerful states.

Outside pressures and agendas can combine with domestic incompetence and corruption to create financial havoc. The stories of several Latin American nations during the late nineteenth and early twentieth century provide such examples. In these instances, economies were not ruined by outlandish schemes like the Darien colony, but through poor management and corruption helped along by old-fashioned imperialism. It was a truly hazardous Caribbean cocktail.

With the exception of the South Pacific, no region has a larger collection of small countries than the Caribbean. From the Bahamas down to Guyana and Suriname, this region has literally been caught in the crosswinds of international capitalism since the arrival of Christopher Columbus in 1492 and the ensuing Spanish quest for gold. More permanent European presences developed during the sixteenth century as the cultivation and export of sugar took center stage. In the twentieth century and into our own time, the Caribbean has maintained itself as a premier tourist destination famed for crystal clear waters and as a hub for offshore financing supported by lenient tax regulations.

Through much of modern history, finance, usually in the form of debt, has been a headache for much of the Caribbean. Indeed, the management, or should we say, mismanagement, of debt frequently jeopardized national sovereignty and led to crises with foreign powers. In some cases, financial mismanagement resulted in outright foreign occupation, complete with troops and administrators as with the American occupations of the Dominican Republic (1915-1924) and Haiti (1915-1934).

It is the purpose of this chapter to examine some of the more dramatic examples of financial crises in the Caribbean during the late nineteenth and early twentieth century, with a focus on the Dominican Republic, Haiti, and Cuba. These were some of the first Caribbean nations to achieve independence and their experiences provide an excellent backdrop for analyzing the weakness of small countries and their governments in seeking to deal with the fickleness of international investors and the powerful governments who supported them.

## The Era of Gunboat Diplomacy

By the mid-nineteenth century, "gunboat diplomacy," the use or threat of military force to back largely commercial claims, was in full swing. "Gunboat diplomacy" was endemic in the Caribbean, but hardly limited to the region. Nations as distant and disparate as Egypt had suffered similar experiences at the hands of British and French financiers in the 1870s.[1] In many ways, much of the early history of Caribbean finance was a jaded affair, driven by mutual greed and little regard for the national good. On occasion, great power foreign policy objectives did clash and financial complications provided legalistic "fig leaves" by necessity.

The rising power of the United States played a key role in Caribbean history during the nineteenth century. The expansion of US power resulted in increased American economic interest in the Caribbean. This process was accelerated by the Spanish-American War of 1898. As a result of its victory, the United States acquired Puerto Rico and Cuba from Spain and, through the Platt Amendment, maintained the right to "legally" intervene in the Caribbean and the Philippines. This increase in American power was soon followed by the development of the Panama Canal. As US influence increased, the smaller countries in the Caribbean came under deeper scrutiny. American policymakers found them lacking in political stability. In 1904, Theodore Roosevelt advanced what came to be known as the Roosevelt Corollary to the Monroe Doctrine of 1823. At the start of the nineteenth century, President Monroe had declared the Western Hemisphere to be an American zone of influence. He announced that any European attempts to deepen their colonial presence or interfere in local affairs would be treated by the United States as acts of aggression. Roosevelt's Corollary added that the United States could intervene in the Americas (including through military means) to ensure political and economic stability. Such declarations rested on the conviction that the United States must uphold law and order in the Caribbean to deprive extra-hemispheric states of an excuse to meddle in regional affairs.[2]

It is important to underscore that the Roosevelt Corollary was the result of another collision between debtors and creditors that degenerated into a challenge to Venezuela's sovereignty. Venezuela at the turn of the twentieth century was a potentially wealthy country. It had considerable size, especially when compared to other nations in the Caribbean, a wealth of natural resources, and fertile soil. What it lacked was infrastructure—the critical component needed by businesses to get their goods to the coast or to distribute them within the country. Consequently, successive Venezuelan governments turned to foreign bankers and investors to raise capital.

In 1899, Cipriano Castro took power as the country's new strongman or *caudillo*. Like others before him, Castro had few qualms about making a substantial part of Venezuela's wealth his own. His combination of ruthlessness, extravagant living, and only a cursory attention to the mundane affairs of state, did not generate a fond opinion of him among foreigners. The US Secretary of State Elihu Root referred to Castro as "a crazy brute" and he is remembered by historian Edwin Lieuwer as "probably the worst of Venezuela's many dictators." When Castro's reckless spending resulted in a difficulty in making repayments, foreign powers, namely Germany and Britain, were ready to pounce.

The European powers threatened a naval blockade of Venezuela. In response, Venezuela appealed to the US for assistance. President Roosevelt's approach was guided by US strategic concerns about the possibility of the Germans gaining a base in Venezuela and a racist view of Latin Americans. Castro's physical appearance and reputation as a carouser did not help. Theodore Roosevelt's biographer Edmund Morris observed: "The fact that Castro was only five feet tall and simian in appearance, confirmed his general prejudice against Latin Americans as political primates, low in the pantheon of nations. To evolve, they must be taught responsible behavior."[3]

Responsible behavior was soon to become the issue for Venezuela and the Atlantic powers. Castro's government lacked responsibility and the European powers, particularly Germany and Britain, were going to provide it. Despite Venezuela's often-tumultuous political history, the Castro's government excesses made repayment of foreign debt and even touchier issue. To force repayment, German ships actually bombarded a Venezuelan port. In the end, the US brought enough pressure to bear on Germany and Britain that they stood down after the declaration of the Roosevelt Corollary. For his part, Castro agreed to a financial settlement with the European investors.

What was significant about the Venezuelan crisis of 1902-04 was that some of the "guidelines" for conduct between large powers and smaller, weaker countries became clear. In spite of the troubles, the wily Castro survived the crisis, the Venezuelan economy did not collapse, and some form of foreign investment resumed. Castro, however, was ultimately a victim of his own brashness. In 1907, he antagonized the Dutch until they seized a Venezuelan port and destroyed part of the South American country's fledging navy. The US again mediated, sending the issue to the Permanent Court of Arbitration at The Hague. The ruling favored the European creditors. Castro refused to pay up, but his excesses and ineptness were clearly costing his country. When Castro left Venezuela for Paris to receive medical treatment for a serious illness (said to be syphilis), his second-in-command, Juan Vincente Gómez, seized power. Castro recovered, but spent his remaining years living as an exile in Puerto Rico.

The Roosevelt Corollary was followed by President William Howard Taft's policy of "Dollar Diplomacy." This put US bankers in touch with debtor governments. Between the Roosevelt Corollary and Dollar Diplomacy, US financial interests advanced deeply into the Caribbean. In many cases, Washington extended explicit guarantees for bankers operating in the region. It was reasoned that the combination of private sector and US government engagement in the Caribbean would help consolidate debt and provide better governments. In turn, countries like the Dominican Republic and Haiti would no longer attract revolutionaries and foreign speculators. Instead they would be able to peacefully pursue stable economic development that would put them out of reach of foreign and domestic subversion.[4] American investors would reap profits and the government would maintain stability in its neighbors. Or so it was hoped.

## Dominican Tales

One of the more interesting stories of Caribbean "high finance" took place in the Dominican Republic. The first place that Columbus set foot, the island of Hispaniola, was to give birth to two countries, Haiti in the west and the Dominican Republic in the east. Haiti was a child of the French Empire, born through a bloody combination of the French

Revolution and a massive slave rebellion. A lengthy period of highly productive, yet heavy-handed plantation agriculture had made the French colony of Saint-Domingue (as Haiti was named at the time) the world's leading sugar and cacao producer, during the 1780s and early 1790s. Yet the slave system was regarded as one of the most brutal in the Caribbean. When the ideas of "liberté, egalité, and fraternité" trickled into the colony from revolutionary France, the results were explosive. Indeed, Count Mirabeau, a keen contemporary observer, noted that Saint-Domingue's white planter class "slept at the foot of Vesuvius." In August 1791, the slaves rose in rebellion, initially led by Dutty Boukman, a high priest of Voodoo. Despite the efforts of both French and British troops over the next several years, Haiti's people, led by the charismatic Toussaint L'Ouventure and Jean-Jacques Dessalines, refused to surrender.

For a country born in rebellion against slavery, the continued existence of slavery next door in the Spanish colony Santo Domingo (later the Dominican Republic) was not welcome, especially since foreign powers were using it as a springboard to attack the Western Hemisphere's only successful slave rebellion. Consequently, Haiti's new rulers opted to invade the Dominican Republic in 1822, staying until they were driven out in 1844. The ongoing Haitian threat hardly led to a stable political environment in the Dominican Republic.

By the 1860s, the Dominican Republic had settled into a political system dominated by the military strongmen. This political system was imposed over a largely agricultural economy, dominated by cattle, tobacco and, increasingly, sugar. One of the most prominent political figures was Buenaventura Báez. A rich property owner and mahogany exporter in Azua, Báez first became president in 1849. As Dominican historian Frank Moya Pons observed: "Báez had an impressive political background. He had been a congressman during the Haitian occupation, one of the secret negotiators of the French protectorate, and had headed the Dominican diplomatic mission that went to Europe in 1845 to garner the political support of England, France, and Spain."[5] He was also a military leader and one of the country's leading businessmen.

Despite Báez's impressive résumé he was to prove sadly inept when it came to the economy. The entanglements he created with foreign creditors would repeatedly compromise the Dominican Republic's sovereignty. However, his first efforts included a reorganization of the country's army and navy with an eye to taking the offensive against Haiti and the ratification of a treaty of recognition, friendship, trade and navigation with the British in 1850. The involvement of the British turned out to be a positive development as London was able to pressure the Haitians to signing a ten-year truce with the Dominicans. This was to provide a period of relative peace between the two countries from 1849-1853—one of the few breaks up to the point. Báez peacefully left office in 1853, passing power over to his long-time rival, Pedro Santana. Political pressure soon forced Báez was soon to flee to Curaçao and then to St. Thomas. It was no mistake that Curaçao and St. Thomas were his destinations as those two islands were the region's major financial centers. In Curaçao, part of the Dutch Empire, the major bankers were Sephardic Jews, such as J.A. Jesurun, who were well known to many local leaders and had connections with European financiers.

Báez returned to the Dominican Republic in October 1856 and quickly launched a campaign against Santana who soon left the island. Although his main rival was gone, Báez still needed to consolidate his political power. The Dominican Republic's government lacked a well-thought out economic policy, was repeatedly invaded by Haiti, and its financial institutions were rudimentary. Capital was in short supply. The merchants in the Cibao region, largely supported by tobacco and cattle income, were one of the few local sources of capital and they did not easily part with their money. Compounding matters, the national currency was worth very little as frequent government resort to the printing press had generated inflation and instability. Indeed, in the 1880s, dollars used to back the national currency were held in bank accounts in neighboring St. Thomas under the protection of the British colonial authorities.

Báez was not above turning to the printing press for a little personal gain. He did so in 1857 arguing that the old money was badly devalued and that there was a dangerous lack of currency to cover the needs of the tobacco dealers.[6] This monetary duplicity came with a cost—a rebellion broke out among those who were at the receiving end of the depreciation—mainly the Cibao tobacco dealers. This quickly led to a costly civil war between the Cibao and Báez. Both sides turned to the printing press to finance their military expeditions, heaping more misery on the Dominican money system. This created a further depreciation of the peso vis-à-vis the dollar, effectively undermining the economy. Eventually Santana made his return and Báez left the country for yet another exile. The economy remained in crisis with the government turning to devaluation to help exports. Complicating matters further, foreign merchants refused the 1859 devaluation and turned to their consuls to obtain a more beneficial exchange rate (at that point 2,000 pesos to the dollar). Not receiving satisfaction from the Dominican government, the consuls departed. In their place came warships from France, England, and Spain, threatening to bombard Santo Domingo if the government did not accept their demands for an exchange rate of 500 pesos to one dollar.[7] The government in Santo Domingo, such as it was, quickly gave in.

The Dominican Republic's political elite remained inept and the economy was hit by one problem after another. Threatened by other countries, including a short-lived private expedition from the US to claim the guano-rich islet of Alta Vela, the Dominicans even briefly returned to Spanish rule in 1861. Abandoning the business of government, Báez slipped off to Spain where he lived a life of relative ease. The Spanish, however, quit the Dominican Republic in 1865, which created more political instability. Báez returned yet again, only to put the country up for annexation by the United States. The Dominican leaders needed money to remain in power and hoped that a deal with their larger North American neighbor would generate considerable personal windfalls. For its part, the administration of President Grant was interested in establishing a naval base in Samaná (on the central part of the country's north coast), and a place to resettle newly freed slaves.[8]

While Báez schemed with the Americans, his need for money was as great as ever. This led to the Dominican Republic becoming entangled in international financial complications. By the beginning of the twentieth century, the country has once more lost its sovereignty. The first loan, in 1869, was raised by Edward H. Hartmont of London, who was a contact of Jesurun in Curaçao. Historian R.W. Logan observed that the Hartmont Loan was "the initial foreign commitment which was to lead to the American receivership of 1905."[9] He also stated that "the terms were not only onerous but scandalous, even for a country devastated by war and allowing for the customary *pourboires* to the members of the government who signed the deal."

The scope of the deal was apparently straightforward—for a loan of £750,000, Báez pledged all of the resources of the country. At the same, the London-based Hartmont & Company received about £150,000 of the bond issue's proceeds. Hartmont was not exactly a man of honor. As one historian noted:

He got the loan listed on the London Stock Exchange by fraud, sold most of the bonds after the Dominican Congress had cancelled the agreement for ample cause—non-fulfillment of terms—and misapplied the greater part of the next sum realized (£372,009,155 Id). Some of this was paid to bondholders as interest on money never received by Santo Domingo, in order to hold the market steady until his own claims for alleged damages come to concession.[10]

There was so much opposition to the loan's terms in the Dominican Republic that the government was forced to cancel the loan contract. Considering that the Hartmont went ahead and issued bonds in the London market, but that the Dominican government refused to pay, the loan went into default by 1872. This, in turn, forced the British government to insist that no further lien be placed on Dominican revenues until the bondholders' interests had been met. The situation became even more farcical when Báez was forced out of power on January 2, 1874 and fled the country yet again. He returned to assume power one last time from 1876 until 1878, when he was ousted for a final time and slipped off to Puerto Rico. He died in Mayagüez in 1924, old, rich and ill with "no interest in returning from exile to live in a country where his very name was discredited and only served to arouse hostility."[11]

## Baéz's Legacies

The external debt issue would dog the Dominican Republic well beyond Báez's final departure. Out of the political upheaval of the 1870s emerged General Ulises "Lilis" Heureaux. Elected in 1882, the new leader came into office with considerable support and hope for political peace and economic prosperity.[12] He remained in power until his assassination in 1889, and is remembered as one of the country's more colorful and brutal dictators. Heureaux's regime was based on a pervasive spy system, a large personal army, systematic corruption, terror, cruelty, and the co-opting of potential opponents.[13] Heureaux changed the constitution to allow him to rule for life. The dictator's hard-fisted rule focused on maintaining the regime and a lavish lifestyle for himself, his family, and his mistresses. Yet he did have some vision. Under his rule the government spent heavily on the construction of roads, bridges, and railroads. He also created a national bank. Despite personal greed, Heureaux understood the need for national development—as long as he received a generous cut.

Heureaux demonstrated cunning in the use of public funds and foreign business interests. Public funds were used to bribe local *caudillos*, while concessions were granted to US and European "businessmen," usually adventurers, to administer projects or partake in international trade and investment (as in mining). These policies helped Heureaux to play the United States and European states against each other, while maintaining his lavish lifestyle.[14]

Although US influence was growing in the Caribbean, European financial interests were still powerful and well established. This was certainly the case of the French, who maintained colonies in Martinique, Guadeloupe, and French Guiana. The Germans, latecomers to imperialism, were eager to expand their interests, while the Dutch remained secure in their colonies of the Netherlands Antilles (the most significant of which was Curaçao) and Suriname. The British continued to be a major financial force.

In his *The Dominican Republic 1850-1900*, Dutch historian H. Hoetink observed: "it can be said in general terms that European financial influence in the country, which continued until the nineties, was based on a network of relations that the Sephardim from the Caribbean maintained in Europe. It is not, therefore, surprising that this group, since it was oriented toward Europe, would resist increasing North American penetration...."[15]

The external debt issue, going back to the Hartmont loan, remained a weak point for Heureaux as it made obtaining any new loans problematic. This became painfully evident in 1887, when Heureaux sent Eugenio G. de Marchena, a Curaçao-Sephardic immigrant, to Europe to obtain new financial assistance.[16] Bondholders of the Hartmont loan were still demanding payment, a position supported by the British government. Being creative, and no doubt concerned about his superior's reaction to coming home with nothing, Marchena was able to secure a secret agreement with Westerndorp and Company of Amsterdam.

Under the terms of the new deal, the Dominican Republic was to issue 30-years gold bonds for £770,000 of which about 38 percent was to pay off the Hartmont loan and Dominican domestic indebtedness, with the remainder held by Westerndorp.[17] To secure the loan, the Dominican government pledged the country's customs revenues, which were to be collected and administered by Westerndorp. This arrangement would allow Westerndorp to receive payments on the loan and reimburse its agents' expenses and commissions (which were 30 percent of total revenues) before turning over remaining funds to the Dominican government. The "secret contract" was ratified in 1888, with Westerndorp assuming its role in the Dominican payments system.

At this juncture, one would have hoped that the Dominican Republic's external debt problems were ended. Sadly this was not to be. Heureaux was soon requesting more funds from Westerndorp—this time for the development of a new railroad. Once again there was a turn to creative accounting—a new 56-year bond issuance for £900,000 was made, secured by a mortgage on the railroad and a second lien of customs revenue encompassing considerable new annual charges. The results, as described by two diplomatic historians, were predictably negative for the Dominican Republic. "Heureaux soon spent the proceeds of the loan, while customs revenues were insufficient to service the two bond issues. Westerndorp refused Heureaux's application for another loan."[18]

Heureaux was not deterred in his quest for foreign money. With Europe seemingly closed to him, he looked north. In the United States, Heureaux was able to connect with a group of American investors, seemingly undeterred by the Dominican Republic's sorry track record with external debt repayments. The North American group formed in 1892 around John Wanamaker, postmaster general in President Benjamin Harrison's cabinet, and New York moneymen, Smith M. Weed and Charles W. Wells. Weed was a prominent New York Democrat and close friend of Grover Cleveland. This group created a loan syndicate under the name of the San Domingo Improvement Company of New York (henceforth referred to as the Improvement Company or SDIC).

American interest in the Dominican Republic increased during the 1860s and 1870s with the development of the sugar industry. Political problems in Cuba drove Cuban sugar cultivators to the fertile lands in the neighboring island. They were soon followed by Italian and US interests in the southern part of the Dominican Republic.

The Improvement Company soon became the heir of the Hartmont loan as in May 1892 bought up the claims of Westerndorp, which "was glad to divest itself"—even at a substantially reduced value of the original bonds. Not shy about wading into the Dominican Republic, the Improvement Company provided new loans to Heureaux. The demise of the Westerndorp clearly accelerated the rise of North American financial predominance.

What was significant about the Improvement Company's involvement in the Dominican Republic was its creeping control over the Caribbean country's national finances. Indeed, as *The New York Times* noted in early 1893 of the deal between the Improvement Company and Westernport: "The San Domingo Government has ratified the bargain with the Holland bankers, by which the American syndicate assumes control of the Custom House and partly completed railroad. Indeed, the Americans have secured concessions which practically put them in control of the finances of San Domingo."[19]

While the Dominican Republic had considerable attractiveness to foreign investors, it was ultimately a financial abyss, conditioned by the personal idiosyncrasies of the country's leaders. This is not to say that there were not well-intentioned individuals, but political institutions remained weak and the *caudillo* tradition of military strongmen established by Baéz and Santana had become deeply entrenched. What this meant was that many of the Dominican national leaders regarded the state treasury as their own. This naturally led to ongoing problems both in the management of national finances and in dealings with foreign creditors. This situation would become even more problematic when conflicting foreign policies entered the scene. This occurred in 1892 with a presidential election pitting Heureaux, who claimed he was tired and disinclined to run, and Generoso de Marchena, his financial agent and a member of the National Bank of Santo Domingo.

Heureaux had allowed considerable concessions to US interests in the Dominican Republic, something opposed by other segments of the country's political and economic elite. Indeed, Marchena became the frontman against US financial dominance, supporting the interests European financiers instead. Marchena's National Bank was owned by French capitalists, who wanted to expand their sway on the island. To counteract US interests, the National Bank created a plan to consolidate the national debt with a new issue of bonds through a European syndicate consisting of German, British, Belgian, Dutch, and Spanish investors.[20]

The National Bank syndicate would also lease Samaná Bay and fortify it within three years. The bay was attractive as a possible naval and coaling base, something of particular interest to an emerging imperial power, like Germany. The National Bank's efforts achieved little except to incur the wrath of Heureaux and the Improvement Company. The realty was that geopolitics had changed in the Caribbean in the 1890s. The United States was now far more oriented to asserting its dominance vis-à-vis external, i.e., European, powers. Heureaux was ultimately content to seek office a final time, pitting himself against Marchena.

Marchena refused to be defeated easily. Through his influence at the National Bank, he managed to have that institution refuse all credit to Heureaux. Allegedly the reason for this was that the president was overdue in repayment of his personal loans to the bank. If that was not enough, de Marchena had the bank freeze Heureaux's other funds at the bank and placed an embargo on the guarantees provided by Heureaux to fulfill his obligations.[21]

Marchena's actions were far more dangerous than an armed uprising—they challenged the economic edifice of Heureaux's regime and his ability to pay those he needed to influence. The dictator's retribution came quickly—Marchena was seized in December 1892 and executed the following year. As for the National Bank, the authorities forced their way into the bank, closed it, and its operations were assumed by the Improvement Company.

But the French were not done in throwing around their political muscle. The French Navy returned in 1895 following the illegal imprisonment and murder of two Frenchmen. Three US warships were sent to counter French influence. To defuse matters, the Improvement Company provided financial indemnification to the French interests affected by the incident and a direct conflict between the US and France was avoided.[22]

Heureaux belatedly recognized that the Improvement Company was fast becoming a problem. By the late 1890s, the company loomed large in the DR's economic life, controlling a substantial share of export revenues and shaping national finances. As the economic power of the Cibao merchants declined (sucked dry by the government) and the influence of sugar interests (many of them tied to New York) expanded, Heureaux had increasingly leaned on the latter for local credit. Eventually these sugar producers demanded repayment, forcing the Dominican leader to raise another loan in Europe for $600,000. This loan went to meet Heureaux's obligations with the merchants and industrialists of the sugar districts. This, in turn, left rancor in the Cibao, ultimately sparking yet another failed rebellion. However, one of the Cibao leaders, Juan Isidro Jimenes, in exile in Paris, met up with a group of young Dominican students, including one Jacobito de Lara.

The chain of events seemed predestined. The young student de Lara returned to the Dominican Republic and with another man, Ramon Cocares, shot and killed Heureaux on July 26, 1899. The assassination took place in Moca, part of the Cibao. According to historian Moya Pons, the *caudillo* was "travelling through the region in an effort to placate the local merchants and convince them to lend him even more money in exchange for new fiscal exemptions and financial privileges."[23]

### After the Strongman…

Heureaux left the country in political crisis with an empty treasury and poor international credit standing. The real crux of the problem was the stranglehold that the Improvement Company had over national finances. After all was said and done with repayments, the government was only receiving $60,000 a month, totally insufficient to run its operations. Complicating matters, the Dominican public resented the Improvement Company and questioned the legitimacy of its hold over customs revenues since it worked under agreements between the dead dictator and a foreign-backed company.

Following Heureaux's death, the Dominican Republic continued to have economic troubles. The reluctance of foreign powers to lend it new money dimmed the prospects of recovery. Several years of inconclusive negotiation finally exhausted the patience of the Dominican Republic's European creditors. In 1904, German, French, Italian, and Dutch warships sailed into Dominican waters to assert their financial claims. The Dominicans turned to the United States, which it asked to assume control of collecting customs revenues. From this position, US authority would only increase. Eventually the combination of US strategic interests and trade propelled Washington's dominance over its considerably smaller neighbor. By the early 1900s, the US strategic framework was clear—the Spanish-American War of 1898 left it with a Caribbean empire of Puerto Rico and, in a less direct fashion, Cuba. The construction of the Panama Canal only reinforced US strategic considerations for political order in the Dominican Republic, which ultimately meant bringing national finances under control. What began as a takeover of the country's customhouses by US agents (who superseded the Improvement Company) morphed into outright political control of the entire country.

Washington policymakers grew increasingly worried about the inability of the company to handle the situation. This meant displacing the more narrow interests of the Improvement Company with the grander goals of the emerging Progressive era. Cyrus Veeser, a noted historian on the SDIC observed: "In place of the narrow, venal goals of the Improvement Company Roosevelt substituted a grand vision of rehabilitation for the Dominican Republic based on the proposition that it served American interests "that all communities immediately south of us should be or become prosperous and stable."[24]

Despite the US desire for order, the country's factional politics could not be contained. In 1911, President Ramón Cácases (himself implicated in Heureaux's assassination), was assassinated. The civil war that followed was only briefly halted by US negotiations. In 1914, President Woodrow Wilson notified the Dominicans that either they select a president or the US would impose one. The country then went from a provisional president to elections that brought about the brief and ineffective presidency of Juan Isidro Jimenes Pereyra. Jimeses, unable to contain the ambitions of other cabinet ministers, resigned in May, 1916 and the US Marines were ordered in to restore order. The marines were able to pacify the country, rebuild and improve the national infrastructure (mainly roads), and help the economy. Of particular note, the military government was instrumental in reducing the external debt and putting the repayments on a regular system. They were also deeply resented—as they were a foreign occupying army—and carried out sometimes brutal campaigns against local rebels. The US occupation lasted until 1924, when an elected government resumed Dominican sovereignty. The legacy, however, was a sour one. Once again, the Dominican Republic slipped from elective government into a long dictatorship under General Rafael Leonidas Trujillo. Trujillo seizer power in 1930 and ruled supreme until he was assassinated in 1961 by the brothers of one of his lovers.

## Haiti's Ill-Fated Slide to Occupation

Haiti's problems with external debt and finance were almost as long lasting and profound as the Dominican Republic's. Very much like its neighbor, Haiti's government had borrowed, defaulted, and borrowed again. Additionally, Haiti was caught up in larger international politics that made it a pawn in the chess game played by global powers, this time between the Germans and Americans.

At the beginning of the twentieth century, Haiti was plagued by weak central governments, rebel groups along much of the Dominican border (some funded by Santo Domingo), and an inefficiently managed economy. Haiti had also suffered as it was one of the few independent non-white governments run by the descendants of African slaves. It was repeatedly snubbed by other governments, including those in Latin America, and was hard pressed to obtain financing. Between 1911 and 1915, Haiti underwent an even more profound round of political disorder than usual. During that period the country had seven different presidents, who either fled into exile or were killed. Rival political factions financed rebel bands of peasants, called *cacos*, who kept the country in a state of chaos.

## Spheres of Influence

Until the arrival of the Americans and Germans, the major power in Haiti was France. Haiti had been a French colony and despite the disruption of relations in the aftermath of the liberation, commercial interests were slowly re-established in the nineteenth century. Some two-thirds of Haitian exports (mainly coffee) went to France in exchange for luxury goods: wine, liqueur, perfume, books, and a limited amount of precision tools. While France dominated in trade it provided financing for Haiti's only bank. One historian observed: "Every loan from 1825 to 1896 was a

French loan, so France still remained Haiti's chief creditor."[25] But things in Haiti were not so simple and German influence began to expand in the early twentieth century.

The local German community had considerable economic and political influence. Despite their small numbers (estimated at 200 in 1910), the Germans had made considerable inroads into Haiti's international trade, owned utilities in Cap Haïtien and Port-au-Prince, the largest wharf in the capital, and a railroad. The last was the Chemin de Fer de la Plaine du cul-de-sac or P.C.S. Railroad. It was an important transportation for the island's sugar industry and a substantial footprint in a small economy. This development was helped along by a willingness of the Germans to become part of the local society. Indeed, many of the Germans married into prominent mulatto families, an action that allowed them to bypass a constitutional prohibition barring foreign land-ownership, an obvious touchy point in the former slave colony.

The German connection also had a financial angle. As one of the few groups with any capital in the Haitian economy, they were a source for a number of high-interest loans. The local Germans also had links to the Keitel banking family in Hamburg. This financial and economic clout in the Haitian political arena became increasingly worrisome to Washington, especially as it was believed that German loans bankrolled the country's successive revolutions and coups.

The challenge for the administration of President Woodrow Wilson was how to deal with the German "threat." To a backdrop of fast-moving international developments, the US State Department encouraged a consortium of US investors, led by the National City Bank of New York, to purchase a controlling share of the new Banque National d'Haïti. Not without significance this was the island-state's sole commercial bank (replacing the bankrupt old National Bank) and a place the government entrusted with the treasury. This brought the Americans into a fierce competition with a rival Franco-German bid. There was considerable politicking between the two groups, behind which the governments quietly leaned on the respective parties. The Americans were to emerge with a dominant share of the new bank, renamed the Banque Nationale de la République d'Haiti. Unfortunately, the purchase, in 1910-1911, coincided with a deterioration in Haiti's political fortunes. Through the ensuing period, the American bankers clung to their new possession, but considering the gut-wrenching nature of political upheaval, they must have wondered why they had bought into Haiti.

## A Bloody Descent

Haiti's political life appeared to be moving toward a little more stability when in February 1915 Jean Vilbrun Guillaume Sam came to power, promising a strongman approach to law and order. The son of former president Tiresias Simon Sam, Guillaume Sam had been one of the leaders that brought Cincinnatus Leconte to power and toppled President Oreste Zamor. He followed Joseph Davilmar Théodore, who resigned after he could not pay the *cacos* who had helped him depose Zamor. Considering that he was the fifth president in five years, Sam was hardly paranoid in believing that there were people out to get him.

Sam followed two strategies: one was to align his interests with that of the United States; the second was to round up political prisoners as a safeguard to political stability in Port-au-Prince. In the later case, he soon had at least 200 prisoners, most of them from the mulatto upper class.[26] A lengthy revolt led by Rosalvo Bobo, who cast himself as a "progressive," made Sam fearful that he would suffer the same fate as those before him. The situation was far from stable. The *cacos* were defeated, but threatened to wipe out Haitians and others who had gathered at the consulates as a final blow. The French cruiser *Descartes* landed marines, who secured the consulates. Bobo remained ready for more fighting and the US sent its own warship. On the morning of July 27, before dawn, Sam's troops turned against him, and someone shot him in the leg. He managed to escape to the French legation. Fearing a general uprising, the leader ordered the execution of the 200 prisoners, which had already been done by nervous guards who reacted to the first shots. The ensuing massacre was recorded by one survivor:

> A flash of red light entered our cell, my comrades were slaughtered, disemboweled, dismembered, reduced to a mass of flesh. "Finish me! Finish me!" shrieked a wounded man.... I see a mass of dead bodies, huddled, faces on the ground, crouching in corners, horribly wounded....[27]

As word seeped out about the executions, Port-au-Prince exploded into an angry mob. Sam ran to the French embassy, which sought to give him diplomatic shelter. The mulatto leadership, however, was not to be halted by diplomatic niceties. After several sorties were repulsed, the angry Haitians eventually entered the embassy and found Sam hiding in a toilet. The former leader was dragged from his hiding place into the embassy's courtyard and hacked to death with a machete. His body was then thrown over the French embassy's fence where the mob took hold of it, tore his corpse to pieces and paraded the parts around Port-au-Prince. Political order evaporated and Haiti plunged into almost complete lawlessness.

The Wilson administration was at a loss. It had backed Sam and now it appeared that Bobo, who had demonstrated a degree of anti-Americanism, would take over. The combination of geo-strategic considerations, economic interests, and political instability thus opened the door for US occupation. Backing up the US position was the landing of 330 marines at the capital on July 28, 1915. They were soon followed by a larger force, which was to remain in Haiti until 1934. Given Haiti's record, some historians have noted that the intervention came not too soon, but surprisingly late.[28]

The point should be made that Haiti represented a geo-strategic concern for Washington, which outweighed any economic interest. With US strategic interests centering on the Panama Canal and heavier economic involvement in Cuba, Puerto Rico, and the Dominican Republic, Haiti continued to be regarded as a disruptive force. Robert Debs Heinl, Nancy Gordon Heinl, and Michael Heinl observed what officials in the Wilson administration confronted: "of twenty-two rulers of Haiti between 1843 and 1915, only one had served out his term of office. Four had died in office. One had been blown up in his palace. One had been overthrown and executed. One had been torn to pieces by his subjects. Thirteen had been ousted by coup or revolution."[29] This does not include the multiple of US and foreign warships sent into Haitian waters in acts of gunboat diplomacy. The additional fact that the Haitian government was unable to service its debt obligations only furthered these considerations. The fateful decision was made to assume control over Haiti's customhouses and national treasury, much as was done in the Dominican Republic.

The US occupation of Haiti effectively interrupted the country's self-rule for almost twenty years. Although it brought a degree of political stability, a limited amount of institution building (namely the military), and a system of roads, the US occupation left a bitter legacy and contributed to the later string of military-supported dictatorships. It also taught the Haitians the dangers associated with international finance through which large and powerful countries could impose themselves on small and weak ones. Haiti's economic weakness had fed its political instability. Plagued by problems in the international debt markets, the country's financial disasters cost it its independence and the lives of thousands of citizens.

## Cuba's Dance of the Millions

Caribbean countries were vulnerable not only to sovereign crises, but commodity ones as well. With economies often focused on the production and export of a hanful of cash crops, they were vulnerable to fluctuations in international markets. The island of Cuba has a long history associated with the cultivation and export of sugar. Indeed, sugar remains one of Cuba's key exports and generators of foreign exchange. Consequently, the ups and downs in sugar prices have played a significant role in shaping the Caribbean country's socio-economic development. Certainly one of the most extreme cases of this was the Dance of the Millions that hit Cuba in the late 1910s and early 1920s. It combined an export boom with a financial bubble that eventually led the Caribbean nation in a deep depression. It also left a longstanding historical memory of the follies of capitalism among the country's population, something that would resurface decades later in the Cuban Revolution.

## King Sugar

Cuba's relationship with sugar began under the Spanish. Although sugar was introduced in the sixteenth century it did not fully take off until the Haitian Revolution in the 1790s removed the neighboring French colony from its position as the world's leading producer. This left a gap in the supply of sugar and sent planters looking for alternative locations to grow the crop. One such alternative was Cuba, then a somewhat sleepy Spanish colony. By the nineteenth century, Spanish capital went into the development of large plantations, linked to European and North American markets and based largely on African slave labor. When Cuba gained its independence following the Spanish-American War of 1898, there was an inflow of US and Canadian capital, which was attracted to the agricultural sector.

One of the key factors in the development of the Cuban economy was the long-term decline in the price of sugar. Causes for this decline ranged from a wider spread of countries producing cane sugar (such as Australia and Fiji) to alternative sources of sugar (i.e., beet sugar produced in much of Europe). The increased supply more than met demand. This pushed pushing out marginal producers, forcing technological innovation, and a sparked search for places that contained comparative advantages, such as fertile soil, adequate water, and access to cheap labor.

In an effort to remain competitive, producers in Cuba shifted from the plantation system and slavery to a heavily mechanized central process, which utilized new technologies to create important economies of scale.[30] The technology arrived in Cuba following the Spanish-American War and was overwhelmingly deployed by US investors who found Washington's protectorate-role on the island attractive. This development made sugar-producing facilities the cornerstone of the industry. Surviving Cuban interests were forced to upgrade or vanish.

Cuba loomed large for US investors by the 1910s. While Mexico was the most attractive point for American investment in the late nineteenth century, the situation changed by 1910 when the longstanding dictatorship of Porfirio Díaz came to an end. Mexico soon slid into the political chaos of revolution. In the wake of this development, US investors opted out of one Latin American cauldron and into a safer, more stable business environment—Cuba. What underscored the island-state's attractiveness—at least to businessmen—was the lopsided political arrangement between Cuba and the United States. Technically a sovereign nation, Cuba had agreed to allow US intervention if instability occurred. This arrangement was embodied in the 1901 Platt Amendment, something that attracted foreign investment in the early twentieth century, but, in subsequent decades, came to symbolize US heavy-handedness. Cuba's geographical proximity to the US also enhanced its attractiveness to American investors.

The inflow of foreign capital and technology also had a regional element within Cuba. Over time, the sugar industry had spread from west to east on the island. This meant that for most of the nineteenth century, the western half of Cuba was more developed. The introduction of new investors and technology changed the socio-economic landscape. In the early years of the twentieth century, the bulk of new money was pumped into the east, in particular the provinces of Camagüey and Oriente. This process left Cuba with two different sugar industries—one in the west populated by independent cane farmers and a railway system constructed around production patterns dating back to the 1830s; another in the east that hit upon largely virgin terrain and had far more leeway to shape its industrial and communications infrastructure. Furthermore, these changes took place in the context of the huge upheaval in international markets that came with the outbreak of the First World War in 1914.

In 1914, the international sugar regime was based on sugarcane production, much of it from the Caribbean and Brazil, with some production in the southern United States, and Australia. Sugar also came from sugar beets, which were concentrated in Europe, in particular, the Austro-Hungarian Empire, Germany, and Russia.[31] Prices were low prior to the war and, in Cuba, some sugar producers were quietly happy to diversify into rum. This process of diversification started well before the early twentieth century, when families like the Bacardis learned how to refine rum. Between raw sugar and rum, Cuba's sugar sector was well structured to benefit from the disruption to come.

When the Austrian archduke, Franz Ferdinand, was assassinated by a Serbian nationalist on June 28, 1914 in Sarajevo—setting in motion a series of events that would lead to the First World War—the fortunes of Cuban and North American sugar producers unexpectedly brightened. As the Austro-Hungarian Empire slipped down the road to war with Serbia, pulling Germany and Russia, then France and Britain into the conflict, the global sugar industry was suddenly cast adrift from its familiar moorings. The advent of submarine warfare and the drain of workers from the fields to the battlefields meant the disruption of sugar beet production in much of Europe.

For Cuba, this meant a bonanza. Demand for Cuban sugar skyrocketed. During the war, the price for Cuban sugar climber sharply upward. Cuban growers had based their industry on a price of two cents per pound before the war. After 1914 they could get as much as five.[32] By 1920, the price had sailed up to 22.5 cents a pound.

### Empires in the Sun

Although part of the Cuban sugar industry was held by US and Canadian interests, there were local players who helped push along the country's sugar bloom and its financial bust. Key among these figures was José "Poté" López Rodríguez, who came from Spain and started his career as a bookstore clerk in Havana in the 1880s. While Poté was known for his interest in books, he had a high degree of business acumen and rapidly built up an empire. In William Belmont Parker's, *Cubans of To-Day*, a who's who published in 1919, Poté was described in almost glowing terms: "Señor Rodriguez, known far and wide as 'Poté', and regarded for his remarkable business sagacity and the prosperity of his enterprises, has made no attempt to enter public life of Cuba but continues to devote himself to his commercial and financial interests." Parker also felt it worthwhile to mention that Poté was known to enter the Presidential Palace "in short sleeves, disregarding the fashion norms at that time that demanded complete suit and stiff collars."[33]

Poté's empire went from owning the bookshop he started, to acquiring a controlling share of Banco Nacional in 1912. This purchase included buying out a number of high-profile US investors, including J.P. Morgan. Poté's holdings included companies involved in labor accidents, street paving, cement, meat production, and printing. Like many of the island's big businessmen, he was also into sugar. In 1915 and 1916 he bought and sold the Conchita and Asuncion mills. Poté did more than flip investments. His holdings also demonstrated productivity. His España mill, for example, increased production from 207,000 bags of sugar in 1917 to 523,000 bags by 1919.[34]

Poté was not the only immigrant to find his fortunes in Cuba. There was a small group of Catalans who found fame and fortune in the Caribbean nation. They included Narciso Gelats (investor/private broker), Emilio Bacardí (distillery owner), Ramón Crusellas (soap manufacturer), and Jośe Marimón. The last began his business life in Cuba as a merchant and worked his way up to become president of the Banco Español de la Isla de Cuba (founded in 1856). In the period before independence, the bank was active in providing drafts and other financial services for merchants. Equally important, under Marimón's guidance, the bank started making loans directly to sugar producers.[35]

Marimón was to emerge as one of the more dynamic local capitalists. In a similar fashion to the US financial titan, J.P. Morgan, Marimón was a consolidator, something critical in the rise of financial capitalism. Under his wings, a large swath of Cuban companies were corralled into trusts. These included hat makers, shoe factories, cracker and candy makers, and paper producers. Not content with an industrial and financial empire, Marimón was also for a period the president of a Santiago utility, an electric railway in Cienfuegos, an insurance company, and like Poté, he headed the Compañía Azucarera Oriental Cubana (a sugar mill). It should also be noted that his bank had stakes in the Cuban Telephone Company, the Cuban Tire and Rubber Company, a coastal shipping company, and the Port of Havana Docks Company (which controlled some of the main warehouses and wharves in the capital city). Between 1914 and mid-1920, the stocks and bonds on the bank's balance sheet more than quadrupled, from $4.3 million to $18.9 million.[36]

The US involvement in the Cuban sugar industry was extensive and the game changed dramatically in 1915 when the Cuban Cane Sugar Corporation was established in New York. This company was led by a Spaniard, Manuel Rionda, and a Cuban, Miguel Arango, both of whom were bankers. Additionally, Rionda was then managing partner in New York of Czarnikow Ltd. of London, the largest dealer in European beet and other sugars.[37] What was to elevate the Cuban Cane Sugar Corporation was its links to Wall Street. Accordingly, Rionda had persuaded

Wall Street bankers in 1912 to purchase a mill on the island. Rionda and Arango upped the ante by forming a syndicate to buy sugar mills and sell securities on Wall Street.

In January 1916, the company's representatives arrived in Cuba, sparking a buying spree that included assets from Poté. Cuba Cane's operation was not to create new mills but to take-over old ones. In many cases the management was left in place, but ownership shifted to the new organization. By 1918, Cuba Cane was the largest sugar enterprise in the world.[38]

During this time, the lucrative sugar industry drew more and more investment from the Cuban banking sector. There was plenty of money to go around and some of it was used to start up new banks. The banking sector's growth began to mimic the sugar industry. As historian Mary Speck observed: "Banks were created and expanded nearly as rapidly as sugar mills. Between 1915 and 1920, about 37 new banks were founded in Cuba."[39] Significantly, some of these were small institutions with less than $10,000 of capital. Others, like the Banco Internacional, were somewhat bigger. By mid-1920 it had $5 million in capital and 104 branches holding $37 million in deposits. Complementing the local institutions, National City Bank (now Citigroup) opened its first office in 1915 and rapidly expanded within five years to 15 branches and $29 million in deposits.

It is also worth noting that Cuban society was a small place; the major political and economic players usually knew each other and had dealings. Poté had easy access to the Presidential Palace as did many of the sugar lords. Access was also available to the foreign sugar executives. The US sugar engineer Hubert Edson was sent to see Mario García Menocal about an absentee *colono*, or landlord. This *colono*, a colonel in the Cuban army and acquaintance of the national leader, was stealing the laborers of other *colonos* who worked with the Alto Cedro sugar factory. The engineer was working with the factory and was sent to the president for assistance in the matter, especially after the other *colonos* were ready to revolt over the matter. As Edson relates the story, he was brought to a large sitting room, the walls decorated with a number of historical paintings and the floor covered by a heavy carpet which the president told him was bought from Tiffany's in New York for $25,000.[40] The two men were seated opposite each other in large leather-covered chairs, from which the conversation came to focus on the delicate matter of what to do with the troublesome colonel. Edson, however, had little to worry about. The Cuban president was quick to agree to the remove the colonel, but insisted that his friend be compensated to avoid any financial loss.

Edson noted that President Menocal's "willingness to accede to our program struck me as odd at the time, but I later learned it was characteristic of him to grant favors of all kinds when they brought no personal inconvenience to him because he figured that the best way to retain friends was to never say no to them. Conversely, he did not hesitate at asking favors for himself without regard for the inconveniences placed on those helping him."[41]

Cuba's president, Aurelio Mario García Menocal, was also part of the Dance of the Millions. Born in 1866, trained as an engineer, and a general in the army during Cuba's War of Independence, Menocal was busy with the sugar industry after the US intervention. Using his engineering skills, he built the Chaparra sugar plantation for the Cuban-American Sugar Company. Under his management Chaparra was soon one of the most productive sugar-producing estates in the Western Hemisphere. From being successful in business, Menocal turned to politics, making an unsuccessful presidential bid in 1908. At his second attempt in 1912, he became Cuba's third president. Forty-six in 1913, he came into office well respected and regarded as able. Some, however, saw him as too close to the United States, where he had attended Cornell University and worked with Cuban-American sugar. His first administration was noted for advances in education, public health and agricultural production. He also created an effective monetary system placing the dollar and peso on par. However, the longer Menocal remained in power the more corrupt he became. His "corrupt" rule and his "cold and calculating" quest for wealth meant that his personal fortune swelled from $1 million in 1913 to $40 million 1921, when he left office.[42]

## A Heady Brew Comes to an End

The combination of sugar wealth and an expanding financial sector with few restrictions as well as the incestuous nature of big business pumped up the Cuban economy into a bubble in 1918-1919; it burst in 1920. This process was described by an American economist in 1928:

> high-powered salesmen, who would sell money to persons who might be easily persuaded to use it. Cuban farmers, who had borrowed of one bank all that they needed to harvest their crop were begged by rival managers to borrow more. They might build a bigger house with their money, buy a car, send their families abroad! Cuban, American, Spanish, British-all were the same.... Wall Street beamed upon it. This was not an irrigation by fertilizing streams of American capital. It was a cloudburst of bank credit which struck Cuba.[43]

The Dance of the Millions was a heady time for Cuba. There were imported cars, and larger homes, marble palaces in the Vedado district of Havana, using the architecture of the Italian Renaissance, Louis XVI, and Florentine Gothic.[44] A luxurious new suburb of Miramar opened with grand houses built around country clubs.

Most Cubans and foreigners operating on the island believed that the sugar boom would continue indefinitely. When an American engineer questioned one of his colleagues about making further investments in land and factories, he was told:

> you evidently do not understand the sugar situation as a whole. If you did, you would not worry about taking over a property at much more than its intrinsic value. We are faced with a long era of high sugar prices, and even if the price was to drop to eight cents per pound for the coming crop, we would make enough money from the crop to pay off the fictitious value set of the property.[45]

When the engineer pressed further, the same man shook his head as though such a possibility was not possible. He stated: "It is the opinion of sugar experts everywhere that prices will continue at a high level."[46]

A commission sent to report on the possible recovery of Europe's sugar industry allegedly reported that the chances of such a recovery were remote and that Europe would have to depend on cane-sugar imports for the foreseeable future. This erroneous view "undoubtedly added fire to the enthusiasm of the optimists operating in West Indies."[47] In fact, the Commission's report represented some unsubstantiated personal opinions and that the Europe part of the investigation was "very cursory," as the commissioners spent "most of their time in riotous living in New York." Cubans and non-Cubans alike expected the surge of capital to continue. The island became transfixed in a mania, with banks wildly extending credit, sugar producers borrowing heavily (to further expand production), and the rest of society greedily along for the ride. The Cuban economy dramatically overleveraged just as parts of the financial sector continued to be undercapitalized. While this worked in an economy on the move, spurred by ever rising sugar prices, it was unsustainable when prices moved down.

At the beginning of 1920, sugar stood at 9 cents a pound in May it reached 22 cents, a spike caused by the lifting of wartime controls in the United States. By December, however, sugar prices plunged, selling for less than 4 cents a pound, a full cent below the estimated production cost of 5 cents a pound. Historian Mary Speck summarized the impact of this chain of developments: "Sugar producers were unable to repay loans (generally made with sugar as collateral) and the banks, new and old, large and small, suddenly seemed vulnerable."[48]

The crisis played out through the second half of 1920. By late summer and early fall it was painfully evident to most that the Cuban economy was in dire shape. Credit, not too long ago so easy to obtain, evaporated. The banks were shaky. Complicating matters Cuba lacked a central bank that could function as a lender of last resort. In early October, the country's business leaders and bankers issued a statement inviting the population to a mass meeting "to solidify the Republic financially and free it from bankruptcy." The result was disastrous. "Instead of a mass patriotic meeting, there was a run on the banks, beginning on 6 October at the once venerable Banco Español and spreading two days later to the upstart Banco Internacional."[49] By October 11, 1920 the government was forced to declare a banking moratorium. The moratorium, however, was only a stop-gap measure and was undermined with loopholes, including one that allowed depositors to withdraw money from their accounts by certified checks.

Between October and December 1920, the Cuban financial system continued to fold. The crisis was exacerbated by the continuing downtrend in sugar prices. Some relief did come at the end of December through a $50 million syndicated loan from American banks. The loan was used by the government to help the Cuban banks finance the producers against the remaining sugar stocks and against the 1920-1921 crop. At the same time, the government moved to assist the marketing and selling the balance of sugar from the 1919-1920 crop. For Cuba's already overburdened domestic banking sector, the efforts were a classic case of "too little too late."[50]

The end results were predictable. Banco Nacional went into bankruptcy and Poté's business empire was shattered. Poté was unable to recover and was found hanging from the balcony on his apartment on March 27, 1921. Commentators debated whether he had been murdered or committed suicide.[51] The other major capitalist in the Dance of the Millions, Marimón, was more fortunate. Faced with the deteriorating conditions, he traveled to Europe to raise capital. He failed. In his absence, public discontent with the financial/industrial class and the economy's plunge made it dangerous for the moneyed class. When Marimón returned to Cuba in February 1922 the public mood was such that he decided not to get off the boat and left the island fearing for his life.

The inglorious end of the Dance of the Millions was a brutal disruption of the Cuban economy. The local financial sector suffered a complete breakdown. Emergency Cuban government measures did little to restore confidence. Twenty banks were forced to close, well over half of the total in the country. The collapse of Cuba's domestic banking sector paved the way for an increase in foreign control: "foreign banks, which held about 20 percent of total loans in 1920, held 76 percent of the deposits and made 84 percent of the loans in 1923."[52]

The economic collapse also had political consequences. Public discontent was widespread. By the time of the November 1920 election, Menocal prudently decided not to run for a third term. Alfredo Zayas, the former vice president under Menocal's predecessor, won in what was probably a rigged election against his former boss, José Miguel Goméz. Clearly the new president, dealing with a pressure to clean up the political situation had little interest in helping Poté or any other sugar baron. Indeed, the US forced a new election in March 1921, which Zayas again won.

Cuba's economic woes were not over. Considering the country's shaky banking system and the mess in the sugar industry, US sugar policies only made matters worse. In April 1921 the US government imposed a new emergency tariff of just over one cent per pound, which obviously hurt Cuban sugar. In the aftermath of the Dance of the Millions, the Cuban economy went through a period of major adjustment. Although the demise of Cuba's entrepreneurial class has probably been overstated, the foreign, in particular, North American role in the Cuban economy did increase. Both the National City Bank and the Chase National Bank received the titles of many mills in return for settlement of debts. At the same time, the financial ties between Havana and Washington increased. In 1923, close relations were initiated between the Cuban Treasury and the Federal Reserve. Indeed, The Federal Reserve Banks of Boston and Atlanta both established a presence in Cuba, with the Atlanta agency issuing notes and the Boston agency conducting actual banking operations.[53]

The crash of the Cuban economy was devastating. Over-concentration on the production of sugar had left the economy of the entire country vulnerable to price fluctuations and international events beyond the control of the Cuban government. Over-eagerness to cash in on the boom during the war, led to a dramatic oversupply of sugar, which caused prices to crash after the peace. The end of the war had come suddenly, but the Cuban sugar sector was so overleveraged and vulnerable that small changes had major effects. Spurred by the prospect of new business opportunities and flush with leverage-based cash, banks and financiers had also expanded massively. They too were vulnerable when sugar prices declined. The balance sheets had been built for uninterrupted economic expansion. In tough times, and without the support of a central bank that could serve as a lender of last resort, they faced catastrophe.

## The Modern Caribbean

Far removed from the Caribbean sun, a group of Haiti's official creditors met in Montreal, Canada in January 2010. Haiti was just beginning its tentative steps toward a recovery from one of history's most devastating earthquakes. The meeting of the Paris Club, led by the governments of the U.S, Canada, Britain, and France, met to discuss the cancellation of Haiti's remaining foreign debt as part of a program to help rebuild the Caribbean country. In June 2009, the World Bank and IMF approved $1.2 billion of debt relief for Haiti, following the devastation of a hurricane and riots over food prices. At the Montreal summit, attention was given to acceleration of the cancellation of remaining Paris Club debt and dealing with outstanding debts owed to Venezuela ($295 million) and Taiwan ($90 million).[54]

The fact that Haiti is still having trouble with foreign debt in the early twenty-first century is a reminder that the risk of leverage is a daily factor in the Caribbean. Other Caribbean nations have faced near-collapses in their economies sparked by a combination of too much debt, poor transparency in financial transactions, and, in some cases, outright fraud. The Dominican Republic experienced a major banking crisis in 2003, which cost the country 15 percent of its GDP and brought a near-collapse in economic life.[55] Jamaica had a major financial crisis in 1995-1996, which left the country a legacy of heavy public sector dependence, painfully slow growth, and fiscal restraints. The root causes for Jamaica's crisis were financial liberalization without "a sufficiently robust prudential and supervisory infrastructure" (according the IMF), the onset of a severe recession, foreign exchange volatility, and a loss of confidence.[56] While the Dominican Republic and Jamaica have had near-collapses, Cuba, with its socialist-caudillo system, out and out defaulted on its external debt during the early 1990s. This increased its reliance on Venezuela in the early twenty-first century for financial and oil assistance.

Although gunboat diplomacy has ended, the threat of economic collapse linked to excessive leverage lingers throughout parts of the Caribbean. Haiti is an extreme case as the forces of nature, human ineptitude, and greed have generated a dismal track record. Small countries remain vulnerable to larger political and economic forces. In a world defined by globalization, particularly in the field of finance, these vulnerabilities are exacerbated. Interconnectedness, however, can also bring additional support to developing economies through debt forgiveness, low-interest loans, and investment in their future. It will remain the task of new Caribbean leaders to leverage these links rather than their balance sheets. They must work with their people and with bankers and industrialists from around the world to make sure that investment develops real growth and not simply quick profits. Shortsighted greed is too vulnerable to the changing wind.

## Notes

1. While the Caribbean was often referred to as the "backyard" of the United States, Egypt and North Africa increasingly came under a European sphere of influence. The British eventually emerged as the primary European power in Egypt through financial affairs. Egypt's ruler at the time, Ismail, was a great modernizer building railways, roads, bridges, telegraph and postal services, and upgrading the school system. The Khedive also had shares in the Suez Canal, largely built with British and French money. While Ismail appeared to preside over an independent and modernizing Egypt, the reality was that he had saddled his country with enormous and unpayable debts. In 1875 Ismail's financial irresponsibility resulted in Egypt's shares in the Suez Canal being bought by the British government under Benjamin Disraeli. The end result of Ismail's financial recklessness and predatory foreign investors was the slow, steady loss of sovereignty. Professor Derek Hopwood observed of Ismail: "his desires and wild tastes were exploited by others an despite his contributions to the development of Egypt his debts ensured its subjection to Europe and eventually to Britain." By 1876 Ismail ran out of money and postponed his payments. From this point Egypt slid into a British protectorate, only to re-emerge from British dominance in the early 1950s. See Derek Hopwood, *Egypt: Politics and Society 1945-1984* (Boston: Unwin Hyman, 1985), pp. 11-12.
2. Brenda Gayle Plummer, *Haiti and the United States: The Psychological Moment* (Athens: The University of Georgia Press, 1992), p. 82.
3. Edmund Morris, *Theodore Rex* (New York: Random House, 2001), pp. 177-178.
4. Plummer, *Haiti and the United States*, p. 84.
5. Frank Moya Pons, *The Dominican Republic: A National History* (Princeton, N.J.: First Markus Weiner Publishers edition 1998, 1995), p. 178.
6. Báez's way of raising money is described by Moya Pons: "After having the seven-member Senate extended the presidential powers to issue money, he authorized the printing of 18 million more pesos on the pretext that the old money was badly deteriorated and that there was a dangerous lack of currency to cover the needs of the tobacco dealers in the Cibao. The new bills were then divided among his favorites and protégés who then travelled to the Cibao to buy as much tobacco and gold as they could. When this scheme was discovered, it was already too late for the Cibao merchants to recuperate their money. The Cibao farmers and merchants who had accepted the old paper money at an exchange rate of 50:1 soon found themselves ruined by the flood of new bills that greatly decreased the value of the national peso. Báez had not been popular in the Cibao since 1849 when he attempted to set up a tobacco monopoly with some French associates, and now the tobacco growers and dealers decided to revolt." Moya Pons, *The Dominican Republic*, p. 191.

7. Moya Pons, *The Dominican Republic*, p. 197.
8. Coming out of the Civil War (1861-1865), the United States was gradually asserting its influence outside of continental North America. Considering the French intervention in Mexico, the Caribbean remained a fluid political region with a number of European powers active in seeking influence or maintaining their possessions, like Britain, France, Spain, and the Netherlands. Consequently, a US naval base in the region had a certain strategic attraction.
9. R.W. Logan, *Haiti and the Dominican Republic* (New York: Oxford University Press, 1968), p. 45.
10. Melvin M. Knight, *The Americans in Santo Domingo* (New York: Vanguard Press, 1928), pp. 16-17.
11. Moya Pons, *The Dominican Republic*, p. 242.
12. G. Pope Atkins and Larman Curtis Wilson, *The Dominican Republic and the United States: From Imperialism to Transnationalism* (Athens, Georgia: University of Georgia Press, 1998), p. 29.
13. *Ibid.*, p. 80.
14. Atkins and Wilson, *The Dominican Republic and the United States*, p. 30.
15. H. Hoetink, *The Dominican Republic 1850-1900: Notes for a Historical Sociology* (Baltimore: The Johns Hopkins University Press, 1982), p. 88.
16. The Curaçao-Sephardic connection was critical to the European connection.
17. Hoetink, p. 88.
18. Atkins and Wilson, *The Dominican Republic and the United States*, p. 30.
19. "San Domingo Is Willing: Agrees to the Scheme of Her American Debt Holders," *The New York Times*, February 11, 1893.
20. Moya Pons, *The Dominican Republic*, p. 272. Hoetink: *The Dominican People*, p. 90.
21. Moya Pons, *The Dominican Republic*, p. 273.
22. Hoetink, *The Dominican People*, p. 90.
23. Moya Pons, *The Dominican Republic* p. 278.
24. Cyrus Veeser, *A World Safe for Capitalism: Dollar Diplomacy and America's Rise to Global Power* (New York: Columbia University Press, 2002), p. 5.
25. Heinl, Heinl, and Heinl, *Written in Blood,* p. 337.
26. Robert Debs Heinl, Nancy Gordon Heinl, and Michael Heinl, *Written in Blood: The Story of the Haitian People, 1492-1995* (New York: University Press of America, Inc., 1996), p. 374.
27. Quoted from Heinl, Heinl, and Heinl, *Written in Blood*, p. 378. Taken from Stephen Alexis, "In Memoriam," *Le Matin* (Paup). 27 July 1932, also *Le Matin*, 29 July 1995.
28. Robert Rotberg, *Haiti, The Politics of Squalor* (Boston, 1971), p. 109.
29. Heinl, Heinl, and Heinl, *Written in Blood* , p. 385.
30. For a detailed account of this and the Cuban sugar industry see Alan B. Dye, *Cuban Sugar in the Age of Mass Production: Technology and the Economics of the Sugar Central, 1899-1929* (Palo Alto, CA.: Stanford University Press, 1998).
31. Sugar beet production is historically a new development. Around 1590 the French botanist Oliver de Serres extracted a sweet syrup from beetroot. Mainstream production took much longer, beginning in Prussia around 1801. The stimulus for more industrial production came in 1807 when the British began a blockade of France. This prevented the import of sugar from the Caribbean. Napoleon was to impose his own embargo on trade with the British. By the end of the Napoleonic wars in 1815 over 300 sugar beet mills were in operation in France and central Europe.
32. Hubert Edson. *Sugar: From Scarcity to Surplus* (New York: Chemical Publishing Co., Inc., 1958), p. 118. Edson began in the Caribbean industry in 1888 and was

to retire only in 1950. This book is a narrative of his experiences in Cuba, Haiti, and the Dominican Republic.

33. William Belmont Parker, *Cubans of To-Day* (New York: G.P. Putnam's Sons, 1919).
34. Speck, "Prosperity, Progress and Wealth," *Cuban Studies,* p. 75.
35. Ibid., p. 72.
36. *Ibid.*, p. 73.
37. Thomas, *Cuba*, p. 538.
38. *Ibid.,* p. 538.
39. Speck, pp. 73-74.
40. Edson, *Sugar*, p. 126.
41. Ibid., p. 128.
42  Thomas, *Cuba*, p. 525.
43  Lealand H. Jenks, *Our Cuban Colony: A Study in Sugar* (New York: Vanguard Press, 1928).
44. Thomas, *Cuba*, p. 540.
45. Edson, *Sugar*, p. 186.
46. *Ibid.*
47. Edson, *Sugar*, p. 187.
48. Speck, p. 74.
49. *Ibid.*
50. Kevin Grogan, "Cuba's Dance of the Millions: Examining the Causes and Consequences of Violent Price Fluctuations in the Sugar Market Between 1919 and 1920," A Thesis presented to the Graduate School of the University of Florida in Partial Fulfillment of the Requirements for the Degree of Masters of Arts, University of Florida, 2004, p. 63.
51. Thomas, *Cuba,* p. 549.
52. Speck, p. 75. As Hugh Thomas stated: "The only credit-worthy institutions were foreign—the National City Bank and the Royal Bank of Canada.... These two banks met their obligations and lived on, greatly profiting as a result." Thomas, *Cuba*, p. 550.
53. Henry Christopher Wallinch, *Monetary Problems of an Export Economy: The Cuban Experience 1914-1917* (Boston: Harvard University Press, 1950).
54. Harvey Morris, Benedict Mander, and Robin Kwong, "Ministers Urged to Cancel Haiti Debt," *Financial Times*, January 26, 2010, p. 2.
55. USAID, Dominican Republic, An Economic Snapshot," December 2005 (Washington, D.C.). http://www.usaid.gov/our-work/cross-cutting -programs/wid/pubs/ Dominican Republic_Economic_Snapshot_Dec 2005.pdf.
56. International Monetary Fund, Jamaica: Staff Report for the 1999 Article IV Consultation, January 2000, IMF Country Report NO 0/8 (Washington, D.C.), p. 5.

# 4

# Austria, Credit-Anstalt, and the Great Depression

In early May 1931, Austria's largest banking house, the Credit-Anstalt, secretly informed the Austrian government that it had sustained massive losses during 1930 amounting to some 140,000,000 schillings ($20 million). The notification was done quietly, away from the eyes of a nervous public and with the intention of staving off a panicked run on the banks. In spite of the attempts at secrecy, by the middle of the month, news of the bank's financial troubles was making headlines across Europe. The bank's losses, reported the international press, came from three major sources: massive debt from the recent acquisition of a competing large bank with a poor balance sheet—the Bodencreditanstalt (which had suffered significant reverses because of the financial crash of 1929); losses from having to write off bad debts (including major loans to industry); and losses from depreciation of Credit-Anstalt's securities portfolio, again a result of the 1929 stock market crash in New York.[1]

Although a single bank, the Credit-Anstalt was a central pillar of the Austrian financial system. It had investments throughout Central Europe and investors throughout the world. To political and economic leaders throughout Europe, Credit-Anstalt was an essential edifice of the financial landscape; it was too big to fail. Massive pressures, however, were pushing Credit-Anstalt in precisely that direction. At the same time, Credit-Anstalt's weakness reflected a broader vulnerability present in the global economy. The troubles of Austria and Credit-Anstalt were symbolic of a world economy about to lurch deeper into what was to become known as the Great Depression. In some ways, Credit-Anstalt's crisis exacerbated the perilous descent that commenced with Wall Street's crash in 1929. If nothing else, Credit-Anstalt's collapse made certain that the depression was more global and protracted than it would have been otherwise.

In spite of its external effects, Credit-Anstalt's collapse was very much an Austria problem with Austrian causes. The dissolution of the Austro-Hungarian Empire in 1919 radically altered the political landscape of central Europe and left the newly formed Austrian nation politically adrift and economically vulnerable. Political extremism, a lack of democratic traditions, and a number of constraints imposed by the victorious powers all contributed to Austrian weakness. At the same time, the crisis was also the result of particular banking practices pursued by Credit-Anstalt: the over-concentration of loans in the hands of a few borrowers, unwise acquisitions (some forced by the Austrian government), and opaque dealings.

Credit-Anstalt's structure had helped create its problems. In the mould of a modern private equity firm, the bank had invested directly (and heavily) in industry. In addition, $75 million of its $250 million deposit base came from international investors.[2] These investors, skittish about the prospects of the Austrian economy and political events in central Europe were among the first to pull their money out. This capital flight created pressure on Austria's currency, its gold reserves, and on Credit-Anstalt's deposit cover.

Still, many of the reasons behind Credit-Anstalt's problems were the result of factors outside of its control: the global depression gripping the entire financial system in the wake of the 1929 stock market crash in New York, Austria's shaky economic foundations (the result of the re-drawing of central Europe after the First World War), the political weakness of Austria's embryonic democracy, and the absence of any international body large enough and strong enough to act to provide Austria the support necessary to avoid a financial meltdown. For Credit-Anstalt it would prove a lethal combination.

The purpose of this chapter is to examine the rise and fall of Credit-Anstalt and its role in the economic collapse of Austria during the early 1930s. Credit-Anstalt's failure was to trigger a major banking panic that spread from Austria to Hungary, to Germany, England, and eventually to the United States. Although Austria was a small nation with a GDP of $1.5 billion and a population of less than 7 million people, the collapse of its banking system proved catastrophic both locally and abroad. As Credit-Anstalt collapsed in Austria, the panic spread to the German banking sector bringing down several important financial houses and precipitating a massive government rescue.

Political instability went hand in glove with the economic pain in both Austria and Germany. Weak and ineffective governments were threatened by totalitarian groups on both the left and right wings. They confronted massive social unrest stemming from currency depreciation and systemic unemployment. Enormous public debts and the burden of war reparations constrained economic policy even further. When faced with a crisis like the failure of Credit-Anstalt, options were limited. Unsuccessful attempts to rescue the financial situation created a revolving door of governments as various parties, each unable to reverse the economic decline, vied for power.

Many of the challenges confronting Austrian and German politicians, financiers, and bankers were related to the particular circumstances prevailing in the two countries in the early 1930s. Defeat in the First World War, reparations, the replacement of the old autocratic empires with unsteady new democracies, and the Global Depression were all major factors. At the same time, the challenges of banks with gruesome balance sheets wracked with debt, of politicians injecting liquidity in a frantic effort to avoid panics and collapse, of wage cuts, bad loans, strikes, civil disorder, and political instability, are as relevant today as they were in the 1930s. These facts make the story of Credit-Anstalt essential reading in the discussion of financial panic in small economies.

## The Rise and Fall of Credit-Anstalt

Credit-Anstalt was founded in Vienna in 1855. The bank's original name was the *Österreichische Credit-Anstalt für Handel und Gewerbe*—the Imperial and Royal Austrian Credit Institute for Commerce and Industry or Credit-Anstalt. The new institution was modeled along the lines of the Parisian Credit Mobilier, with interests in long-term industrial loans as well as short-term deposits.[3] Although the Rothschilds were closely associated with what was the empire's first major financial institution and at times contributed leadership, with the active encouragement of the government, Credit-Anstalt was the major instrument of the country's wealthy business elite in national economic development. It is important to underscore that the formation of Credit-Anstalt was an indication that the Hapsburgs were increasingly more comfortable with *laissez-faire* precepts in economics, limiting itself to infrastructure and commercial agreements.

The linkage to the Rothschild banking empire was important to Credit-Anstalt. Credit-Anstalt was a complement to the Jewish financier family's other branches in Germany, Britain, France, and Italy. Credit-Anstalt was formed at a time when the Rothschilds were focusing on Vienna as the main support for their investments in central European railroad construction. Railways were a booming industry in mid-nineteenth century Austria, and the Rothschild's were determined to prevent rival banking families from gaining access to this lucrative business.[4]

For the Rothschilds, the choice of Vienna was a natural one. The city on the Danube, and Austria more generally, sits astride some of the most important communications systems in Europe. It connected southern Germany, northern Italy, and the Adriatic.[5] Vienna was a major cosmopolitan capital and the center of the powerful multinational Habsburg Empire that had dominated central Europe for centuries.

The Rothschild family patriarch, Meyer Amschel Rothschild (born 1744), began his career as a "court Jew" and rose to prominence in Frankfurt as a money lender.[6] Meyer had considerable vision and sent his five sons to different cities in Europe to establish a network of banks, based on family ties. Rothschild branches were soon operating in Frankfurt, Vienna, London, Naples, and Paris. The Viennese branch was established by Salomon Mayer von Rothschild in 1820. The official name of the new firm was S.M. von Rothschild, which was largely involved in financing government projects. The firm did exceedingly well. Its adroit handling of rail finance and political sensitivity in the imperial capital helped it to become an important part of the Habsburg Empire's financial network. Rothschild financing was integral to large-scale projects such as Emperor Ferdinand's *Nordbahn*, Austria's first steam engine powered rail system.

The Rothschilds's success in the Habsburg Empire was quickly reflected in the ability of the family to climb the social ladder. This was evident as early as 1822, when Salomon was granted the hereditary title of baron by Emperor Francis II. The Viennese Rothschilds' financial influence took another major step forward when Salomon's son, Anselm von Rothschild, organized and largely financed the Credit-Anstalt. This rapidly expanded into the most significant bank in the Habsburg Empire with branches in Prague, Budapest, Brno, Kronstadt, Trieste, and Lemberg. For the next three-quarters of a century, the bank would be the dominant force in Austrian finance. Credit-Anstalt had the advantage of being the biggest bank in the one of the most significant empires in the world, dominating much of central Europe and the Balkans. Although it might be somewhat grandiose to say that the business of Credit-Anstalt was the business of the empire, the statement is not far removed from reality, especially considering the access enjoyed by the bank's management to the top tiers of the imperial government.

It was hardly surprising that the dismemberment of the Habsburg Empire following its defeat in the First World War dramatically reduced the scope and stability of institutions like the Credit-Anstalt. The global conflict had brought four empires to ruin: the Austro-Hungarian, the Russian, the Ottoman, and the German. Even the victorious powers like France and Britain faced a financial reckoning, having spent hundreds of millions and borrowed hundreds of millions more (almost all of it from the United States) in order to achieve victory. To compensate themselves, they levied massive reparations from Germany and Austria. These reparations would not only help the victors replenish their financial losses, but, as was hoped by France in particular, would render Germany incapable of waging another war.

While the economic terms of the peace were harsh, the political terms were revolutionary. The entire structure of Europe was redrawn. An independent Poland emerged for the first time in more than one hundred years. The territories of Alsace and Lorraine were returned to France from the now defunct German Empire. The Austro-Hungarian Empire was also dissolved and four new countries were created: Austria, Czechoslovakia, Yugoslavia, and Hungary. Credit-Anstalt would have to find its way in a completely different world.

Austria emerged from the First World War as a shadow of itself. Under the terms of the Treaty of St. Germain-en-Laye (1919), the former metropole of the polyglot Austro-Hungarian Empire was shorn of most of its territory and became one of several small, central European states. The army of the "Republic of German Austria," as the new state was called, was reduced to a volunteer force of 30,000 men. Like Germany, the new Austrian government was forced to pay heavy reparations to the victorious allied powers. An imperial center no longer, Austria's economy changed dramatically. In addition to the territorial losses and reparation payments, the peace agreement also included prohibitions against closer economic and political ties with the new German Republic leaving Austria economically adrift and vulnerable.

The order created by the victorious allies failed to live up to its own principles of liberty and national self-determination, severing Austria's six and a half million German-speakers from another four million who ended up in the new non-German states of Hungary, Yugoslavia, and Czechoslovakia. Austria was expressly forbidden from unification with Germany and any move in this direction was vehemently opposed by the allies, particularly by France.

The new creation, soon renamed the "Republic of Austria" faced massive economic challenges. Riots, strikes, and armed battles in the street caused by unemployment and political infighting, became a regular feature of life between late 1918 and early 1920. As in Germany, extremism both from the left and from the right undermined the effective exercise of democracy. In the years immediately after the war, Allied food aid was necessary to sustain many Austrians as inflation and the collapse of wartime savings bonds bankrupted much of the country's middle class.[7] Territorial truncation left Vienna in particularly dire straits. Like many imperial metropoles, it had relied on the periphery for basic goods. Coal and industrial materials came from Bohemia (part of the new Czechoslovakia), food supplies from Hungary. Neither new country felt much sympathy for the old imperial capital, nor had they much desire to provide assistance without a price and Austria was hardly in a position to pay.[8] The basic necessities became rare and expensive.

The political system had changed too. The rule of the Habsburgs, Austria's monarchs since the thirteenth century, ended in 1918. Although the empire had developed a parliament and political parties during the reforms of the nineteenth century, real authority had remained within the imperial palace and with the empire's bureaucracy. In fact, the Habsburg state had been one of the most reactionary and authoritarian in Europe, leaving the new republic with no tradition of exercising political power through elected governments. This meant a weak democratic tradition, a poor understanding of parliamentary dynamics, and a penchant for strong political figures.

When Emperor Karl I, the last Hapsburg ruler, was officially banished from Austria in 1919, Austria's political system was ill-prepared for the future. Autocratic rule was replaced by a fledgling democracy, rent by political divisions and swamped with economic difficulties. The 1920 parliamentary elections brought a weak coalition government to power, which struggled to make any headway against the myriad problems confronting the Austrian state. It was not until 1922 that Ignaz Seipel was able to form an effective center-right government. Seipel's government provided a more unified face to the outside world and provided Austria the opportunities to go in search of economic assistance abroad.

Seipel served two terms as Austria's chancellor: 1922-24 and 1926-29. Described as "very tall, stoop-shouldered and beak-nosed," he was a Roman Catholic priest, ordained in 1899.[9] Before the war, he taught moral philosophy at the universities of Salzburg and Vienna. With the end of the empire, Seipel emerged as one of the leaders in the Christian

Democratic Party. Deeply conservative, he worked hard to keep the Social Democrats out of office. This policy led him depend more and more on nationalist and right-wing forces to maintain his power. Nevertheless, by 1922 Seipel was seen by many Austrians as a savvy political player capable of pulling the country from its troubles.

In the disjointed times that followed the end of the war, inflation spiraled. Economic hardship raised the age-old question of closer relations with Germany, but the allies would have none of it. In 1922, Seipel secured a supervised loan from the League of Nations in order to prevent bankruptcy. Austria paid a heavy cost for the loan as it promised that the question of *Anschluss* (unification with Germany) would be postponed for twenty years, that a League of Nations commission would supervise Austrian finance (a humiliating circumstance for this once world power), and that an immediate reform would be undertaken so that the budget would be balanced in two years.[10] Opposition to the agreement was widespread, in particular to the clause pertaining to *Anschluss*. Nevertheless, the League of Nations program was relatively successful in stabilizing the Austrian economy. Buoyed by the loan, and the creation of a new currency, the schilling, in March 1925, the Austrian economy enjoyed a brief recovery (marked by a fall in inflation) during the second half of the 1920s. There was little cause to hope, however. The fundamental weaknesses of the system remained; Austria was simply building on sand.

This "sand" factor was evident in the banking system. Although the general economy appeared more stable by the mid-1920s, the banking system still struggled. The break-up of the empire, the creation of new countries and the difficult nature of economies through much of Central and Eastern Europe created an unsettled banking environment. As trade and industrial relations within the former empire sought to find a new equilibrium, old banking relationships came under strain. New competitors rose, some of them closely affiliated with the new national elites.

Yet, the brave new world of banking did not turn out as expected. Dr. Max Sokal, manager of the *Wiener Giro-und Kaessen-Verein* in Vienna observed in 1921: "It was prophesied of Austrian Banks, that after the collapse of the Austro-Hungarian Monarchy they have greatly to reduce their establishments on account of the diminution of their sphere of action, the vastness of their organizations being wholly out of proportion to the requirements of crippled Austria."[11] Yet, many of the banks that survived the war and the end of the monarchy went in entirely the opposite direction—expansion. As Sokal observed further:

So far this hypothesis [of contraction] has been disproved by facts. The banks very soon had to extend their business, to increase their staff, to enlarge their premises; and the turnover of the last financial year, where balance sheets are already available, shows a consideration surplus over that of preceding periods, a surplus, which is, of course, partly accounted for by the steady depreciation of the Austrian currency.[12]

The banking landscape faced its own painful new realities. Austria's new neighbors (and former subjects) instituted regulations restricting the operations of foreign banks. In Czechoslovakia, branches of foreign banks were limited to five years of operation and subject to numerous conditions during that time. This struck directly at institutions like Credit-Anstalt that had previously conducted business across central Europe. Moreover, the collapse of Austria's currency, the kronen, in the wake of the aftermath of the war had "stimulated dealings in foreign exchanges in Austria."[13] Austrian banks thus became vulnerable not only to the weakness of the Austrian currency, but also to the fact that foreign funds could be drained from their accounts at a whiff of instability.

Sokal's analysis in 1921 highlighted a number of vulnerabilities for the ever-expanding Austrian banks: their debt exposure, their political limitations placed on their operations, their reliance on foreign investment, and the depreciating Austrian kronen. These unstable economic and monetary conditions were to bedevil the banks for years to come. Any expansion of operations left institutions over-exposed in terms of operational costs and lending risks. At the very best the Austrian banks remained fragile throughout much of the 1920s. In 1924, two large banks, the Central Bank of the German Savings Bank and the Postal Savings Bank both failed. Although the damage of these failures was contained, the signal of more bad things to come was there for anyone willing to look beyond the surface. It was in this shaky environment that Credit-Anstalt continued to expand.

It should also be noted that Austrian politics contributed to the poor business environment. Although Ignaz Seipel was to remain the major force in Austrian politics through the 1920s, the political arena was hardly settled. His party maintained a majority in the parliament, but the Social Democrats, and the left remained a major force in the nation's political life. In fact, the Socialist party was particularly strong in the nation's capital, which was referred to at times as "Red Vienna." Both the left and right developed their own armed wings, which often  transformed political disagreements into street violence.

As in Germany, the Austrian right developed significant paramilitary forces in the form of the *Heimwehr* (Home Guard) and the *Heimatschutz*

(Homeland Defense). Composed of a heterogenous mix of religious conservatives, anti-Marxists, hardliner Royalists from the army, and unrepentant pan-German nationalists, these groups were based largely outside of Vienna. By the mid 1920s, these right-wing militias became more ideologically cohesive due to the influence of the rise of Italian fascism. Under the leadership of Prince Ernst Rudiger von Starhemberg the *Heimwehr* morphed into a far-right political party supporting *volkish* notions of German identity and vehemently opposing communism. In the 1930 parliamentary elections, a new right-wing government emerged, minus the *Heimwehr*. This government embarked upon negotiations with Germany over a customs union in March 1931. It was with this political backdrop that Credit-Anstalt entered its final days.

Although Credit-Anstalt's position deteriorated rapidly in the spring of 1931, its problems had not occurred overnight. They were the result of a chain of events reflecting both the political and economic weaknesses of Austria. Economic recovery, such as it was, during the 1920s only brought Austria's economy back to its 1913 levels by 1929. Inflation and currency pressure remained a major concern for the government even after the introduction of the schilling in 1925. One financial historian argued that the Austrian government, in fact, "had no economic policy" and watched ineptly as inflationary pressures pushed wages up 24 percent from 1925 to 1929. The government's social benefits bill also bloated out of control, rising from 258 million schillings to 383 million schillings over the same period. The government had no choice by to raise taxes, constricting economic growth even further.[14]

The hopes of any manner of recovery were firmly dashed in 1929 with the crash of the American stock market in New York. In two trading days, October 28 and 29, the market on Wall Street plunged from 298.97 to 230.07 a decline of slightly more than 23 percent. Entire fortunes were wiped out; companies were bankrupted. While stories of brokers leaping to the deaths from windows are in all likelihood fabrications, there were several recorded suicides. The financial carnage spread from Wall Street and rippled through the entire US economy. The banking sector and the government appeared powerless to contain or repair the damage; in fact, the tightening of liquidity by the authorities proved fatal. The stock market decline continued, reaching an all-time low of 41.22 in July 1932.

In 1931, Austria was firmly mired in the global depression. Business activity and industrial production had already contracted sharply between 1929 and 1931. By 1931, Austria had been in recession for approximately

18 months.[15] Austria's economic troubles had created major problems for Credit-Anstalt. During Austria's contraction, the bank, faced with mounting government pressure, had agreed to absorb the country's second largest bank, the Bodenkreditanstalt. Bodenkreditanstalt was insolvent and faced significant exposure to Austria's shrinking industrial sector. The acquisition made Credit-Anstalt the largest financial institution in the country with total assets that exceeded "all other Austrian joint stock banks combined."[16] Credit-Anstalt was so large, in fact, that its balance sheet equaled the expenditures of the Austrian government.[17] This bloating of Credit-Anstalt was the primary reason why politicians regarded it as "too big to fail" and were forced to exhaust all courses in an attempt to save it.

Despite the economic crisis, there is reason to believe that Credit-Anstalt's difficulties went back further in the decade. Evidence from the bank's records suggests that Credit-Anstalt was manipulating its balance sheet from as early as 1925, reporting profits that "were not really earned."[18] The challenging economic conditions of the 1920s resulted in Austrian bankers taking greater risks in search of profits. Regulation was minimal, and after the dislocation and hardships of the war, investors were desperate for a return to profitability.

Credit-Anstalt made its losses for 1930 (some $20 million) public on May 11, 1931. The losses practically wiped out the bank's equity.[19] Credit-Anstalt was now at the mercy of Austrian law and the Austrian government. Simply stated, Austrian law required any bank with losses of more than half its capital to close down. Credit-Anstalt's position was untenable.[20] It needed an immediate injection of liquidity if it was to avoid collapse. In a series of secret meetings, the Austrian government scrambled to bail out Credit-Anstalt with the help of emergency loans from leading foreign banks and international financiers. By some estimates, the bank had responsibility for the credit of almost two-thirds of the country's industries.[21] Although this figure is disputed,[22] the bank did control 50 percent of Austria's deposits to the tune of $250 million.[23]

The Austrian government, now headed by Chancellor Otto Ender, scrambled to assemble a bailout package. On May 29, the Austrian parliament voted to guarantee Credit-Anstalt's liabilities and "credits to ease its financial difficulties" were supplied "partly from abroad and partly by the Austrian Government."[24] Support loans were also pledged by the Rothschilds and the Austrian National Bank.

Domestic and international investors were not mollified by the emergency measures. The public reaction was one of nervous agitation. As one observer stated:

Day after desperate day frightened depositors swarmed around the threatened institution, talked earnestly with each other and with officials who worked overtime reassuring the public. Every depositor who refused to be reassured got his money, but the currency of Austria had to be inflated to keep Kreditanstalt open and paying out.[25]

Investors' confidence in the Austrian banking system had been fundamentally shaken. Over the weeks that followed, tens of millions of schillings were withdrawn as banks throughout the country came under pressure. In response, the Austrian central bank "injected some 235 million schillings [$33.57 million]" of liquidity between May 7 and June 1 "causing note circulation to rise by more than 25%." Fear spread that Austria might be facing an inflationary crisis similar to the hyperinflation that had rocked Germany in 1923.[26] By June 6, the Austrian National Bank's cover for the total amount in circulation amounted to 57.1 percent, down from 67 percent only two weeks before. The Austrian government could not afford to keep Credit-Anstalt afloat on its own; it needed help from abroad.

Over the two weeks between May 14 and May 31, telephone calls and telegrams crisscrossed Europe and the Atlantic, Washington, Berlin, London, Paris, Geneva, and Vienna discussing how to pull Austria away from the precipice of financial ruin and political collapse. After all the wrangling, the Bank of International Settlements, supported by the Bank of England, "arranged a loan of 100 million schillings ($14 million) from the ten largest central banks." As economist Charles Kindleberger lamented, "the niggardliness of the sum and the delay together proved disastrous."[27] None of the central bankers involved had had any experience with a crisis on this scale. Their response was dilatory and feeble. By June 5, the Austrian National Bank had blown through the loan and was requesting more funds. $40 million [280 million schillings] of its $110 million [770 million schillings] in gold reserves had drained away. Austria's entire banking system was "under threat" and its currency "under siege."[28]

Internationally, the Austrian government continued to seek additional funds while appealing for a customs union with Germany as another strategy to prop itself up. France played a key role in pressuring the Austrian government to abandon the customs union as a condition for financial assistance. While negotiations for a new loan continued, the Austrian government refused to abandon the customs union and fell. At the Bank of England, Governor Norman unilaterally forwarded Vienna another 50 million schillings [$7 million] for one week as a stop-gap measure.[29]

Credit-Anstalt's vulnerability soon started to ripple through other banks and financial institutions with devastating effect. One example was the case of the historic private bank of Auspitz, Lieben & Co. According to the American publication, *Time* magazine, Credit-Anstalt began actively calling in as many of its loans as possible, including a loan with the Auspitz, Lieben & Co.[30] The bank, like Credit-Anstalt, had suffered from the New York crash and the early stages of the Depression. It was in no state to pay up. Upon receiving news of the loan call, the company's chairman, Stephen Auspitz attempted to commit suicide by jumping into the Danube. He was, however, held back by friends. His partner, Dr. Ludwig Schiller, was less fortunate. Schiller went to the banks of the Danube and shot himself. Seven days later, his body was pulled out of the river a hundred miles from Vienna.

What happened at Auspitz, Lieben & Co. that put the company in such dire straits? According to the firm's officials, since 1924 they were making large bets to put the bank on firmer financial standing. Sadly, their speculations failed. As a *Time* magazine reporter noted:

> They speculated against the French franc, were fooled and lost heavily when Raymond Poincaré stabilized and rehabilitated the money of his country. Second they invested in Dutch industrials, lost more. Third they got in on the Wall Street boom, making so much that, even though they lost much in the crash, Wall Street gave them no coup de grace.[31]

It was reported that once Stephen Auspitz regained his composure, he sold his "priceless" collection of Italian paintings, which had featured on loan during an exhibition in London the year prior. The turmoil to hit Auspitz, Lieben & Co. was not unique to that institution, but repeated at other financial firms throughout the country. Credit-Anstalt's insolvency, it seemed, was only the tip of Austria's financial iceberg.

In Austria, the Ender government promptly sent emissaries to Berlin and London as well as the Bank for International Settlements, seeking further assistance. Feelers also went out to Germany for the establishment of a customs union. France refused any move in this direction. With plans for a customs union scuttled, the reception in Berlin was neither warm nor fruitful. In London, however, the Rothschild connection provided some utility. The British branch was moved by the plight of its brother house in Vienna and urged the powerful Bank of England Governor Montagu Norman to provide additional support. A British consortium was formed, offering $60 million. However, the consortium demanded that for bailing out Credit-Anstalt, it wanted its $60 million to be guaranteed by the

Austrian Treasury. This, in turn, created a political squawk as earlier creditors also demanded the government guarantee their loans.

The Chancellor and his cabinet went into a lengthy meeting that went until 2:30 am. When the meeting finished, Ender emerged to announce to correspondents: "No limit is fixed by a bill which we shall introduce in Parliament today. The State assumes liability for whatever new credit may be required by Kreditanstalt."[32] The chancellor was pressed about the rights of the "old creditors," who were said to have put up $110 million, and responded "A great exaggeration!" The parliament quickly passed the Ender bill.

By the middle of June, the political fallout began. On June 17, the minister of the interior resigned, triggering the resignation of Chancellor Ender and the entire cabinet. As *The Times* reported, "the fall of the government is more immediately the consequence of the Credit-Anstalt crisis and the assumption by the government of greater responsibility than the minister of the interior thought he could answer for to his supporters."[33] Ender had managed to contain the financial panic, but his political support evaporated. The poor treatment of the old creditors damaged the chancellor's reputation and many Austrians were unsettled at the state assuming the burden of the failed financial institution.

The political fallout continued. Nationalists were furious over the abandonment of the customs union with Germany. In September, the *Heimwehr*'s fascist leader, Walter Pfrimer, attempted a coup in the style of Mussolini's famous "march on Rome." Its planning and execution were so poor, and Pfrimer so unimpressive as an orator and leader, that even the weak government of Ender's successor, Karl Buresch, was able to suppress the putsch with ease. Still, Austria lacked leadership powerful or capable enough to reverse the downward trend.

Austria's economy, like its politics, continued to deteriorate. In 1931, with the banking crisis ranging, unemployment was 20 percent. It continued to climb, reaching a crippling high of almost 40 percent by 1934. The government's continuing budget crisis (with revenues deteriorating with the massive loss of jobs) meant that many of the unemployed had to make do without benefits.[34]

As confidence in the government shrank, measures to restore the confidence and balance sheet of Credit-Anstalt were afoot. In early July, the bank's new Director-General announced plans to reduce the salaries and pensions of leading figures within the bank. In October, 25 of 28 directors and deputy-directors were dismissed. Another former director was charged with fraudulent bankruptcy and cashing bad checks. Having fled to France, the Austrian government asked for his extradition. Like Credit-Anstalt, Austria itself planned belt-tightening measures. In the budget for 1932, the number of plays at the State Theatre and Opera House would be reduced. Free rail passes would be cancelled. It was hardly a pure austerity budget, but it was trying to nudge Austria in the right direction in the teeth of massive unemployment and a global depression. In many ways it was too little, too late. Buresch's austerity measures failed to convince Austrian voters and he was replaced as chancellor in May 1932 by fascist leader Engelbert Dollfuss. Dollfuss was an outspoken opponent of Adolf Hitler, choosing to model his party and leadership style on Benito Mussolini instead. Together, the two fascist leaders hoped to provide a counter to the ambitions of both Hitler and Stalin.

Austria's economic decline, dramatic though it was, was still less than Credit-Anstalt's. Within a few months, the bank had gone from being one of the largest and most powerful financial institutions in Austria to a government-controlled bankruptcy case. Savings deposits had dropped 74 percent, checking deposits, a stunning 80 percent between March and August 1931. Credit-Anstalt's share of all deposits in the Austrian banking sector as a whole had contracted from 16.3 percent to only 4 percent over the same four-month period.[35] The fall had been nothing short of spectacular. Worst of all, Germany, Austria's neighbor and the world's third largest economy was about to face a crisis similar in nature, but far larger in size. In Germany, the political aftershocks would be of a far more devastating nature too.

## The Storm Out of Vienna

Credit-Anstalt's failure sent shockwaves through the European banking system and the world economy. Indeed, the Bank of England's Harry Siepmann, a senior advisor to Governor Norman, stated: "This, I think, is it, and it may well bring down the whole house of cards in which we have been living."[36] As governments and institutions scrambled to cope with the crisis, write off bad debts, restructure balance sheets, and inject liquidity into Austria's collapsing economy, the Great Depression took root. In neighboring Germany, the panic spread through the banking sector causing a rash of bank failures. The political fallout in Germany was also severe. The National Socialist, or "Nazi," Party fed off people's fears and disaffection to score a major success at the polls in the summer of 1932. By the start of 1933, democracy in Germany was dead and Adolf Hitler firmly in power.

While the collapse of Credit-Anstalt was a thunderbolt to Austria's small economy, the wider financial crisis developed slowly and had begun before the bank's troubled balance sheet became public knowledge. While a complete financial meltdown was avoided—barely—the panic of 1931 brought down several major European banking houses, Austrian democracy, and Germany's Weimar Republic.

Austria's troubles caused immediate pressure on the German banking sector. A great deal of German capital was tied up in Austria but, more importantly, the financial world "had never drawn much of a distinction between the banking situation in Berlin and that in Vienna." Investors were quick to conclude that "if the main Austrian bank was in such serious trouble, it was very possible that a German bank might soon follow."[37] German gold reserves began to hemorrhage. As part of the terms of its loan from the international community, the Austrian government had secured a moratorium on its debt, rumors spread that Germany was seeking a similar halt to reparations payments.

The political situation in Germany teetered on the brink of revolution. Chancellor Brüning declared a state of emergency on June 5 and used his emergency powers to enforce new austerity measures: civil service salaries, military pensions, unemployment benefits, and welfare services were slashed. Taxes were raised. Not surprisingly, there was public outrage. Nazi and communist agitation was at a fever pitch; open street battles among social democrats, Nazis, and communists became a daily feature of life. Brüning made plans to counter a potential popular revolt.[38]

Economically, the German state was on treacherous ground. Over half of the country's gold reserves were lost during the first three weeks of June to the tune of $350 million.[39] Scrambling to stave off collapse, the United States announced on June 20 that it would forgive $245 million war debt from its allies if they would suspend $385 million in German reparations.[40] France, which had not been consulted, refused to cooperate with the American plan. In a desperate series of last-ditch negotiations the Americans and the French met in Paris between June 25 and July 7 to hammer out a deal. The settlement conceded the partial suspension of German reparations and that France would lend back reparation money immediately to Germany.[41] The odd compromise came too late.

In Austria, the failure of Credit-Anstalt had precipitated an attack on Austria's currency and the draining of its gold reserves, forcing its government to seek an international aid package. In Germany, an attack on the currency and the draining of its gold reserves precipitated a run on one of its largest banks and a general banking panic. The *Darmstädter und Nationalbank* (Danatbank), like all German banks, was put in a weak position by the fallout over the failure of Credit-Anstalt and the general decline of the German economy. Danat also had the particular misfortune to see a massive loan (corresponding to some 40 percent of its equity) fail at exactly the time of the Credit-Anstalt crisis. Under enormous financial pressure, Danat had only stayed afloat through recourse to the Reichsbank discount window. Now, with its reserves sinking fast, the Reichsbank became reluctant to discount the bills necessary for Danat to survive. By early July the situation had reached a breaking point. Like their Austrian colleagues, Danat Chairman Jacob Goldschmidt and Reichsbank President Hans Luther appealed to Montagu Norman for funds from the Bank of England. On July 13, it was clear that Danat would be unable to open its doors. Germany's president, Paul von Hindenburg, declared a two-day bank holiday.

German banks re-opened on July 16 in a brave new world: "foreign credits were blocked and the discount rate was raised from 7 to 10 percent." A new guarantee corporation (without the Danatbank) was formed along with an Acceptance and Guarantee Bank to replace foreign credits and access funds through the Reichsbank discount window.[42] "All payments on Germany's short-term foreign debt were suspended. All foreign exchange had to be turned over to the Reichsbank and all movements of money out of Germany were tightly regulated—the practical equivalent of going off gold."[43]

The economy continued its downward spiral. During the last six months of 1931 production contracted another 20 percent. GDP for 1931 totaled an anemic 67.1 billion marks, down from 81.9 billion in 1930. Unemployment stood at 16.7 percent. Disillusionment with the world community, international finance, the government, and with democracy itself was growing by the day. Germany's democratic regime, unpopular for signing a humiliating peace treaty after the First World War, for presiding over the hyperinflation of 1923 and the start of the Great Depression, was destroyed by the banking panic of 1931. These forces of frustration found expression during the national elections of July 31, 1932. The Nazi party, previously a fringe element of agitators scored spectacular successes. Their vote more than doubled, from 18 percent of voters in the 1930 elections to 37.8 percent of the vote in 1932. As a result, 230 Nazi deputies, including Adolf Hitler, took their place in the Reichstag as the largest single party in assembly.

## Painful Legacies

Credit-Anstalt's failure left a number of bitter legacies in Austria and beyond. First and foremost, the collapse of the financial system fatally undermined the Austrian political system. It revealed the weakness of the government to deal with the financial and ensuing economic chaos, causing a period of political instability. A successful rescue would have required considerable outside assistance—something that was not forthcoming despite the obvious significance of the bank. Some official multi-national rescue might have prompted panicked investors to return gold to the central banks in exchange for interest-bearing assets, begun to reduce their demand for liquidity (a problem throughout Europe and the United States), and taken some of the steam out of the ballooning panic. Indeed, the correspondent for *The Economist* in Berlin believed that a rescue of Credit-Anstalt by a major international financial institution might have halted the panic and prevented contagion. He observed:

> It was clear from the beginning … that such an institution could not collapse without the most serious consequences, but the fire might have been localized if the fire brigade had arrived quickly enough on the scene. It was the delay of several weeks in rendering effective international assistance to the Credit Anstalt which allowed the fire to spread so widely.[44]

Local European banks and the international community had both failed to organize an effective rescue. Reaction from Britain, France, the United States, and the Bank of International Settlements, relating both to Austria and later to Germany had been slow, uncoordinated, and crippled by national divisions. In the end, the sums raised were simply too small and came too late to prevent economic and political chaos from engulfing both Austria and Germany.

The price for this failure in the financial world was high. As Austria's banking failure infected Germany, so Germany's failure infected Britain and central Europe. American banks suffered as well. Panic in the Austrian and German banking systems was the final straw for the democratic regimes in both countries. Massive unemployment, inflation, disillusionment with international finance, and prejudices that Germany was held captive by a cabal of world bankers opened the way for Hitler to attain power.

Credit-Anstalt remains one of the more often overlooked stories in terms of its connection to the spread of the global depression in the early 1930s, its role in transforming the Austrian political landscape, and the dangers represented by a large bank in a small economy operating with little transparency and disclosure. The banking panic highlighted the weaknesses in the international financial system and in the banking sectors of Austria, Germany, England, and America. For countries already staggered by the stock market crash and the beginning of the Great Depression, Credit-Anstalt's collapse accelerated a knockout blow that would only be overturned with the economic expansion of the Second World War. Politically, the fallout was equally dramatic. Nurtured by financial hardships, bank failures, and massive unemployment, radical political parties, foremost Germany's Nazi party gained power. Credit-Anstalt did not ensure the election of Hitler, but it lifted the lid to a series of events that pushed Europe and the world into their worst economic downturn and their most destructive conflict.

## Notes

1.   *The Times*, Wednesday, May 13, 1931; p. 21; Issue 45821; col. G.
2.   Liqquat Ahamed, *Lords of Finance: The Bankers Who Broke the World*, London: Penguin Books, 2009, p. 405.
3.   Robin Okey, *The Habsburg Monarchy c. 1765-1918, From Enlightenment to Eclipse*, New York: Palgrave Macmillan, 2001, p. 169.
4.   Niall Ferguson, *The House of Rothschild: The World's Banker. 1849-1999*, London: Penguin Books 1998, pp. 86-7.
5.   Karl R. Stadler, *Austria*, New York: Praeger Publishers, 1971, p. 21.
6.   For more information on the Rothschild family and banking see Niall Ferguson's two-volume history: *The House of Rothschild: Money's Prophets: 1798-1848*, New York: Viking Press, 1988, and *The House of Rothschild (Vol. 2): The World's Banker: 1849-1999*, New York: Diane Publishing Co., 1999; Frederic Morton, *The Rothschilds, A Family Portrait*, New York: Atheneum Publishers, 1962; and Amos Elon, *Founder: A Man and His Time*, New York: Penguin, 1997.
7.   Steve Beller, *A Concise History of Austria*, (Cambridge: Cambridge University Press, 2009), p. 203.
8.   Ibid., p. 203.
9.   "Austria: Three-Room President," *Time*, December 17, 1928.
10.  Barbara Jelavish, *Modern Austria: Empire and Republic, 1815-1986*, Cambridge: University of Cambridge Press, 1987, p. 175.
11.  Max Sokal, "Austrian Banks," *Annals of the American Academy of Political and Social Science*, Vol. 98, Supplement: Present Day Social and Industrial Conditions in Austria (Nov., 1921), pp. 34-40.
12.  Ibid., p. 34.
13.  Ibid., p. 36.
14.  Charles P. Kindleberger, *The World in Depression, 1929-1939*, University of California Press, 1986, p. 144.
15.  Aurel Schubert, *The Credit-Anstalt Crisis of 1931*, (New York: Cambridge University Press, 1991), p. 24.
16.  Barry Eichengreen, *Golden Fetters: The Gold Standard and the Great Depression, 1919-1939*, (New York: Oxford University Press, 1992), p. 265.
17.  Ibid., p. 265.

18. Schubert, p. 25.
19. Ahamed, p. 404.
20. Niall Ferguson, *The House of Rothschild: The World's Banker. 1849-1999*, London: Penguin Books 1998, p. 465.
21. Eichengreen, p. 265.
22. Ferguson, p. 465.
23. Ahamed, p. 404.
24. *The Times*, Friday, May 29, 1931; p. 20; Issue 45835; col. E.
25. "Austria: Black Week," *Time*, June 8, 1930. http://www.time.com/time/printout/0,8816,741788,00.html.
26. "Danatbank," David Moss, (Harvard Business School, 2009), p. 10.
27. Kindleberger, p. 147.
28. Ahmed, p. 406.
29. Kindleberger, p. 147.
30. "Austria: Black Week," *Time*, June 8, 1931. http://www.time.com/printout/0,8816,74188,00.html.
31. Ibid.
32. Ibid.
33. *The Times*, June 17, 1931; p. 14; Issue 45851; col. F.
34. Beller, p. 221.
35. Schubert, p. 27.
36. Quoted in Ahamed, p. 404.
37. Ahamed, p. 407.
38. Thomas Ferguson and Peter Temin, "Made in Germany: The German Currency Crisis of July 1931," *Research in Economic History* 21 (2003), pp. 5-6.
39. Ahamed, p. 410.
40. Ibid.
41. Ibid., p. 413.
42. Kindleberger, p. 152.
43. Ahamed, p. 419.
44. Quoted from J. Bradford DeLong, "Slouching toward Utopia?: The Economic History of the Twentieth Century," February 1997. http://econ161.berkely.edu/TCEH/Slouch_Crash14.html.

# 5

# When Finland Almost Failed

In the early 1990s, Finland experienced a dramatic financial and economic crisis. Finnish GDP shrank in each year between 1990 and 1993, reducing per capita GDP by nearly 15 percent. The crash was even more pronounced in the domestic job market. Between 1990 and 1994, Finnish unemployment grew an astonishing 418.75 percent, increasing from 3.2 percent to 16.6 percent. This chapter focuses on Finland's crisis and tries to explain how such a profound economic downturn could strike such an affluent country in the Organization for Economic Cooperation and Development (OECD). Simply stated, a period of financial deregulation led to a credit-fueled asset bubble that ran headlong into an external shock—the stunning and unexpected end of the Soviet Union. The collapse of the Soviet Union disrupted longstanding and highly significant trade relations for Finland. For the country of five million, the combination of damaging external events and unstable internal practices formed a perfect storm that sank much of the banking system and swamped the economy with corporate bankruptcies. Unemployment spiked, and large fiscal deficits created fears that the hitherto stable Nordic country might be forced into a sovereign default.

As two Finnish economists later observed: "The Finnish depression of the 1990's has been the most serious economic crisis in its peacetime history. It is more severe than the depression of the 1930's [for Finland] in terms of many indicators, and in fact it is the perhaps most severe crisis of any OECD economy."[1] Finland's descent was also sudden. Dr. Pauli Järvenpää, who served as the director general of Finland's Department of Defense, wrote in November of 1990 that at the beginning of the new decade: "a general overview of Finland's situation in Europe produces an image of remarkably continuity. No fundamental changes

87

of policy direction are in the offing, and the nation appears to be more at ease with itself than ever."[2] Järvenpää's assessment was fundamentally based on politics and national defense, but it represented the general utopian attitude in Finland on the eve of the crisis.

Although conditions in Finland in the early 1990s were depression-like, the government was able to halt the crisis through a combination of policies. Social expenditure was raised with heavy intervention in the financial sector (including the forced merger of major banks). The economy was dramatically restructured, setting the stage for a sustainable recovery later in the 1990s that carried on into the next decade. The fall of the Soviet Union, which at first damaged Finnish exports, soon had positive political effects as Finland, formerly prohibited by the Soviet Union from closer ties with Europe, was able to begin a period of economic integration with its capitalist neighbors.

Nonetheless, the crisis in the early 1990s was a traumatic experience for Finnish society, leaving a profound historical memory of a country that almost failed. How could such a stable, developed economy have fallen so quickly so fast? How did internal and external factors collude to such devastating effect? How did the Finnish government react to the collapse and eventually rescue the situation?

### Building the Bubble

Finland is a country of a little over five million people. Sandwiched between Sweden and Russia, in the northernmost reaches of Europe, it has a lengthy coastline along the Baltic Sea. Its northern elevation makes for cold seasons and difficult agriculture, but airflows from the Atlantic, the Baltic Sea, and the country's inland waters mean temperatures can average as much as ten degrees higher than for other areas at similarly high latitudes. Agriculture in Finland traditionally counts for between 3.0-3.5 percent of GDP, while industry, especially related to the lumber sector, is the single largest contributor with between 25 percent and 30 percent. This nation also has a unique language, a member of the Finno-Ugric language family, which includes Estonian and Hungarian.

Long caught between Swedish and Russian imperial ambitions, Finland became an independent grand duchy within the Russian Empire in 1809. After the Russian Revolution in 1917, the Finns revolted against Russian control. A brief civil war of White (Tsarist/Republican) versus Red (Communist) forces was fought in Finland as it was in Russia. In Finland, however, the Whites, supported by Germany, won and established an independent republic. Finland's early independence remained precarious due to pressure from the newly formed Soviet Union, which supported the Finnish Reds in their neighbor's civil war and had a strong dislike for the White regime on its doorstep.

Fears of the Russians were once again at the forefront in 1939 when Soviet troops, seeking to secure their northern flank in the upcoming world war, invaded Finland. During the "Winter War," fought between late November 1939 and March 1940, Finland displayed remarkable resilience in the face of overwhelming Russian forces. The Finns were eventually defeated and forced to sign a peace treaty giving massive economic reparations and 11 percent of their territory to the Soviets. They did, however, inflict heavy casualties on the numerically superior Russians and were able to maintain their independence. During the Second World War, Finland sided with Nazi Germany against the Soviet Union in order to regain its lost territory. As the war eventually turned irrevocably in favor of the Allies, the Finns concluded a separate peace with the Soviet Union, resulting in some loss of territory, but avoiding Soviet occupation. The twelve percent of Finland's population living in the lands ceded to the Soviet Union chose, en masse, to resettle themselves elsewhere in Finland.[3]

At the end of World War II, Finland's position was again precarious. It had few allies and a hostile and victorious Soviet Union on its borders. Through careful maneuvering, Finland, once again, managed to avoid Russian occupation. The cost of this was Finnish neutrality during the Cold War. It did not join the North Atlantic Treaty Organization (NATO) or the European Coal and Steel Community (the first step towards the modern European Union). After quietly taking approximately $120 million of American aid under the auspices of the Export-Import Bank and the World Bank, it refused further American financial assistance under the Marshall Plan.[4] At the same time, Finland's trading relations would be dominated by the Soviet Union. These compromises were a prelude to the development of strong links between the Finnish and Soviet economies. With the collapse of the Soviet Union, this relationship would come to haunt Finland.

After modest growth in the decades after World War II, Finland began a process of liberalizing its economy in the 1980s. This was stimulated in part by the process of globalization and a convergence in Europe and North America about the role of free capital flows and banks. Along side of this, ideas of liberalizing and export-oriented economic reforms gained traction. In Finland, the banking sector and international capital flows had been heavily regulated. Indeed, there was a suspicion that free capital flows would leave the Finnish economy open to international turbulence as had happened, to some extent, during the Great Depression. Yet, the Finnish government was keenly aware of the reforms many other countries were implementing to deregulate their financial sectors, including neighboring Norway and Sweden. Consequently, the Finnish government moved to deregulate the banking industry and capital flows.

The short-term response to the liberation of Finnish capital markets was an inflow of foreign credit. Foreign direct investment into Finland increased nearly tenfold between 1983 and 1990 rising from $84 million to $812 million. In percentage terms, the expansion was only incremental, rising from 0.2 percent of Finland's economy to 0.7 percent. The real effects of liberalization were local. During 1986-1989, as foreign credit flowed in, domestic liquidity expanded. In turn, this capital created an investment boom and an asset price bubble. At the same time, exports took off, helped along by improved terms-of-trade, Finland's full membership in the European Free Trade Area (EFTA) in 1985, and rapid European growth from 1986-1989. Total Finnish exports (f.o.b.) increased from $13.62 billion in 1985 to $26.57 billion in 1990.[5] For many investors, the credit fundamentals were enhanced by a stable debt to GDP ratio (of around 25 percent), full employment, sound public finances, very low public debt (11.3 percent of GDP in 1990), and political stability. In a sense, Finland in the late 1980s appeared to be a place where the stars had correctly aligned, attracting both domestic and foreign investment.

The Finns themselves recognized the fortunate state of affairs. Dr. Pauli Järvenpää, the director general of Finland's Department of Defense, wrote in an article from late 1990 that the "country has never been so prosperous as it is today." Gone was the sort of pessimism expressed in the country's national anthem "poor is our land and will stay so forever." Instead, Finns felt "fortunate and privileged to be living in Finland."[6] And why not? In 1989, Finland's national income per capita ranked third trailing only Switzerland and Japan.[7] The good times were rolling.

But the boom had a downside. The expansion of output, consumption, and investment came with consumer price and asset price inflation. This became problematic as inflation and currency appreciation increased Finnish price levels. Inflation moved forward steadily: 6.5 percent in 1989, 6.1 percent in 1990, and 4.1 percent in 1991. By 1990, Finnish price levels were 40 percent higher than the OECD average. At the same time, there was a noticeable widening of the current account deficit over a very short period of time, raising the issue of sustainability. The current account deficit exploded from a little more than $69 million in 1986 to more than $6.96 billion in 1990. Even more worrisome was the expansion of private sector debt. While public sector finances were sound, Finnish business found borrowing easy, both from domestic and external banks. After all, credit was cheap and access easy. This translated into private sector debt climbing from roughly 225 percent of GDP in 1987 to a little under 400 percent in 1990 and 1991. While Finland's currency, the markka, remained strong, this was not a problem, but any major depreciation ran the risk of dangerously pushing up the external debt burden. Furthermore, the increasingly aggressive behavior of business and banks shook up Finnish society, leaving some to feel that in moving away from the "old economy" to the "new economy" a "casino" mentality had taken grip of the country.[8]

Finland's banking sector would ultimately be the Achilles' heel of the country's economy. The banking system had three major types of deposit-taking institutions—commercial banks, savings banks, and co-operative banks. In 1980, this combination accounted for 88 percent of loans in Finland; by 1990 it was 100 percent, with commercial banks and savings banks growing at the expense of the cooperative banks.[9] Three commercial banks, MeritaBank, KOP and SYP, and Skopbank—the "central bank" of the savings banks—were the dominant players. It was the handful of large commercial banks that offered a wide range of financial services and the banks' direct equity stakes in nonfinancial companies.[10] Skopbank, in particular, blurred the lines of established banking practices. It acted as a traditional lender, but also as a partial owner in industry. At the same time, it was playing a dangerous game investing in the Finnish stock market. Skopbank's lending/ownership activities smacked of the shortsighted and dangerous practice of self-lending.

There were also a handful of smaller commercial banks and savings banks. In many regards, Finland had a banking system typical to many other small-to-medium-sized economies—a clutch of large institutions with access to international capital markets, complemented by a constellation of smaller banks, largely geared to local community needs. Commercial banks were focused on the corporate sector, while cooperative banks concentrated on households and small businesses. An additional factor was that prior to the liberalization reforms of the 1980s, the banking environment was defined by credit rationing and the absence of price competition. Along these lines, relationship banking was critical.

The challenge for Finnish banks was how to manage a brave new world of deregulation and newfound access to capital. In many regards, the snug old world of Finnish banking relationships came undone as strong economic growth and a boom mentality led to new demand for lending as well as new applicants for credit. As Finland's financial system opened up more and more, it appeared that demand for credit was unlimited. Bankers felt that such a shift in sentiment spelled bigger profits. In the rush to make money in this radically changed business environment, many bankers ended up with what would become a toxic mix of poor lending practices, poor governance, lack of internal controls, a focus on market-share rather than profitability, and currency and maturity mismatches in the banks or with their borrowers. At the same time, banks were taking excessive risks with other peoples' money. As Stefan Ingves, a Norwegian bank regulator commented in 2002, "distorted incentives" existed for bank owners during the run-up to the crisis. By and large, the bank owners did "not have enough capital at stake." For their part, the bank managers carried "little personal responsibility for the excessive risk they [were] taking."[11] Finnish bankers, like so many of their counterparts in different times and nations, were seduced by an apparently endless buffet of easy money.

Complicating matters were the weak regulatory and supervision framework in Finland. As is the case in many systems, regulators often lag behind the innovations of financiers. The change in the banking system in Finland certainly created such a situation. Finnish banking went from existing in a business environment that was a relatively sleepy backwater with well-defined controls to an open, more rough-and-tumble system. The idea of the banks to function as public utilities morphed into bankers pushing the margins for profit. Finnish bank regulators, like their counterparts in other countries, were caught behind the learning curve. The result was a lack of transparency and disclosure, poor accounting and auditing practices, and concentrated lending. Deceptively robust on the surface, the system was extremely fragile.

### Taking the Plunge

Finland's debt crisis was triggered by three major external factors that underscored domestic weaknesses. These factors included: rising European interest rates (especially those in Germany following re-unification), pressures in Finland's banking system, and the collapse of the Soviet Union, which was disastrous for Finnish-Soviet trade. All of the aforementioned factors combined with high local interest rates (10.9

percent in 1990), over-indebtedness of the Finnish corporate sector, and a horribly over-extended banking system. While Finland enjoyed the excesses of marching into the bubble, the consequences of its bursting were abrupt, long-term, and painful. Finland went into only what can be described as a depression.

New restrictions came into effect on monetary policy even before the crisis hit. These combined with events in the broader European markets to put pressure on the Finnish currency. In early 1989, the government revalued the markka and began defending the currency "against speculative attacks." This policy "kept nominal and real interest rates high and made short rates volatile."[12] By 1991, German re-unification raised interest rates throughout Europe, putting further pressure on Finland's debt burden.

Finland's economic hardships (the story may be getting familiar by this stage) were triggered by turmoil in the banking sector. In Finland's case, this took the form of the collapse of the country's fourth-largest commercial bank—Skopbank. Skopbank had engaged in weighty amounts of bad lending across a number of markets. It had damaging exposure in industry and real estate, and had lost large amounts of money investing in the stock market. Through 1990, the bank, already unable to raise sufficient funds in the interbank market, had been forced to get overnight lending from the Bank of Finland to ensure liquidity.

As the broader economic environment worsened, in 1991 it all began to unravel. Skopbank announced itself illiquid in September 1991, and the Bank of Finland felt forced to intervene. The Bank of Finland guaranteed Skopbank's liquidity and purchased its "problem assets" for 9.5 billion markkas. An additional cash injection of 2 billion markkas was also provided.[13] The rescue process deepened. The government formed two asset management companies to sort out the mess: one took possession of Skopbank's industrial holdings, the other, its real estate exposure. As might have been expected, Skopbank's management was replaced. In all, the Bank of Finland injected 14 billion markkas in 1991 and 1992. Still, the bank was not entirely out of the woods. With Skopbank owned by the Guarantee Fund and its industrial and real estate positions managed by the Bank of Finland through holding companies, the slow road out of the red began. By 1994, Skopbank had received an incredible amount of support amounting to 3 percent of Finland's entire GDP—some 15.2 billion markkas.[14]

The catalytic role played by the demise of the Soviet Union was also significant. Finland's large eastern neighbor was, after all, its major trade partner and a key region for Finnish overseas investment. Although Finnish exports to the Soviet Union had dropped from 20 percent of total exports in 1986 to only 14.5 percent in 1989, the USSR remained Finland's primary export market.[15] When the Soviet Union encountered rising economic problems in the late 1980s, the negative impact on Finnish business was still manageable. The demise and fragmentation of the Soviet Union in 1990, however dealt the Finnish economy a significant blow as the scope and scale was well beyond what any business management teams expected. Suddenly what had been a standard feature of the Finnish economic landscape transformed into a bewildering economic freefall, complicated by political uncertainty in Moscow exemplified by the failed hardliner coup in August 1991 and the emergence of an entire new crop of countries, each seeking to restructure their economies among the ruins of the old order. For many Finns, the spread of political instability was close to home and held up the specter of the Russian civil war. After the fall of the Soviet Union in 1991, trade with Russia experienced a sudden drop of almost 70 percent.[16] Trade with Finland's two other major trade partners, Britain and Sweden, fell by over 10 percent, furthering complicating the situation.

At the same time, there were more straightforward economic challenges. The Finnish economy had long been able to get by with less value-added products sent to the Soviet Union, many of which products were non-competitive with other Western economies. Now, Finland's major export market was gone and the Nordic country was forced to compete with more cost-efficient Western economies. The sharp drop in exports had a negative impact across most sectors, striking at corporate balance sheets, and pushing up unemployment, which more than doubled from 3.2 percent in 1990 to 6.6 percent in 1991.

The problem for the Finnish banks was clear. The rapid expansion of credit led to problems in the banking sector when the economy entered into a downswing and asset prices plummeted.[17] On top of this, very high real interest rates drained liquidity. As the downturn gained momentum and corporate bankruptcies rose (a situation worsened by the currency's depreciation), the banks radically cut lending and developed a bunker mentality. While the bankers sought to guard their capital, the sharp reduction of liquidity created a downward spiral that only made conditions worse. The impact on banks' balance sheets was devastating. Nonperforming loans shot upwards from low and very manageable levels in the mid-1980s to 9.3 percent of total exposure in 1992, even after 3.7 percent had been written off as loan and guarantee losses.[18] The most significant default rates were in the services, real estate and construction sectors. Almost half of the banks' real estate exposure was either written off as credit losses or was nonperforming in 1992.[19]

High interest rates and the implosion of Soviet trade were major factors in sparking Finland's crisis, and the situation was worsened by the initial inability of policymakers to understand the macroeconomic consequences of declining asset prices. For many Finns, the turn of events, with the destruction of wealth and credit losses, came as a rude surprise. Indeed, the early policy responses of attempting to balance the budget by higher taxes and expenditure cuts further dampened private demand and employment. The fiscal matter was most pronounced in 1992-1995 when social benefits were frozen or reduced and labor taxes raised (1992-1995) via income taxes and employers' contributions (this meant real after-tax incomes were sharply cut). Having already doubled to 6.6 percent in 1991, the unemployment rate doubled again to 11.7 percent in 1992 and just kept rising, hitting 16.3 percent in 1993 and 16.6 percent in 1994 before moderating slightly to 15.4 percent in 1995. Rising unemployment eroded the government's tax base, and debt-GDP reached the 15 percent range by 1993. Finland had moved "from the group of low-public-debt countries to the group of medium-debt countries" in just a few years.[20]

## Finland in Context

Finland was not the only Nordic country to be hit by a severe financial crisis in the early 1990s. Although the impact of the Soviet Union's demise was not as significant to Norway and Sweden, both of those countries encountered considerable problems with financial deregulation and boom-bust economic cycles. In many regards, Norway and Sweden shared a similar set of problems (though in slightly different forms): bad banking, inadequate market discipline, weak banking regulation and supervision, and inadequate macro policies.[21] At the same time, the depth of the banking and economic crises were not as severe in Norway and Sweden as it was in Finland.

Sweden, like Finland, had embarked upon financial deregulation. It had, earlier in the 1980s, modernized its industrial sector and did not have the vulnerability of trade with the Soviet Union. However, deregulation led to a construction and lending boom, which meant an overleveraging of parts of the Swedish economy. The trigger for Sweden's crisis was the uptick in European interest rates, stimulated by Germany's re-unification and speculative attacks on its currency, the Swedish krona.

Norway's experience was different from both Sweden and Finland. First and foremost, Norway's economy went into a slowdown mode as early as 1986 due to a decline in international oil prices. Norway, it should be remembered, is one of the world's largest oil and gas producers. In response to the downturn in energy markets, the Norwegian krona was devalued by 6 percent and restrictive credit policies were introduced.

Despite Norway's economic slowdown, its banking system was opened up. Yet, problems appeared in Norway as early as 1986-87 with finance companies, as a number of them went bankrupt due to a slowdown in the property sector. In 1988-89, Norwegian banks were hit by substantial loan losses related to bad banking and excessive lending by some small and medium-sized banks. Initially it was thought the banking system could ride through these problems. However, this changed as loan losses mounted in 1990 and 1991, when even some of the largest Norwegian banks indicated signs of financial trouble. This was especially the case in 1991 when loan losses unexpectedly leaped to 6 percent of GDP.[22] As in Finland, a surge in corporate bankruptcies and defaults added to the carnage.

Despite the difference in external factors, Swedish banks hit the wall in 1993, when nonperforming loans rose to 11 percent.[23] Close to 75 percent of defaults came from nonfinancial enterprises, dominated by real-estate-related entities. The impact of Sweden's crisis was so comprehensive and memorable that *The New York Times* commented 16 years later: "The country was so far in the hole in 1992—after years of imprudent regulation, short-sighted economic policy and the end of its property boom—that its banking system was, for all practical purposes, insolvent."[24] Both the Swedish and Norwegian governments were forced to put together rescue plans.

## Fixing Finland

In the early 1990s, the Finnish government confronted a crisis of a similar magnitude to that of the late 1930s and 1940s, when the country fought two wars against the Soviet Union and faced a bleak post-war geopolitical and economic landscape. Despite Finland's membership in such organizations as the OECD, the European Free Trade Area (EFTA), and the Bank for International Settlements (BIS), the 1990s crisis found the Nordic country in a position of relative isolation. The OECD was a policy-talking shop at best; EFTA was limited to trade matters and lacked any financial support institutions, and the Bank for International

Settlements had a very limited history of financial rescues. At the same time other Nordic countries were undergoing a similar type of crisis. Finland clearly had the bad luck to get into a major financial/economic crisis at a time when the Soviet Union had imploded and a brave new world of economically struggling nations was being born.

The economic crisis reverberated into Finland's political life. The implosion of the banks, contraction of economic activity, and spike in unemployment left most Finns in a state of shock and anger. While the bankers were an obvious focus for public scorn, the country's ruling party was to suffer the consequences of what many perceived as a poor public stewardship.

The Finnish Social Democratic Party had long dominated the country's political life; since 1937, they were only out of power once between 1957 and 1966. Indeed, the party held the Premiership through much of the 1970s and well into the 1980s. Even after 1990, when Harri Holkeri of the conservative National Coalition became prime minister, the Social Democrats were part of the ruling coalition. This broad left-right government was rare by Finnish standards and despite what might have been a difficult political marriage elsewhere led to manageable governments.[25]

The uniqueness of the Holkeri government reflected that the usual comparatively peaceful and stable political life of the country (despite a number of minority and caretaker administrations) was entering a more difficult period. Indeed, Holkeri was the first conservative prime minister since 1946 and the 1987 election placed Conservatives in government for the first time in 20 years. Adding to the changed landscape in the late 1980s was the absence of the Centre Party from the government ranks for the first time since 1945.

The growing tensions in the Finnish political spectrum became more acute when the Holkeri government pushed through another round of economic reforms. Although much of the Finnish society was willing to go along with earlier reforms in the late 1980s, the country's economy was becoming frothy and doubts were emerging as to the extent of change. Complicating matters, Finnish domestic demand was rising, which caused imports to increase and swelled the trade deficit to around 10 percent. The result of all this was open conflict between the government and the central bank over monetary policy (to devalue or not), a threatened general strike, the resignation of one member of the Cabinet, and the resignation of another minister from Parliament—a shocking and unprecedented event by Finnish standards.[26]

Considering the horrific nature of the economic collapse, eventually the Holkeri government resigned, prompting elections. A more openly rightist coalition under Prime Minister Esko Aho emerged, composed of the Centre Party, the conservative National Coalition Party and the Swedish People's Party of Finland, which together amassed a little under 50 percent of the vote. The new prime minister's party, the Centre Party, became the repository of voters from small and rural municipalities. The party was formed around the ideas of decentralization, free will, free and fair trade, small enterprise, and the subsidization of agriculture.

Finland's new prime minister was Esko Aho. Only 36 years old at the time of his election, he was the youngest prime minister in his country's history. He started his long career in politics in 1974, when he served as the chairman of the Youth Organization of the Centre Party. In 1978, he became a presidential elector, and from 1979 to 1980 he was political secretary to the Ministry of Foreign Affairs. First elected to parliament in 1983, he was the leader of the Centre Party by 1990.

The economic landscape facing the Aho administration was daunting. Indeed, the crisis was aggravated by the ill-conceived policy to link the Finnish markka to the European currency unit or ECU, in 1991. This was a hasty response to Sweden's move to join the ECU, but failed to protect the markka against speculation. This left Aho in a precarious position. The prime minister initially sought to forge a consensus to deal with the situation, but industrial exporters favored devaluation and unions opposed it. Conditions continued to deteriorate, a situation marked by capital flight. The central bank was ultimately forced to intervene by raising short-term interest rates, and moving the exchange rate bond up 14 percent against the ECU, effectively devaluing the markka, helping exporters but hurting holders of foreign debt—like the banks.[27]

The government's approach to the banking crisis was to launch a comprehensive restructuring. This entailed the merger of the two largest commercial banks, KOP and SOP, into a new institution called Merita. The next step was to merge Mertia with a Swedish bank, Nordbanken, which became Nordea. The rationalization of the banking sector helped restore some degree of life to the sector, but one third of the bank staff lost their jobs. At the same time as the restructuring was initiated, the central bank lowered interest rates. The change in monetary policy was critical from the standpoint that another year of steep recession would have caused even greater credit losses than experienced.

While saving the banking system was a priority, the government also moved to stimulate export expansion and reflation. This entailed the earlier-mentioned depreciation of the Finnish markka, a productivity shift and wage moderation oriented to improve competitiveness. The impact of these policies became evident in 1992-1993 with a strong rebound of exports and industrial production. At the same time, this process was not going to be easy. Domestic demand clearly lagged as many Finns still were feeling the impact of the crisis on their wallets. However, lower interest rates enabled asset price reflation and an increase in consumer spending beginning in 1994. Finland's crisis, which witnessed a considerable cheapening of the country's assets and the government's pro-active stance in restructuring the economy, functioned to attract foreign investment, something that helped the recovery gain pace. The stock market's main indicator, the HEX-index quadrupled in the period between 1993 and 1998.

Achieving an exit from the crisis was not easy. The majority of Finns confronted a decline in their lifestyles and considerable angst was evident in society. The government also did not always get its way. Big pension cuts faced stiff resistance and the threat of a general strike forced the national leadership to back off. Additionally, the financial rescue rankled many Finns who felt they endured the costs, but that many benefits went to restore foreign investors. Historian David Kirby noted: "This costly rescue operation may have helped restore national confidence in Finnish financial institutions, but it caused deep resentment in the public at large, forced to bear the burden of cuts in services and real earnings, and faced with mounting unemployment."[28]

Finland's economic restructuring eventually set the stage for a period of strong growth. Between 1994 and 2000 GDP expanded at an annual rate of 4.7 percent, followed by an average of 3.5 percent between 2001 and 2007. Such robust, uninterrupted growth was enviable by any OECD standard and even to emerging markets. Equally significant, unemployment fell from 18 percent to 10 percent between 1994 and 2000 and returned to a more manageable 6 percent in 2008. Rounding out the picture, Finland did an excellent job in terms of fiscal consolidation and fulfillment of the EMU criteria in 1997. The government was able to generate record surpluses in 2000 and 2007, while implementing tax cuts and steady growth in expenditures.

Another government policy that was to bear fruit for Finland's longer-term economic recovery and competitiveness was investment in technology. Considering the need to consolidate state finances and the cost of bailing out the banking sector, the idea of looking ahead and focusing on technology as a means to restructure the Finnish economy was both courageous and visionary. Despite the drastic nature of the economic landscape, the Aho government actually increased R&D spending, roughly by 70 percent between 1991 and 1995. Over the 1990s, Finland developed a strong technology sector, spearheaded globally by Nokia, one of the world's dominant players in the mobile phone industry.

The main instrument of Finnish government investment in the long-term development of the economy was TEKES (the Finnish Funding Agency for Technology and Innovation). As the OECD was to later comment on the Aho government's gamble on R&D technology: "The government decision to complement macroeconomic stabilization measures with sustained investment in infrastructure, education and incentives for structural changed helped put the Finnish economy on a stronger, more knowledge-intensive, growth path following the crisis."

One of the outcomes of the economic/financial crisis and subsequent restructuring and reorienting of the country was Finland's joining the European Union. This was one of the more successful policies pursued by the Aho administration, taking place in 1995. This was a significant step as it clearly signaled that Finland's days of neutrality were over and that it had every intention to be more fully integrated with the European economy. Symbolically, Finland joined at the same time as Austria and Sweden, the first new members after the end of the Cold War.

## Conclusion

Finland's crisis of the early 1990s was one of the first systematic crises in an OECD country since the 1930s. In the words of a Norwegian bank regulator: "The Nordic banking crises were…eye-openers. How could such problems occur in otherwise well organized managed economies and financial systems?"[29] This excellent question would obviously elude policymakers in larger and more powerful economies as well as other small economies in the years ahead.

Finland's experience holds both promise and peril. The downward lurch was sudden and deep causing severe damage to a previously stable and prosperous economy. To many observers, it came as a complete surprise. At the same time, Finnish policymakers were able to stem the negative spiral, rescue the banking sector, and eventually restore a degree of order. There were, however, no simple fixes. Finland paid a high price to put its finances in order proving that in the face of such extreme downturns, there are no short cuts. Significantly the Finns did not approach the crisis with the view that someone else was to blame, that external support was essential, or that the country faced a national income garnishment that was to last their lives. In many regards, the Finns' handling of the crisis reflected a societal tendency of self-reliance and willingness to confront and overcome challenges. Finland's experience proves that when confronted with massive shocks, deleveraging takes time. Good policy decisions always matter. A broad societal consensus and the will to implement the necessary measures are essential to tackling problems of significant scope and scale.

## Notes

1.  Quoted from Seppo Honkapohja and Erkki Koskela, "The Economic Crisis of the 1990s in Finland" *Keskusteluaiheita*—Discussion Papers, The Research Institute of the Finnish Economy (Helsinki) 9/8/1999, p. 3. Also see Liisa Halme, Head of Unit, Rahoitustar Kastus, Financial Supervision Authority, "The 1990s Banking Crisis in Finland: Main Causes and Consequences, Lessons for the Future."www. finanstilsynet.no/archive/f-avd-word/01/024L115009.doc.
2.  Pauli O. Järvenpää, "Finland: An Image of Continuity in Turbulent Europe," *Annals of the American Academy of Political and Social Science*, Vol. 512, (Nov., 1990), pp. 125-139, p. 137.
3.  Ibid., pp. 125-139, p. 126.
4.  Pekka Kalevi Hamalainen, "The Finnish Solution," *The Wilson Quarterly* (1976-), Vol. 10, No. 4 (Autumn, 1986), pp. 59-75, p. 67.
5.  Economist Intelligence Unit, Country Data for Finland.
6.  Järvenpää, "Finland: An Image of Continuity in Turbulent Europe," *Annals of the American Academy of Political and Social Science*, pp. 125-139, p.126, pp. 134-5.
7.  Ibid., p. 126.
8.  See Professor Osmo Suovaniemi, M.D., Ph.D., President + CEO of Biohit Plc., "Being an Investor in Finland," www.biohit.com/upload/dia/literature/BeingInvestorInFinland.pdf.2005.
9.  Burkhard Drees and Ceyla Pazarbaşioğlu, The Nordic Banking Crises: Pitfalls in Financial Liberation?, International Monetary Fund, (Washington, D.C.) Occasional Paper # 161, (April 1998), p. 5.
10. Ibid., p. 6.
11. Stefan Ingves, director, Monetary and Exchange Affairs Department, Seminar on Financial Crisis, Kreditilsynet, The Banking, Insurance and Securities Commission of Norway, Oslo, September 11, 2002, "The Nordic Banking Crisis from an International Perspective." p. 2.
12. Honkapohja and Koskela, "The Economic Crisis of the 1990s in Finland," *Keskustleluaiheita*, p. 405.
13. Charles Albert Goodhart, *The Central Bank and the Financial System*, (London: MIT Press, 1995), p. 381.
14. Burkhard Drees and Ceyla Pazarbşioğlu, *The Nordic Banking Crises: Pitfalls in Financial Liberalization?* (Washington DC: The International Monetary Fund, 1998), p. 31.
15. Järvenpää, "Finland: An Image of Continuity in Turbulent Europe," *Annals of the American Academy of Political and Social Science*, p. 136.
16. Honkapohja and Koskela, "The Economic Crisis of the 1990s in Finland," *Keskustleluaiheita*, p. 405.
17. Ibid., p. 15.

18. Drees and Pazarbaşioğlu, *The Nordic Banking Crises*, p. 23.
19. Ibid., p. 24.
20. Honkapohja and Koskela, "The Economic Crisis of the 1990s in Finland," pp. 401-436, p. 417.
21. Ingves, "The Nordic Banking Crisis from an International Perspective," p. 7.
22. Drees and Pazarbaşioğlu, *The Nordic Banking Crises*, p. 23.
23. Ibid.
24. Carter Dougherty, "Stopping a Financial Crisis, the Swedish Way," *The New York Times*, September 22, 2008. http://www.nytimes.com/2008/09/23/business/worldbusiness/23Krona.html.
25. See Staffan Marklund and Anders Nordlund, "Economic Problems, Welfare Convergence and Political Instability," in Mikko Kautto, Chapter 2. Matti Heikkilï, Bjorn Huinden, Staff on Marklund and Niels Ploug, eds., *Nordic Social Policy: Changing Welfare States* (London: Routledge, 1999), p. 43.
26. Kenneth Newton, "Political Support Social Capital, Civil Society, and Political and Economic Performance," UC Irvine: Center for the Study of Democracy, August 22, 2006, p. 7.
27. David Kirby, *A Concise History of Finland* (New York: Cambridge University Press, 2008), p. 291.
28. Ibid., p. 293.
29. Ingves, "The Nordic Banking Crisis from an International Perspective," p. 11.

# 6

# Albanian Pyramid Schemes

In the cold days of late January 1997, Albania teetered on the brink of collapse. Chaos reigned as massive rioting was directed at an apparently inept and corrupt government over the failure of a number of nation-wide pyramid schemes. The southern part of the country fell under the sway of rebels and criminal gangs who focused on looting and the destruction of property. By the start of March, the government had been forced to resign and a state of emergency was declared. Unable to end the violence, the Albanian government welcomed an Italian-led United Nations peacekeeping force of 7,000 troops to disarm the militias and restore order. Before some semblance of normalcy was restored, nearly 2,000 Albanians had lost their lives. Large numbers of arms remained unaccounted for and parts of the country were in dire need of reconstruction. Nearly $1.2 billion in assets had been wiped away from a population of only 3 million. Albania's hopes of emerging from the post-Cold War world as a modern European state had taken a major step backward.

The idea of a "failed state" emerging just south of the already fragile former Yugoslavia, was seen as a direct threat by policymakers throughout Europe, particularly in Athens and Rome. Washington and Moscow, erstwhile rivals in the region, were also concerned. The root cause of Albania's trouble was financial, coming in the form of highly popular and poorly regulated finance companies that were eventually revealed to be involved in "pyramid schemes." A pyramid scheme offers well above market-rate interest rates (return on investment) by taking in capital on ever-expanding levels. Some of the new capital is then pumped back to pay off earlier investors. Pyramid schemes work when investors hear about the high rates of return from earlier investors and are recruited to invest. The numbers of individuals brought into the scheme is important as each old member is rewarded to recruit more, pushing the number of investors up exponentially. The constant inflow of new money is needed to sustain payments to existing investors. The schemes take a big cut of the capital flow and at some point the "management" flee or if confidence departs, the scheme unravels, usually with a spectacular collapse. In such a model, growth inevitably exceeds the target population.

Ponzi schemes are a little different. While momentum is critical for both, pyramid schemes play on growing ranks of investors, but Ponzi schemes focus more on a central pool of funds. One IMF study gave the following definition: "Ponzi schemes often grow larger than pyramid schemes as they can take in unlimited amounts from a single individual and can continue to operate indefinitely, as long as payments demanded by investors from the scheme do not exceed payments by investors into the scheme."[1] Financial fraud, in both the forms of pyramid and Ponzi schemes range in sophistication and size. The Albanian schemes like similar ones in Jamaica, Suriname, and Russia during the 1990s were fairly simple. Bernie Madoff's 20-year and estimated $50 billion swindle in the United States, involved a more complex system of smoke and mirrors.[2] Simplicity, however, was no obstacle to spreading the scheme throughout Albania. At their peak, the value of the pyramid scheme liabilities in Albania amounted to almost half of the country's GDP and about two-thirds of the population invested in them.[3]

What makes Albania such a compelling story is how one of Europe's most Stalinist countries emerged from its long night of state-dominated economic life and plunged into a period of free-wheeling capitalism. While the same could be said for much of Eastern Europe following the collapse of the Soviet Union in the early 1990s, the repercussions were not as dramatic as they were in Albania. In Albania, the entire socio-economic landscape suffered a massive upheaval and the very idea of the nation temporarily appeared up for grabs. The sad fact is that the culprits of this national tailspin were a handful of speculators who were able to manipulate the political elites as well as the public, whipping them into a frenzy of misguided investments that ended in catastrophe.

### Emerging from Enver Hoxha's World

Long under the heavy-handed rule of dictator Enver Hoxha, Albania began to emerge from its Stalinist straightjacket following his death in 1985. Without a doubt, Hoxha left a legacy of economic backwardness on his country. During the later part of his rule, he had become something of a joke for creating a "Stalinist oasis" within prosperous, capitalist

Europe. While the rest of the world took steps toward globalization in the 1970s and early 1980s, Hoxha's last years in power were marked by a strict isolation and a policy of self-sufficiency.

Born in 1908, Hoxha rose through the ranks of the Communist Party during the 1940s, steered his country out of the Yugoslav orbit, and was a strong believer in the collective economic policies of Joseph Stalin. When Stalin died in 1953, and the Soviet Union moved away from some of the more rigid policies, relations with Moscow deteriorated and Hoxha looked to Mao Zedong's China for assistance. As trade and assistance from China mounted, Hoxha moved away from the Soviet orbit. In 1961, he dismissed Soviet Premier Nikita Khrushchev a "revisionist, an anti-Marxist, and defeatist."[4] Hoxha's focus was increasingly on maintaining ideological purity through: the elimination of private property, collective economic approaches, and the dominance of the leader and party over everything else.

Feeding Albania's population was an ongoing problem, political freedom was lacking, and relations with the outside world were defined by an aggressive and trigger-happy border police. Nevertheless, Hoxha's regime did manage to bring a degree of literacy to the population. Like Stalin, he was a firm believer in the cult of personality and cultivated such titles as Supreme Comrade and Great Teacher. Backing his claims to supremacy was the *Sigurimi*, the Albanian secret police, who imprisoned thousands in forced-labor camps, carried out executions and purges and made certain that Western European culture was kept out of the country. At the same time, churches and mosques were closed and religious practice was strongly discouraged. Beards—regarded as Islamic—were banned.

But even supreme dictators are human. Hoxha had a heart attack in 1973, which left him physically impaired. Although day-to-day functions were handed over to his loyal henchman Ramiz Ali, Hoxha remained the force behind the throne. When he died in 1985, he was not deeply mourned. As Miranda Vickers and James Pettifer noted:

> Although many of his closest collaborators were well aware of his faults and limitations, he remained at the apex of the pyramid; for many Albanians he was a little revered and often hated father figure, whose ideology was of little or no appeal, especially to the young. Yet it was he who had put Albania on the map as a modern industrial country in contrast to the near-medieval conditions prevailing at the time.[5]

Hoxha left a country ill-prepared and apprehensive about rejoining the outside world. Indeed, the IMF noted that Albania, which quickly shifted from neo-Stalinism to a market-based economy, "started its transition as Europe's poorest and most isolated economy."[6]

Albania's post-dictatorship political culture was also rudimentary. Although the Hoxha years were officially communist in ideology, Albanian politics remained dominated by clans. Clans provided influential informal networks throughout the communist party, the nation's bureaucracy and the military. This situation was further complicated by partisan spillovers throughout the country. The authoritarian nature of the Hoxha regime functioned to mask these differences and kept them under control. When the authoritarian edifice crumbled, clannish and regional influences rebounded in the country's political and socio-economic life and would complicate the way to a more open and democratic society.

## A Turn to Market Economics

The post-Hoxha communists in the late 1980s made tentative steps to open up Albania. The country joined the International Monetary Fund, removed travel restrictions, and sought external expertise to help implement reforms. In 1991, the Sigurimi was dissolved and replaced by the National Information Service (NIS). In the 1992 elections, the communists were voted out of office and the Democratic Party, with 62 percent of the vote, replaced them. The communists won only 2 percent of the vote and the socialists 25 percent, much of it in the south of the country. Dr. Sali Berisha became the first non-communist leader of Albania since King Zog in the 1930s. Berisha's handling of the economy and relations with the financial sector were important as to how Albania's crisis evolved.

Born in 1944, Berisha became a cardiologist, taught at university, and for a period was the Communist Party's secretary general. He was also one of the few members of Albania's elite to travel abroad, spending time in both Paris and Copenhagen. With the changes occurring in post-Hoxha Albania, Berisha emerged as a leader of the opposition by 1989. He was a steady voice for creating a competitive multi-party political system and participated in the December 1990 student demonstrations that pushed the communist government to finally allow more than one political party. He quickly became the leader of the newly formed Democratic Party, which served as an important springboard, first to the parliamentary victory in 1992 and, then to the presidency. He also was an effective speaker at campaign rallies. As Albanian commentators Miranda Vickers and James Pettifer observed: "Berisha had become an effective performer at these large-scale events, and with his superficially attractive personality, good looks and media schooling he made a much more favorable impression than old-style ex-communists speakers."[7]

Berisha presided over a country with an economy that can only be described as rudimentarily capitalistic. Most reforms by the prior communist government following Hoxha's exit were cosmetic and ineffectual. The fateful decision was made to radically overhaul the economy, which meant a comprehensive and socially uprooting experience for many Albanians. The reforms included the complete liberalization of the exchange rate, an opening up (mainly to the West) of the trade regime, a re-writing of investment and property-ownerships rules and regulations and wide scale privatization of small and medium-sized state-owned enterprises. Albania also became a member of the Council of Europe in 1995 and developed close cooperation with the European Union and the United States. Critical to the outreach to the West and the modernization of the economy, the Berisha administration adopted European standards. It also introduced a Constitutional Court and High Council of Justice, both standard to Western Europe, but clearly not part of the old communist edifice.

Berisha's objective was to bring Albania in from the cold and make it part of the global economy. This entailed developing a close relationship with United States, but was hindered by a less positive reception from the European Union. European apprehensions about a close embrace were partially related to what was perceived as the tainted underbelly of the Berisha government. Part of this came from Albania's growing role in the global drug trade. According to Vickers and Pettifer: "The war in former Yugoslavia prevented heroin produced in Istanbul from being transported to Western Europe via Belgrade, but there was a more secure route though Albania and Kosovo."[8] While it undermined Albania's attempts at partnership with Europe early in the 1990s, the country's criminal connections were to be front and center during the crisis later in decade.

Another snapshot of Albania's growing linkages to international crime was provided by the US government's Bureau for International Narcotics and Law Enforcement Affairs 1998 International Narcotics Control Strategy Report. It was noted in the mid-1990s that money laundering was widespread and that the primary source of illegal proceeds were narcotics trafficking, organized crime, terrorism, arms trafficking, alien smuggling, corruption, prostitution, and the counterfeiting of local and US currency. The report went on to point to the expansion of linkages to organized crime groups from Italy, Greece, and Macedonia. Alien smuggling, in particular, was a growing problem between Albania and Italy. Indeed, Italian criminal money was finding its way into Albania during the mid-1990s, roughly around the time when the Balkan country was opening up its borders and economy. Rounding out the picture were indications that Islamic terrorist groups were active in Albania; using narcotics trafficking and money laundering to finance their operations throughout the world.[9]

It should also be noted that Albania had a couple of financial scandals that, with hindsight, are clear forerunners of the pyramid schemes. As early as 1991, the Albanian-Swiss company, Sejdia, collected substantial amounts of US dollars from credulous Albanians promising the payment of high-interest returns, and then disappearing with the initial investments.[10] The other fraud, called "Arsidi," involved four Albanian bank employees and a French citizen, who misappropriated $1.6 million during the negotiations on the Albanian public debt with foreign banks.[11] Although these scandals were hardly critical to the national economy, they pointed to the fertile ground for financial fraud in Albania.

Allegations of corruption persistently swirled around the government. Perhaps one of the most damaging allegations was that Albania was used as a transit point for goods (mainly oil and its by-products) to get around an economic embargo against Yugoslavia set up by the United Nations. Accusing fingers pointed to a ghost company linked to Berisha and his minister of defense Safet Zhulali.[12] Whether or not these allegations were accurate remains open to dispute, but they would not go away and were a factor in growing public dissatisfaction with Berisha. This became painfully evident to the Albanian leader when he lost a referendum in November 1994 over a draft constitution that critics said would augment his powers. It was in this politically polarizing environment that Albania's pyramid schemes gained traction.

Albania's pyramid schemes were rooted in the country's "informal economy," also called the "black," "underground," or "parallel" economy. The informal sector operates outside of government regulation and supervision and is geared to evading taxation, circumventing onerous red tape and bureaucracy, and dealing with inflexible labor markets. It can be broadly defined as everything from legitimate services paid for in cash but unreported (and therefore untaxed) to multi-million dollar drug deals and arms sales.

As the communist system unraveled in Albania and capitalism was introduced, the informal sector quickly expanded. This occurred because the old regime imposed substantial obstacles to business development and elements of the old bureaucratic regime lingered. Along the same lines, legal institutions were deficient, resulting in public funds being used inefficiently and economic opportunities being missed.[13] Consequently, the transitional period following the end of communism was a major impetus for an expansion of the informal economy. Additional economic and financial factors such as the United Nations embargo on Yugoslavia, a high level of unemployment, the closure of several former state enterprises and the privatization of others, a weakness of the state and its regulatory institutions and the extended contacts with neighboring countries all contributed.[14]

The expansion of the underground economy extended to the financial sector, where there was little experience with commercial banking, business development, customer service, and deposit insurance. The result was a banking system that was bypassed by many Albanians as a place to put their money, while they were limited in their lending ability due to very strict limits on providing credit. There was also a reluctance to support new and potentially risky private companies.[15]

From an Albanian banker's experience there was a good reason to be cautious. The country's three earliest banks—the Savings Bank, Commercial Bank, and Rural Bank as well as the Small and Medium Enterprises' (SME) foundation—were hurt by poor lending practices and the upheaval in the country's economic and political life. In 1996, the banks reported that more than 30 percent of their loans were not being serviced on time.[16] Between rising bad loans, diminishing deposits, and tortuous government regulations, the banks husbanded their capital.

With bank-based lending only a trickle, Albanians were forced to turn to the other traditional place in a capitalist economic system to raise capital—the stock market. Although the Tirana stock exchange opened in May 1996, there was little to attract local or foreign investment. Part of the problem was a lack of investment worthy companies and part of it was a lack of stock market culture. This left the emerging capitalist economy starved of capital.

Another factor that contributed to the expansion of the informal sector was the improvement in national savings. Despite the economic and political upheaval in the surrounding Balkans, Albania saw capital enter the country from the contraband trade and foreign aid. There was also a flow of emigrant remittances from the Albanian diaspora. Because of these developments, household savings went from around nil before the collapse of communism to $350 million in 1995, $600 million in 1996 and $700 million in 1997.[17] With money in their pockets for the first time in generations, ordinary Albanians were looking for investment opportunities.

Considering the condition of the formal banking and financial systems, the informal credit system based of family ties and financed by worker remittances beckoned. Among the first wave of schemes were Vefa and Sude, both of which appeared in 1992. These schemes started in the southwest of the country, where most emigrant workers came from and which generated the largest per capita remittance inflow.[18]

In clannish Albania, the excitement about the new companies, with names such as Xhafferi and Populli, soon expanded out of control. Part of the problem was a lack of experience with finance sector companies of any type on the part of the population as well as the government. Indeed, the government largely turned a blind eye to the informal financial sector. At the same time, claims of quick enrichment through investment in such schemes were exceedingly attractive.

How exactly did the Albanian pyramid companies work? Jarvis provides an apt description:

> in a typical pyramid scheme, a fund of company attracts investors by offering them very high return; these returns are paid to the first investors out of the funds received from who invest later. The scheme is insolvent—liabilities exceed assets—from the day its opens for business. However, it flourishes initially, as news about the high returns spread and more investors are recruited by the earlier ones. Encouraged by the high payouts, and in some cases by showcase investments and ostentatious spending by the operators, still more people are drawn in, and the scheme grows until the interest and principal due to the early investors exceeds the money paid in by the new investors.[19]

Although the pyramid game dominated, not every company in the sector was limited to financial fraud. Vefa moved beyond the financial sector into trade, tourism, transport, and food processing.[20] It came to operate more than 200 businesses and employed 10,000 people. Indeed, Vefa's beginnings were humble and built up around the fortunes of Vehbi Alimucaj. A former army sergeant during the communist regime and allegedly related to Berishi, he started his business career in 1993 by selling soap from a decrepit building in Tirana. Within a year, his company had six employees, fixed capital of $542,000 and an annual profit of $639,000.[21] Vefa was boosted by Alimucaj's move to attract large numbers of investors by offering  monthly interest rates of between 6 and 12 percent. His well-established political connections and involvement as a Democratic Party fundraiser gave him a further aura of invincibility.

While Alimucaj claimed to invest the money in a number of productive businesses, the reality was that the former sergeant was busy transferring the money out of the country. According to a Radio Free Europe report on January 1, 1997, Vefa's balance of accounts indicated debts of $458 million, while the proper business activities generated revenues of only $2.12 million. In the run-up to January 1997, those facts remained unknown and people were not asking about the company's operations.

Vefa was not alone in moving pyramid/ponzi money into the real sector and augmenting the nation's productivity. Other pyramid companies moved into agriculture, medicine, and other light industry. Moreover, the "foundations" made investments in the construction of supermarkets, office complexes, and fuel stations.[22] Political connections and marketing helped the pyramids become a truly significant force in the Albanian economy. The former helped in getting a number of Ponzi firms time on state television. As economist Dirk Bezemer noted: "Importantly, the absence of warnings from the government, the frequent appearance of pyramid managers and government officials side by side at public meetings and on television, and the association of pyramid managers with the Democratic Party lent state credibility to the schemes."[23] There would be serious repercussions for the blending of reality and perception, the seeming government approval was something that would end in explosive fashion.

By early 1996, the frenzy for pyramid investing was at its peak. Vefa, Gjallica, Xhafferi, and Populli became prime places for Albanians of all ages to place their hard-earned savings. It is estimated that Xhafferi and Populli between them had nearly 2 million depositors—nearly two-thirds of Albanian's 3.5 million people.[24] By November 1996, the face values of the schemes' liabilities were $1.2 billion, a sum larger than the country's foreign exchange reserves. The investment mania had reached new heights, with both urban and rural populations sucked into schemes that promised wealth beyond their dreams. Reaction was extreme and widespread: "Albanians sold their homes to invest in the schemes; farmers sold their livestock. The mood is vividly captured by a resident who said that, in the fall of 1996, Tirana smelled and looked like a slaughter house, as farmers drove their animals to market to invest the proceeds in the pyramid schemes."[25] As one Albanian who lost $20,000 in the collapse of Vefa recalled: "We sold our apartment to invest more when the monthly interest rate was increased to 8 percent. Now my whole family is in Greece trying to save enough money to build a house in Tirana."[26]

The rise of the pyramid schemes badly distorted the Albanian economy. Money entering the country from Albanians working abroad tended to head directly into the informal financial sector. In many ways there was little incentive to work in the real economy considering the high interest rates offered by the pyramid schemes. But a crisis was looming. As Pettifer and Vickers observed: "It was a time of Weimar-like optimism, but the dance was on the edge of the cliff."[27]

There were warnings about the danger. The World Bank publicly alerted Albania in mid-1996 and the IMF followed in October. Considering the frenzied market conditions and the nonchalance of many government officials, if not their outright involvement, the warnings only belatedly resulted in any action. Finally in January 1997, right before the storm broke, the central bank, the National Bank of Albania, under intense IMF pressure, took the initiative of tightening regulations vis-à-vis non-regulated financial institutions. This was accomplished by ruling that the "money firms" were limited to daily withdrawals of US $300,000 from their official accounts. This was done to put a brake on the movement of hot money through the financial system and prevent a run on the schemes. Needless to say many of the fund managers complained, realizing that such an action would undermine an already sagging level of confidence.[28]

## A Painful Collapse

By early 1997, the pyramid schemes were no longer sustainable. Despite the involvement and implied support of President Berisha's government, the bubble burst. Citizens called the bluff of the pyramid companies, which now collapsed like so many dominoes. Following the central bank's action in January, Gjallica announced dates to repay principal, but was unable to do so. It was soon followed by Sude. Adding to the sense of drama on January 18, Sude's top manager was arrested. Vefa and Kamberri also indicated that they were having repayment problems. The coup de grâce came when the government suspended the foundations' bank accounts.

Public anger was expressed on January 19 in Tirana by a demonstration, organized by the Socialist Party and other opposition groups. The government used the police to suppress the demonstration, which did little to reduce tensions. Indeed, the Berisha administration's tough tactics of imposing jail sentences and fines on the protesters set the stage for a rapid breakdown in Albania society.

The rising tide of public discontent and the increasingly deteriorating financial landscape pushed the government into belated action against the financial corruption. On January 21, the Berisha administration officially launched an investigation of the pyramid schemes. It was a classic example of shutting the barn door after the horses had run out. At the same time, the authorities started to seize the assets of the financial firms. This was followed two days later by a banning of pyramid schemes. An address by Berisha to his supporters on January 28, when he assured the crowd that the government was working to "pay their money back, penny for penny," did little to calm matters.[29]

Public order started to dissolve in late January as parts of the country, especially in the south, openly rebelled against the Berisha government. Large-scale protests broke out in the town of Shkodër and quickly spread. Although the government was finally cracking down by the jailing of the presidents of Xhaferri and Populli and the interrogating the presidents of Vefa and Kamberri, many Albanians were furious about the government's response, especially considering the identification of many officials with the informal economy and the tainted companies.

The erosion in the legitimacy of the Berisha government in the eyes of many citizens had begun earlier. By 1995, the administration was increasingly accused of corruption and strong-arm tactics. According to a US State Department report, human rights abuses had occurred, including beatings, prolonged pre-trial decisions, and occasional restrictions on freedom of speech and the press. While these actions did not in themselves make Berisha a dictator, it demonstrated an authoritarian tendency in how the president and his government operated. But there were a number of other actions that eroded Berisha's credibility—the passage of a "genocide" law before the May 1996 elections to preclude anyone who found to have "collaborated with the former communist regime" from holding political office until the year 2002. The May 1996 elections were marred by reported cases of ballot fraud and intimidation by the police vis-à-vis voters and a protest in Skanderbeg Square was violently broken up by authorities. There was also the expulsion of a judge, raising serious concerns over the independence of the judiciary.

Berisha also appeared to be active with patronage via the Democratic Party and government posts. As the American Institute for Defense Analyses observed of the situation in 1995-1996: "There was growing concern that the Democratic Party was awarding jobs based solely on party affiliation. The socialist opposition was accused of clinging to the 'old way' and was systematically discriminated against by the Democratic Party. Supporters of the Socialist Party were purged from government organizations. This left many capable people jobless and dissatisfied with the government.[30] The combination of political heavy-handedness, the use of force, and blatant cronyism left Albania in the run-up to the financial crisis a deeply polarized society. When the financial roller-coaster ride came to an end, the country was ripe from an even more profound political upheaval.

Another major problem was a breakdown in military discipline. Initially deployed to guard public buildings and restore order, the rank and file soldiers were badly torn by the societal polarization. Many within the military had family or friends who were about to lose their savings. Additionally, the Berisha government increasingly appeared inept and dictatorial, especially when it declared a state of emergency. When public discontent turned violent, the military, with a few exceptions, melted away. The political stage was open to anyone with guns and willing to use them.

An estimated 2,000 people were killed in the ensuing chaos, damage to property was extensive, and real GDP contracted by 8 percent in 1997. Finally, Italy, fearing a massive outflow of Albanian refugees, sent in troops through a United Nations mission to help restore order. Earlier requests for help from the Organization of Security and Cooperation in Europe (OSCE) and West European Union had fallen on deaf ears and were complicated by political considerations.

Years later the government and international auditors remained at a loss as to where all the money went with the pyramid schemes. Although the Albanian economy had gradually recovered, many families still felt the repercussions of one of the worst bouts of speculation in the country's history. In a 2000 report prepared by the professional services firm PricewaterhouseCoopers, it was concluded that the 17 schemes that operated until their collapse in early 1997 were "thoroughly dishonest businesses."[31] Accordingly it was revealed that the vast bulk of the money was taken out of the country in trucks bound for Greece and other countries. Although $50 million to $100 million was discovered in overseas bank accounts in Greece, Turkey, Macedonia, Germany, the United Kingdom, and the United States. It remained doubtful that any of it would return. Simply stated, Albania lacked bilateral agreements that would allow this money to be given back to investors. It was also uncovered that some of the companies were involved in narcotics trafficking and money laundering.[32]

## Putting Albania Back on Track

Albania's socio-economic and political meltdown was a profound experience, leaving the small Balkan country dependent on external forces to restore law and order. Italian troops were eventually supplemented by forces from France, Greece, Turkey, Spain, Romania, Austria, and Denmark. This helped stabilize the situation and allowed a government of national reconciliation, under socialist Prime Minister Bashkim Fino, to take office. In late June and early July 1997 the country held parliamentary elections, which occurred without controversy. Fatos Nano, a socialist, became the new prime minister.

In the aftermath of the 1997 collapse, the government sought to deal with the guilty. One of those to be caught up in the "search for justice" was Vehbi Alimucaj, the owner of Vefa. Following an investigation, helped along by Deloitte and Touche, it was revealed that Vefa defrauded at least 92,000 Albanian investors out of $255 million. The company only had assets of $33 million.[33] It was uncovered that Vefa was involved in weapons smuggling, money laundering and other illegitimate businesses. Indeed, when creditors started to demand their money back in early 1997, Alimucaj transferred large sums out of the country. Accordingly, in January and February, he loaded helicopters belonging to Vefa with packages of money and brought them to a factory in the port city of Vlora. From there the trail went cold.

But other money trails were discovered. Between February 19 and June 26 some $2.28 million was transferred to a Greek lawyer (Dionis Bulukos) who ran a bank account for Alimucaj in Greece. Swiss investigators uncovered an account under the name of Alimucaj's son, Edmont, for $1.1 million at the Union Bank of Switzerland, Alimucaj's brother-in-law Dhimeter Cico came under investigation by the Greek authorities for "keeping, hiding, and accepting money of criminal origin," and there were probable links between Alimucaj and another pyramid scheme operator, Hajdin Sejdia (who was latter extradited to Switzerland where he faced trial for fraud).[34] As for Alimucaj, Albanian courts were to sentence him to 20 years in prison for stealing $325 million of investors' money and for arms trafficking. There were also persistent allegations that he was closely linked to organized crime in Italy. He was to serve part of the sentence, but ended up in a hospital due to problems with diabetes.

The Albanian government, with international help, introduced reforms to strengthen the state and the regulatory system. Money laundering was made illegal, better bank supervision ewas implemented, – and international law enforcement and financial regulatory ties were strengthened. Additionally, the government implemented reforms to improve public administration. Along these lines, in 2002 the government adopted a new wage structure for the top civil servants to help deal with issues like attrition and low motivation.[35]

In the general elections of July 2005, Sali Berisha returned to power. The long eight-year rule of the socialists had ultimately left a bad taste in the mouths of many Albanians, enough to make them overlook Berisha's somewhat tainted past. By the first decade of the twenty-first century Albania had largely recovered from the pyramid schemes. Although Albania remains troubled by the international narcotics trade and organized crime, it is doubtful that the country will suffer a crash similar to the one caused by financial fraud as it did in the 1990s.

## Albania in Context

Albania was not the only other small country to be hit by financial fraud in the form of Ponzi or pyramid schemes in the mid- and late 1990s. Grenada, Colombia, Lesotho, and Suriname are all examples of small economies that fell prey to scams offering easy money to investors.

In Suriname in the mid-1990s, for a three-year run, thousands of people put millions of dollars into Roep Inc., which offered annual rates of return of 120 percent and was believed to have more capital than all of the commercial banks in the country. Another rival company, Johwin Inc. was also started. Both companies attracted local Surinamers, but also politicians and thousands of Surinamers living in the Netherlands (the former colonial power).

What was interesting was that the two heads of Roep Inc., Roep Ramtahalsingh and Henk MacDonald, were at pains in March 1997 to make a distinction between their operation and those in Albania that crashed less than two months before. In particular, in Albania each investor was required to bring in three other investors, but in Suriname, investors made a deposit and got 10 percent returns monthly.[36] At the same time, the company promised that people would earn back their original investment in 10 months. Suriname's central bank was not as positive, with Otto Ezechiels, a managing director stating in May 1997: "Everything will go well until no more deposits are made, and then the near-bankers will not be able to continue paying the interest and there will be a collapse."[37] By June 1997, Suriname's pyramid scheme collapsed. Although this hurt the general economy, the impact was not of the same scale and scope of Albania's experience.

Ponzi and pyramid schemes have not disappeared. While Albania and Suriname moved on from large-scale acts of financial fraud, Jamaica was hit by Ponzi schemes during the mid-2000s. Most of the schemes claimed to be investing in a variety of assets including real estate; a large number purported to be involved in foreign exchange trading. There were even some schemes that were allegedly conduits to invest in other better-known schemes. As a group, these companies were not licensed or registered with the authorities, offered returns significantly higher than those offered by regulated entities, and some paid referral fees for bringing in new investors. Two of the best known of these schemes were OLINT Corporation and Cash Plus Limited. Both Cash Plus and OLINT were to cost Jamaicans dearly. For example, the firms took in invested funds of J$22 billion (US$260 million or 2 percent of GDP) during 2004-07 from 35,000 to 45,000 investors.[38] According to a January 2000 Caribbean Policy Research Institute study, the combination of Jamaican financial fraudsters took in investments of 12.5 - 25 percent of GDP, with a typical investment of around J$200,000 to J$300,000 (about US$2,800-$4,100).[39] OLINT was active in Jamaica, but spread its operations to St. Kitts and Nevis, Turks and Caicos, Grenada (via a conduit called SGL Holdings Inc.), Dominica, and St. Lucia. All of these activities were closed by local authorities, but were clearly detrimental to regional economies.

In a 2009 International Monetary Fund Working Paper, entitled "Ponzi Schemes in the Caribbean," the authors identified the following as consequences of this type of financial fraud, which clearly reflects the Albanian experience:

- Undermining confidence in financial markets;
- Diverting savings from productive to unproductive uses and, in some cases (like Albania's), from the domestic economy to overseas destinations, with a balance of payments impact;
- Incurring fiscal costs, if bailouts occur;
- Diverting deposits from banks and increasing non-performing loans if loan proceeds were diverted into schemes;
- Causing swings in consumption driven by paper profits or early withdrawals;
- Causing socio-economic strife if a sufficiently sizeable number of households are exposed to sudden losses; and
- Undermining the credibility (or legitimacy) of political authorities, regulators, and law enforcers for failing to prevent open frauds and money laundering or for supporting other illegal enterprises by scheme's operators.[40]

Many of the above were clearly evident in Albania in the 1990s, a reflection of both the globalization of financial ties and financial crime.

## Conclusion

Albania's initial experience with financial liberalization was a disaster. During the 1990s, Albania experienced an ill-fated combination of a rocky transition from communism to a market economy, overlaid with a troubled experiment with a more open political system complicated by corruption and the authoritarian tendencies of the country's president. In a very basic sense, the weak institutional environment, the very political nature of economic decision-making, official corruption, and widespread public ignorance left one of Europe's least market-experienced country's vulnerable to the blatant manipulation of a handful of unscrupulous individuals. In Albania, there was no tradition of financial supervision, prudent investment supported by due diligence, or history of past scandals. Consequently, Albania stumbled into a large-scale crisis ill-prepared and fragile from a set of internal and external pressures. Indeed, Albania's very survival as a modern nation state briefly devolved from Albanian hands as the country ended up a ward of the international community. In this sense, the scale of the disaster was as great as that which befell the Dominican Republic because of its financial misdealings and Scotland after its doomed venture in Darien.

## Notes

1.  Ana Carvajal, Hunter Monroe, Catherine Pattillo, and Brion Wynter, "Ponzi Schemes in the Caribbean," *IMF Working Paper,* (2009), p. 6.
2.  Christopher Jarvis, "The Rise and Fall of Albania's Pyramid Schemes," *Finance + Development,* (March 2000), Vol. 37, No. 1, p. 1. Publication of the International Monetary Fund.
3.  Ibid.
4.  Miranda Vickers and James Pettifer, *Albania: From Anarchy to a Balkan Identity,* (New York: New York University Press, 2000), p.79.
5.  Ibid., p. 10.
6.  International Monetary Policy, "IMF Approves Emergency Post Conflict Assistance for Albania," Press Release 95151, November 7, 1997 (Washington, D.C), p. 1.
7.  Vickers and Pettifer, *Albania,* p. 79.
8.  Ibid, p. 135.
9.  International Narcotics and Law Enforcement Affairs, *1998 International Narcotics Control Strategy Report,* (Washington, D.C.: US Department of State, 1998).
10. Cyrille Fijnaut and Letizia Paoli, eds., *Organized Crime in Europe: Concepts, Patterns, and Control Policies in the European Union and Beyond* (Dordrecht, The Netherlands: Springer, 2004), p. 556.
11. Ibid.

12. Roger Boyes and Eske Wright, "Drugs Money Linked to The Kosovo Rebels," *The Times*, (London), March 24, 1999.
13. Klarita Gërhani, "Politico—Economic Institutions and the Informal Sector in Albania" in Dirk J. Bezemer, editor, *On Eagle's Wings: The Albanian Economy in Transition*, (New York: Nova Science Publisher, Inc., 2009), p. 86.
14. Ibid.
15. Ibid., p. 87.
16. Ibid., p. 89.
17. C. Elbirt, "Albania under the Shadows of the Pyramid Schemes," *Transition*, (World Bank), October 1997; p. 9.
18. Dirk Bezemer, "Growth but Not Development: The Ponzi Economy and Its Lessons," in Bezemer, ed., *On Eagle's Wings*, p. 21. Also see his "Post-Socialist Financial Fragility: The Case of Albania," *Cambridge Journal of Economics* 25: 1-23 (2001).
19. Jarvis, p. 1.
20. Bezemer, *On Eagle's Wings*, p. 22.
21. Bruce Sterling, "Life as an Albanian Ponzi Scheme Model," Radio Free Europe/Radio Liberty, Prague, Czech Republic, Vol. 4, No. 42, 6 June 2000.
22. Ibid.
23. Ibid.
24. Bezemer, *On Eagle's Wings*, p. 22.
25. Ibid.
26. John Mason and Kerin Hope, "Albanians See Their Pyramid Savings Funds Lost and Gone," *Financial Times*, August 17, 2000, p. 2.
27. James Pettifer and Miranda Vickers, *The Albanian Question: Reshaping the Balkans*, (London: I.B. Tauris & Co. Ltd., 2007), p. 4.
28. Bezemer, *On Eagle's Wings*, p. 23.
29. Quoted from Edward Smith, Jr. and Edwin Pechous, "Crisis Management and Conflict Resolution in the Late 20th Century Europe: Albania—A Case Study." Institute for Defense Analyses, Alexandria, Virginia, p. 133.
30. Ibid., p. 127.
31. John Mason and Kerin Hope, "Albanians See Their Pyramid Savings Funds Lose and Gone," *Financial Times*, August 17, 2000, p. 2.
32. International Narcotics and Law Enforcement Affairs, *1998 International Narcotics Control Strategy Report.*
33. Jane Perlez, "Hunger Strikers Back on Albanian Who Defrauded Thousands," *The New York Times*, March 29, 1998. http://www.nytimes.come/1998/03/29/world/hunger-strikers-back-an-albanian-who-defrauded-thousands.com.
34. Radio Free Europe.
35. Volleer Treichel, "Stabilization Policies and Structural Reforms in Albania since 1997—Achievements and Remaining Challenges," in Bezemer, ed., *On Eagle's Wings*, p. 47.
36. "Thousands Are Investing in Pyramid Scheme Called 'Monetary Time Bomb'," *The Victoria Advocate*, May 22, 1997. p. 8.
37. Ibid.
38. Carvajal, Monroe, Pattilb, and Wynter, *Ponzi Schemes in Caribbean*, p. 16.
39. Caribbean Policy Research Institute, "Investigating Informal Investment Schemes in Jamaica," (Kingston: Caribbean Policy Research Institute, 2008).
40. Carvajal, Monroe, Pattillo, and Wynter, "Ponzi Schemes in the Caribbean," *IMF Working Papers* (2009), p. 5.

# 7

# Volcanoes, Icelandic Banks, and McDonald's

For most of the planet in early 2008 the names of Iceland's three largest banks, Kaupthing, Landisbanki, and Glitner, were, if anything, amusingly different. Indeed, Kaupthing sounded like anything from a farming tool to a ritualistic Viking weapon. Reality was something altogether different—and tragic for the vast majority of Icelanders and investors in those banks. In the first decade of the twenty-first century, the ambitious over-reach of bankers at Kaupthing, Landsbanki, and Glitner came very close to sinking the island-state's economy. The massive build-up of debt, well above the size of Iceland's gross domestic product (GDP), caused a brutal reckoning in late 2008, when the three banks were taken over by the Icelandic government, and the Internet banking assets of Kaupthing were seized and transferred to ING in the United Kingdom under a 2001 anti-terrorist law. This action was to trigger an almost total freeze on banking transactions between Iceland and the rest of the world. Iceland's freewheeling economy was brought to a screeching halt. It can be argued that this was one of the world's worst all-time financial disasters to be inflicted on a sovereign country.

How did Iceland become one of the first epicenters in what was to become an extended European sovereign debt crisis? After all, Iceland repeatedly appeared in statistical data as one of the more affluent countries in the world. By the early 2000s, it had gained a reputation for its aggressive young entrepreneurs blazing a trail into financial circles in Europe, the Middle East, and North America. It was also known for its in-demand fashion models and its own peculiar brand of rock music. In 2007, the North Atlantic island-state was ranked as the most developed country in the world by the United Nations' Human Development Index. Iceland's glory, however, was short-lived. By 2009 its population was shell-shocked, its banks nationalized and shrunk, entrepreneurs either in hiding or out of Iceland and economic prospects gloomy. In 2010, one of Iceland's long dormant volcanoes erupted, spewing an ash cloud that temporarily shut down air traffic over the North Atlantic and much of Europe. Iceland, it appeared, was under a cloud, both figuratively and literally.

What happened in Iceland was a rapid and overly aggressive overseas expansion of banks and entrepreneurs who came of age in the era of easy money. The problem was that as Iceland's business elite expanded there was a weakness in risk management, compounded by a clan-like closeness between many of the country's major financial players including those in government and at the central bank. On top of this, there was an almost blind faith in the magic of the marketplace. Add to this mix getting caught out by foreign investors armed with sharp credit skills, Iceland's banks were ultimately revealed as easy to wound and, over time, vulnerable to the worst thing that could happen to a financial institution—the loss of investor/depositor/counterparty bank confidence. As 2008 progressed it became increasingly evident that fewer investors were willing to invest, depositors to deposit, customers to conduct business, and other banks to extend them credit in any form. The hand of external forces was all over the squeeze of the Icelandic economy, but the Icelanders had also made themselves vulnerable and international market forces proved to be punishing, relentless, and unforgiving. In many ways, Iceland's financial and economic crisis in 2008-2010 was like one of the Icelandic sagas depicting the hard vengeance exacted in the brutal and unpredictable world of the Vikings.

### A Viking Culture in the North Atlantic

Icelanders have a reputation for being independent and self-sufficient. After all, the island-state sits in the North Atlantic, with sparsely populated Greenland its only a neighbor. Iceland itself has more than once been described as a "volcanic rock," due to its rugged terrain and active volcanoes. Some 79 percent of Iceland's land area consists of lakes, mountains, glaciers, mountainous lava desert, and tundra. The country's saving grace is the Atlantic gulf stream, which moderates the climate, and plentiful hot springs. Due to their climate, Icelanders have demonstrated a historical heartiness.

Iceland was originally founded between A.D. 870 and A.D. 930 by Norwegians, who had arrived via Britain, Ireland, Orkney, and the Hebrides. They brought with them Celtic wives and slaves and were fleeing a number of blows against the Viking world. The party that settled Iceland was not a meek group; survival depended upon boldness, independent thinking, and adaptability. Asgeir Jonsson, the head of research and chief economist at Kaupthing Bank, observed: "In the Icelandic mind, success is the reward for personal daring, ingenuity, improvisation, and an eye for the main chance—just as it was in the Viking times."[1]

Over time Norway's hold over Iceland faded and that of Denmark became dominant. The Danes would hold sway over Iceland until 1944, when the Icelanders took advantage of Denmark's occupation by the Germans to declare themselves an independent republic. Danish rule had largely been defined by keeping the country as an agricultural producer and fishery. When the opportunity came, Iceland was quite happy to remove distant Copenhagen from its imperial role. Iceland, which had been occupied first by the British and then the United States to preempt a German takeover during the Second World War, quickly become a founding member of the North Atlantic Treaty Organization (NATO).

One of the offshoots of World War II was that Iceland developed a close relationship with Washington, which maintained a base on the island in the Cold War. This was important, as US support was helpful when Iceland asserted its control over its fishing grounds in the 1972-1973 Cod War against the United Kingdom. The UK backed down in that conflict and relations improved from that point forward, though the memory would no doubt linger in official London. Fishing remained central to Iceland's economy through the 1970s, but in the 1980s concerns arose about overfishing. There was also considerable international pressure against Iceland over its ongoing commitment to whaling. In 1989, in particular, Iceland discovered that severe overfishing resulted in a collapse of cod stock. This came at a critical turning point in Iceland's history and at a time when the global economy was also changing.

## Iceland Calling

One offshoot of Iceland's economic transformation was the evolution of its banking system from a sleepy inward-looking clutch of financial institutions into turbo-charged financial entrepreneurs seeking to cut a large swath in global finance. Icelandic banking was long the domain of the government. Throughout the nineteenth century and the first half of the twentieth century, state banks dominated the scene, largely an extension of the island's fishing industry and the Danish government. Little changed with independence. It was only in the 1980s that Icelandic banking stirred and this was due to the push of external forces, namely the new wave of conservatism from the United Kingdom under Margaret Thatcher and the United States under Ronald Reagan. The free-market mantra that stirred Finland, Sweden, and Norway to transform and liberalize their financial systems also went to work in Iceland. The impact of such different thinking cannot be downplayed. Long in thrall to a more communal system, partially dictated by the island's challenging physical environment and isolation, the idea of individual responsibility, entrepreneurship and wealth had a tremendous appeal to the more youthful segments of the population looking for something different. Indeed, there was a certain resentment over the nanny-like nature of the state—beer was banned until 1989 and television (owned by the government) was turned off on Thursdays to provide families time to talk, sing, and read books.[2]

The 1989-1990 recession was in many ways a catalyst for change in Iceland. The dire state of the fishing industry raised a fundamental question as to what direction the country's economic development was to go. Agricultural production was increasingly efficient, but limited by geography and climate. What the country did have in abundance were well-educated people, who were increasingly global in their outlook. To transform Iceland into a different economy it needed to open up and become more market-oriented. The Icelandic economist Asgeir Jonsson noted: "As the nation struggled, a growing consensus turned away from the Scandinavian welfare-state model with a large public sector and an active state. Instead the focus turned to the Thatcherite, free-market reforms of Britain."[3]

Iceland embarked upon considerable economic reform during the 1990s. The role of the state was reducedby privatizations (including in the banks), financial markets were liberalized, and the country's corporate tax rate was reduced. The capital account, which was closed after the failure of Islandbanki in the 1930s, was reopened. Additionally, Iceland joined the European Free Trade Area (EFTA) in 1994, which gave it better access to a number of European markets. All in all, by the end of the twentieth century, Iceland had become one of the most open OECD economies, with a business class comfortable with the idea of assuming risk by expanding overseas. Indeed, many among Iceland's business elite came to see overseas expansion as the only way to expand their potential for profitability considering their home country's limited population size of a little more than 300,000.

One of the key forces in the transformation of the Icelandic economy was David Oddsson, who was strongly influenced by the works of the

University of Chicago's free-market economist Milton Friedman. A man who was to be Iceland's longest serving prime minister, Oddsson's imprint on his country was substantial. Born in 1948, he was the son of single mother and raised by his maternal grandparents. Oddsson was a charismatic, intelligent, and ambitious young man. As the Icelandic economist Jonsson observed: "His gifts of persuasion were remarkable; whether he was addressing private meetings, large public gatherings, or the entire nation on TV, he could move even the most stubborn and negative audience to cheer once he had spoken."[4]

Oddsson's early career was very much in the public eye. While reading law at the University of Iceland, he worked in a variety of jobs, including assistant to the director of a small theater, produced a popular radio comedy show, worked as a political commentator for a newspaper, and was a director of publication at a publishing house. In 1974, he competed for and won a seat on the Reykjavik Municipal Council for the Independence Party. That party was established in 1929 as a conservative organization, which over time favored membership in NATO and opposed Iceland's joining the European Union.

Oddsson and a number of other young free-marketers formed an increasingly influential strong wing of the Independence Party, favoring the liberalization of the then heavily state-dominated Icelandic economy. This was an important group as it included people like Geir Haarde (who followed Oddsson as prime minister) and Hannes Holmsteinn Gissurarson (a professor of political science at the University of Iceland and strong advocate for free-market policies). Holmsteinn Gissurarson was to become a close adviser to Oddsson during his years as prime minister and had a hand in securing the visits of foreign free-market economists such as Milton Friedman. Holmsteinn Gissurarson was particularly influenced by these economists as reflected in two of his works, *The Fish Stocks in the Icelandic Waters: The Property of the Nation or of the State?* (1990) and *How Can Iceland Become the Richest Country in the World?* (2002). The second book emphasized the importance for Iceland to move in the direction of becoming an international financial center, with low corporate rates and a stable political environment. It also looked to Luxembourg and Ireland as two countries that were similar to Iceland and had achieved a relatively high degree of affluence. With Oddsson out in front, Holmsteinn Gissurarson was to be a supportive voice in the ear of one of the country's strongest political leaders.

Oddsson's political career was impressive. He became the mayor of the nation's capital, Reykjavik, in 1982, a position that he held until

1992. In 1991, he became the leader of the Independence Party and was able to form a coalition government with the Social Democrats in the aftermath of the 1991 elections. During this period, Oddsson, as prime minister, launched some reforms to help move the economy out of what was a prolonged slump. In the 1995 elections, Oddsson and the Independence Party jettisoned the Social Democrats for the more right-wing Progressive Party. It was this combination that accelerated the reforms that greatly liberalized the economy.

There was another important aspect of Oddsson's rise to power; he did not ruffle the feathers of the country's traditional elite. Journalist Roger Boyes identified the old-moneyed families as "the Octopus," controlling many of the old-economy businesses and meeting behind closed doors to discuss the country's future direction. He noted that this clique "had grown together with the political class becoming the closest thing to a ruling elite a small island could have."[5] While the old elite was willing to deal with Oddsson, they were not pleased with the newer class of wealthy young Icelanders whom they regarded with disdain, though initially useful in raising the island's wealth.

One of the most significant acts of the Oddsson governments was the privatization of two of the country's banks, Landsbanki and Bunadarbanki, an act that was to have far-reaching consequences. The decision to do this was taken in 2002 and ultimately had a distinctly political feel to it. In October, the government's 45.8 percent of Landisbanki was sold to Samson Holding, a company owned by three Icelanders who had sold a beer factory in Russia to Heineken for $400 million. Two of the team, father and son Bjorgolfur Gudmundsson and Bjorgolfur Thor Bjorgolfsson, bought out the third man and emerged as the owners of Landsbanki. Although the deal was initially held up by Icelandic banking authorities (the Financial Services Agency or FSA) over concerns relating to the leveraged nature of the father and son's holding company, the background of the father in earlier business dealings and the lack of any banking experience, the sale was eventually consummated.

It is important to note that both Gudmundsson (born in 1941) and his son Bjorgolfur (born 1967) were risk takers. The father had been the managing director of a shipping company, Hafskip, which defaulted in 1985. In its wake it took down the Utvegsbanki (Bank of Fisheries), which resulted in a legal mess that saw Gudmundsson detained and charged with bookkeeping offenses. Despite this he was savvy enough to buy an obsolete factory in the north of Iceland and transport and assemble it in St. Petersburg just as the Russians were shifting to greater consumption of beer over vodka. The son had a business degree from New York University and liked to invest in Eastern Europe using an investment bank, Straumur Burdras. The Landsbanki deal was to make both men exceedingly wealthy. Jonsson noted: "The son became Iceland's first official billionaire in 2005; in 2007 he was ranked as the 249th-richest person in the world by *Forbes* magazine, with a net worth of $3.5 billion. His father—799th on the list—had achieved notoriety in England as the owner of West Ham, a soccer club in London."[6]

Bunadarbanki was put up on the bloc next, going to the S-group. This was an alliance of investors linked to the Progressive Party. Although they also lacked any banking experience, they were well connected with the junior member of the country's ruling coalition.

One of the other young entrepreneurs to stride onto the Icelandic stage was Jón Ásgeir Jóhannesson, one of the owners of the country's third largest bank, Glitner. Journalist Roger Bayes suggests that Jóhannesson and others were a hybrid of adventurers and pioneers of an aggressively entrepreneurial culture, complete with a linkage to the Viking past. He noted that Jóhannesson had something for names and Norse mythology: "a ten-foot-tall statue of a Viking, with a Fender Stratocaster guitar strapped to his back, adorned his London office. When he eventually bought a bank, it was named Glitner, the hall in heaven where all disputes are reconciled."[7]

Jóhannesson was not born to great wealth and his family background was decidedly humble. His father had worked at a slaughterhouse and was a grocer in a supermarket chain. What was interesting was that young Jóhannesson was very focused on the dynamics of making money, apparently at a young age. He was to attend a business college. According to Boyes, the catalyst in his life was when his father lost his job in the late 1960s: "To be laid off was to be let down by the government and the authorities. In Jon Asgeir's eyes, his father has been stripped of his manhood."[8] This set the stage for father and son in 1989 to open up an inexpensive food supermarket close to Reykjavík harbor. The father-son team had a simple, yet highly effective business model—drive hard bargains with importers and sell in bulk with small profit margins. Considering Icelanders long paid high food prices, the Bonus food chain soon became popular, so popular that the traditional reretailer, Hagkaup supermarkets, bought a 50 percent stake.

Jóhannesson was not done. In fact, he was only just starting. Along with Hannes Smarason, Jon Asgier formed a close-knit group composed of Baugur (a holding company) and the FL group, which had stakes in

Sterling Airlines, Iceland Express airline and Glitner, and parts of British high-street retailers.

But for all of the excitement at Landsbanki and Glitner, the real star of the emerging Icelandic banking scene was Kaupthing. Through their investment company Exista, the brothers Lydur and Agust Gudmundsson bought Kaupthing. The significance of this bank to what happened in Iceland was captured by the economist Jonsson (who worked at that august institution): "A single, independent investment bank—Kaupthing—kicked off international expansion in Iceland, and its influence over the rest of the country's banking system cannot be overstated. Its success led to a wholesale-funded, outward orientation and growth in banking assets that had no precedent."[9] Kaupthing was the first to take advantage of the liberalized financial system in the 1990s, becoming the first Icelandic bank to establish a foreign equity fund and become a leading asset management and brokerage house.

Kaupthing also led the way to expanding business overseas, first to Luxembourg and then into the Faroe Islands, Denmark, New York, Sweden, and Switzerland. By the mid-2000s the bank's website advertised Kaupthing as a "Northern European bank offering integrated financial services to companies, institutional investors and individuals." Additionally, Kaupthing (by 2008) was then "among the seven largest banks in the Nordic region in terms of market capitalization." That achievement of becoming one of the largest banks in the Nordic region was built on a series of strategic acquisitions including the UK merchant bank Singer & Friedlander in 2005 and FIH Erhvervsbank in Demark in 2004. Kaupthing was also willing to lever up to make their acquisitions, while their pushiness into the upper rungs of Nordic banking ruffled local feathers.

The new generation of Icelandic businessmen represented a sharp break with the conservative business practices of the past and were quite different from the country's traditional economic elite. Much of this was rooted in a more aggressive attitude to risk, though risk-taking clearly was one of the country's bedrock social characteristics. Iceland's president, Ólafur Ragnar Grímsson, stated of the entrepreneurs in March 2009: "Their success hailed a new era in the economy of Iceland, a nation which over a thousand years—in fishing, in agriculture—was brought up with a sense of risk taking."[10]

One of the most significant developments that came with the emergence of a generation of younger entrepreneurs was the embrace of risk-taking. Attached to this was an eagerness to be part of the global economy. This combination of risk-taking, pro-globalization attitudes, and market orientation came to permeate Iceland in the 1990s and early 2000s. It is important to underscore that the rise of the risk-taking culture in Iceland came at a time of easy money and an intellectually supportive system of central bankers, like Alan Greenspan in the US, and political leaders, from Thatcher and Reagan to Bill Clinton and George W. Bush, Tony Blair in the UK and Bertie Ahern in Ireland. The easy money part of the equation often served to camouflage risk or downplay problems associated with excessive leverage. At the same time, Iceland's leading bankers enjoyed strong political connections, adding to their confidence.

Although Prime Minister Oddsson was not entirely comfortable with the young Vikings, President Grímsson and his wife, Dorritt Moussaieff, came to symbolize the close linkages between government and business. Unlike the prime minister, the president's role was limited, providing Grimsson more time to pursue the promotion of the country. The president, a former leftist parliamentarian and political science professor, was a visible promoter of the entrepreneurs who, in the words of one journalist, "gobbled up European department stores, banks, supermarkets, even a Premier League football club."[11] As for Dorritt, she was all glamour and had a penchant for the high-life. One observer described her as a "wealthy gadabout with a phalanx of celebrity friends; an exotic pedigree (born in Israel, she claims to be a descendent of Genghis Khan), a byline in *Tatler*, the British society magazine; and a designer-jewelry business that includes a boutique in London's Park Lane Hilton."[12] To put it mildly, Dorritt found it easy to access the young Viking entrepreneur business elite as they traveled in many of the same circles.

Iceland's first couple became one of the country's major promoters and thus stimulated a close relationship with the new wealthy. As Condé Nast's Joshua Hammer stated of the first couple's activities: "Moussaieff and Grímsson both befriended magnates like Jón Ásgeir Jóhannesson—whose investment company, Stodir, was a major shareholder in Glitner, the country's third-largest commercial bank—and Jóhannesson's beautiful blond wife, Ingibjörg Pálmadóttir, an interior designer and owner of Reykjavik's ultra-trendy 101 Hotel."

Beyond the closeness of Iceland's business and political elite, the stage was also being set for the financial meltdown by a number of policy moves. In 2001, the central bank released Iceland's currency, the krona, to float against other currencies. International investors looking for a carry trade (borrowing money at a lower interest rate and putting it into another currency with higher rates) turned to the krona seeking a high yield. One outcome of this new demand was currency appreciation, which did not help exports. Armed with a strong currency, Icelandic corporate raiders started buying sprees in the UK and Nordic countries, acquiring department stores, banks, and pharmaceutical companies. In 2003, the Oddsson government adopted an expansionary fiscal policy and lowered income taxes. The impact was to kick off a domestic consumption boom, which in turn began to suck in imports (made cheaper by the strong currency). At roughly the same time, housing began to pick up. This situation was further accelerated in 2004 by the government allowing higher mortgage ratios on public loans for homes. One outcome of this was a rising household debt that reached more than two times personal income by 2007.

Iceland's boom was running full throttle by 2005. During that year a number of foreign governments issued krona-based Glacier bonds. These bonds quickly attracted foreign currency speculators, as Iceland was a highly rated country, with a rapidly growing economy, and increasingly well known for its high-flying entrepreneurs. By 2006, Iceland reached the highpoint of its free-market experiment. During that year the banks opened up high-interest savings accounts, most notably Kaupthing's Icesave, geared to draw in foreign deposits. Yet some of the glow was already fading from the Icelandic juggernaut.

## The Fall

Iceland's hard-charging banks left a trail of financial tidbits for the sharks of global finance—shorters. Although the Icelandic banks were profitable and busy expanding throughout the Nordic region, the UK and into the European continent, they were also big borrowers. What helped the Icelandic banks and investment firms was that asset prices kept moving upward. Consequently, the Icelanders benefited from asset inflation, which made them appear profitable and brilliant. It also gave the Icelanders a certain swagger as developments in financial markets continued to convince them of their market savvy. But the writing was on the wall. In early 2006, a report on Iceland by Danske Bank, Denmark's largest bank, indicated that the pace of growth by the island's financial system was too rapid and most likely heading into a crash. While many Icelandic bankers reacted angrily to this assessment, blaming it on Danish sour grapes from the island-state's declaration of independence from Copenhagen in 1944, others in the financial community, particularly within the hedge fund world took notice.

Although it is difficult to prove, there were ongoing stories about international hedge funds and other investors buying credit default swaps to short Iceland's banks. There was one story in particular that remained constant—a group of foreign investors coming to Iceland and drinking considerable amounts of alcohol and berating those whom they met. This left an enduring impression on Icelanders that forces from the outside world were out to get them. In March 2008, Iceland's central bank announced that the country's banks were under attack by "unscrupulous dealers."[13]

By early 2008, Kaupthing, Glitner, and Landisbanki were swimming in a sea of bad news. Bank management teams felt besieged by hordes of short-sellers (mainly US and European hedge funds), actively seeking to force failures. This situation was worsened by the growing turbulence in international capital markets. Adding to the problem was that Iceland's banks and their free-wheeling management teams were not well loved in the major markets they had pushed into, with Denmark, Norway, and Sweden the most evident repositories of this sentiment.

The problem was that Iceland had allowed a very oversized banking system to develop. The International Monetary Fund (IMF) noted that the banks increased their assets from being worth slightly more than 100 percent of Iceland's GDP to being worth close to 1,000 percent of GDP. This worked while international markets were going up (including the value of Icelandic bank investments), but it was disastrous when those same markets faltered and easy access to liquidity evaporated. All told, Iceland's audacious experiment in free-market capitalism resulted in a banking system that, in IMF parlance, "significantly outstripped the authorities' ability to act as a lender of last resort when the system ran into trouble."[14] Simply stated, the debts and liabilities run up by Icelandic banks were well beyond what the country's central bank had in terms of foreign exchange reserves.

In early 2006, Iceland's banks, currency, and stock exchange were aggressively shorted by foreign hedge funds. The banks were particularly vulnerable to credit default swaps (CDS), a contract through which the buyer insures a certain financial party against default by paying a certain premium. CDS was to be used extensively to short Icelandic banks. Although the financial system survived 2006 (with the so-called Geyser crisis), the problems refused to go away. Beginning in 2007 the fundamental solvency of the three banks was called into question, a number of foreign investors returned to short Icelandic bank bonds and by early 2008 it was impossible to raise new capital. Complicating matters, the global financial system underwent a profound deterioration. Bear Stearns was absorbed by JP Morgan in March, but international markets remained considerably volatile with significant doubts over a number of major companies worrying investors. Despite some tough talk from Prime Minister Geir Haarde, Oddsson's replacement as head of the government, the pressure on Iceland's banks and currency remained significant through the summer of 2008 and into September. Rumors surfaced (and were later verified) that the three banks over the 12 months leading into the October meltdown were busy shorting the krona, something that many Icelanders felt as a betrayal.[15]

In one week in October 2008, Landsbanki, Kaupthing, and Glitner were taken over by the Icelandic authorities, ironically outlasting Bear Stearns and in the case of Kaupthing, Lehman Brothers in the United States. In the midst of the crisis came a flashback to the Cold War and a reminder that geopolitics have not entirely gone away. In early October, word got out that Russia was thinking of providing a 4 billion euro loan to Iceland. Russia's ambassador apparently informed the Icelandic central bank governor Oddsson that help was on its way. This was subsequently denied by the Russian government in Moscow and was never lent. However, the mere fact that this was discussed and had some visibility reflected that Iceland was willing consider assistance from anyone who would provide it, while Russia no doubt savored the possibility of giving the US a nudge in the ribs over its assistance to countries like Ukraine and Georgia, traditionally in the Russian sphere of influence.

The damage to the Icelandic economy was considerable. Real GDP contracted close to 11 percent in 2009; inflation rose from 5.0 percent in 2008 to 12.4 percent; and the country experienced a problem with importing goods because of the plunge in the country's currency. The currency situation was greatly complicated by the UK government's use of an anti-terrorist law to seize Kaupthnig assets. Faced with these myriad difficulties, Iceland also became the first Western European nation forced to turn to the International Monetary Fund in 30 years. Not surprisingly, a groundswell of public opinion forced the ruling government out of power in April 2009. One more humiliation came in the form of McDonald's, the fast-food provider, announcing in late October 2009 that it was leaving Iceland due to the prohibitive costs associated with importing food. Iceland's woes continued through 2009 and into 2010.

## Dealing with the Consequences

The survival skills of Icelanders were severely tested during the end of the first decade of the twenty-first century when the country's once high-flying banking system imploded and the national economy paid the price in terms of severe GDP contraction, high unemployment, and real concerns over the ability of the country to pay for imports. The government fell and a new government was elected to deal with an economic crisis considered worse than in the 1930s. Indeed, some observers likened the situation to the country suffering a nervous breakdown and undergoing a period of serious introspection. Gestur Geirsson, a managing director of Samherji, Iceland's largest fish company, stated in 2010 about the illusion that his country could be a financial empire spread across the north: "I won't lie. I was up for it when it was going on. Now we know of course that it was crazy, and we're angry with government about how it ended up."[16]

The consequences of the rise and fall of Icelandic banks will to take a lengthy period to sort out. The economic fallout was brutal, ego bruising, and extensive, revealing the vulnerability of a small country seeking its way in a global system. At the same time, the economic collapse came like an old-fashioned naval broadside—a broadside of economic cannonballs ripping into the high-life of finance, models, aggressive risk-taking, and ambition. At a fundamental level, the economic collapse brought a focus on what Iceland's pervasive societal mores were to be. Although the freewheeling market ethos was to linger in certain quarters, most Icelanders had come to regard the "free market" idea with trepidation.

Iceland turned to the European Union (EU) with an application in July 2009 against a backdrop of despair and the hope that integration into a larger economic body would help protect it from the ups and downs of international capitalism. But even the prospect of EU membership is complicated as it entails Iceland adhering to a common EU fishing policy. The place of fish in Iceland's history and economy is central; there is a deep concern that the decisions made on fishing would be taken in Brussels and not necessarily in the interests of Iceland. In some ways there is a fear of a small country being taken advantage of by larger countries in a different manner.

Another consequence of the economic collapse was assigning blame. There was political fall-out and criminal investigations. Throughout 2009, Iceland's financial authorities investigated and in turn handed over cases of financial manipulation to a special prosecutor. In August, Gunnar Andersen, director-general of the Financial Supervisory Authority, stated his agency was convinced that "serious" manipulation had taken place and vowed to root out the perpetrators.[17] Of particular interest were possible links between Iceland's former biggest bank, Kaupthing, and loans to a Caribbean-based company controlled by Kevin Stanford, a British retail entrepreneur. The issue is that Kaupthing and other Icelandic companies developed particularly close relations with several high-profile UK-based entrepreneurs and companies as they expanded overseas. Stanford was a business associate of the Baugur retail company, whose UK investments stretched from House of Fraser to Hamley's toys and which borrowed heavily from Kaupthing.

The Icelandic government uncovered how Kaupthing lent heavily to some of its largest shareholders, sometimes with meager or no collateral. While this does not fit good practices, the government was suspicious that some of those loans were used to buy more shares in Kaupthing with the object of propping up its stock price.[18] The link between possible wrongdoing and public backlash was caught by the *Financial Times'* Andrew Ward: "Pressure is mounting on investigators to root out wrongdoing as the Kaupthing revelations stir public anger towards the business and financial elite blamed for crippling Iceland's economy."[19] One outcome was an investigation launched by the Icelandic government, which examined the activities of the country's bankers. One result of this was the arrest of the former CEO of Kaupthing, Hreidar Mar Sigurdsson. According to the special prosecutor, Sigurdsson was suspected of a number of violations, including embezzlement, violations of the law on the trade of stocks, and the law on limited companies. The conclusion of the Special Prosecutor's office was that the banks were emptied from within by their owners and that much of the responsibility lies with them and the governors of the banks.[20]

Another finger was pointed at the ineffective role played by Iceland's central bank. The central bank had three governors, one of whom was the former Prime Minister Oddsson, who was the chairman. The widely accepted idea, at least in the western sense, is that the central bank is supposed to be absolutely impartial. Considering Oddsson was the head of the central bank, his longstanding role as a free-market reforming national leader, and deep-seated personal animosity vis-à-vis a number of the young Vikings, undermined the impartiality of the central bank. There is also the perceptual issue—by having a political figure assume such a key position, the question had to be asked what was his economic or financial expertise, both of which appeared lacking before and during the crisis. This was made evident by the stark fact that the Icelandic state had allowed its banks to grow to such a point that it was impossible for the government to provide either an explicit or implicit guarantee. In a very real sense, Iceland's banks were allowed to become too big to save. Related to the failings of the government and central bank was the ultimately non-viable business model embraced by Glitner, Landsbanki, and Kaupthing.

In a 2000 paper on Iceland's financial problems by economists Willem Builer and Anne Sibert, four factors indicated the problems facing the North Atlantic economy: (1) a small country with (2) a large banking system, (3) its own currency, and (4) limited fiscal capacity. As the economists accurately noted:

> With most of the banking system's assets and liabilities denominated in foreign currency, and with a large amount of the short-maturity foreign-currency liabilities, Iceland needed a foreign currency lender of last resort and market maker of last resort to prevent funding illiquidity or market illiquidity from bringing down the banking system. Without an effective lender of last resort and market maker of last resort—one capable of providing sufficient liquidity in the currency in which it is needed, even fundamentally solvent banking systems can be brought down through either conventional bank runs by depositors and other creditors (finding liquidity crises) or through illiquidity in the markets for its assets.[21]

What was interesting about the Buiter and Sibert paper was that they were invited in the first half of 2008 to visit Iceland and conduct their study. The paper was sent to the Icelandic bank in April 2008 with the title of: "The Icelandic banking Crisis and What to Do About It: The Lender of Last Resort Theory of Optimal Currency Areas." According to the authors, their "Icelandic interlocutors considered our paper to be too market-sensitive to be put in the public domain and we agreed to keep it confidential."[22]

## Out of the Ashes?

For the government of Johanna Siguarórdóttis, elected in May 2009, the Icelandic landscape was devastating. The new prime minister and her government rapidly embarked upon repairing the damage. Under the left-of-center government, a program was implemented to introduce a 30 percent contraction in government finances over the following three years, with extensive cuts to infrastructure spending and wages; an agreement was reached with the IMF on economic targets and the recapitalization of the banks; a stability pact was reached with social partners; and loan agreements were finalized with several countries as part of the IMF program. Iceland officially started negotiations to join the European Union.

One of the major sticking points for Iceland's recovery, however, pertained to the legacy issues of IceSave saving accounts of Landsbanki, which had attracted hundreds of thousands of British and Dutch savers with high interest rates. Under proposed settlement agreements with British and Dutch governments, Iceland is expected to shoulder most of the compensation—a sum equal to about 50 percent of the country's GDP. Although assets against this debt would reduce the burden, it remained substantial, especially for a country seeking to recover from its worst economic crisis since the 1930s. And then there was the smoldering resentment in how the British government treated Iceland and its banks in the midst of the 2008 crisis. According to the Icelandic prime minister: "Last October, when Iceland was in deep crisis, UK authorities froze the assets of Landsbanki, and placed the bank (and for a while Iceland's government) alongside terrorist organizations on the official UK Treasury list of entities subject to asset freezing. Kaupthing Bank, which had been granted a government loan amounting to 5 percent of the GDP, then collapsed after its subsidiary in London was seized by the Financial Services Authority. Despite a critical report in April by the House of Commons Treasury Select Committee, no satisfactory explanations have been given for the UK's actions.[23]

Iceland's prime minister also indicated that in August 2009, the Dutch government opposed IMF support, because of IceSave.[24] This was a particularly loaded charge, considering that an agreement over IceSave accounts was being debated in Iceland's parliament. All of this led Siguarórdóttis to state: "It is hoped that the people of large countries such as the UK and the Netherlands are aware of the lasting impact their governments can have on small countries such as ours at a time of great distress."[25]

The IceSave issue did not to go away. In fact, it descended into farce. In early 2010, the center-left government painstakingly worked out an agreement with the British and Dutch over Icesave. With an eye to IMF conditionality and the need to resolve the block to EU membership, the parliament passed the deal (though holding their nose at the onerous terms). The bill then went to the country's president to be signed into law.

The country's president upon reflection of widespread public anger over the terms of the deal refused to sign the bill. Instead the president put the matter to a national referendum on March 6, 2010, where 93 percent of voters rejected the government-agreed settlement. While this provided an outlet for angry Icelanders, the lack of an agreement with the UK and the Netherlands jeopardized IMF rescue money. This, in turn, weakened Iceland's creditworthiness, which only served to further reduce access to international capital markets. Talks resumed, but were inconclusive.

While the settlement of the IceSave issue was unresolved as of late 2010, the legacies of the financial crisis are expected to be a long term problem. One result was a dent in Iceland's reputation as a destination for foreign investment. In a survey conducted in the summer of 2009 with more than 60 large European financial institutions, more than 90 percent said they were "unlikely" or "highly unlikely" to invest again in Iceland.[26] The same survey also noted that the overwhelming majority expected a prolonged period of instability in Iceland's financial sector and the authorities did not treat international creditors fairly.

On the non-financial side the most notable development from a foreign investor was McDonald's, which announced in October 2009 that it was closing its three outlets because the country's financial crisis made it too expensive for its franchise. The restaurants imported the goods from Germany, which during the crisis doubled in costs due to the falling value of the krona. Jon Gardar, the owner of Lyst, which ran the franchise, stated: "It just makes no sense. For a kilo of onions, imported from Germany, I'm paying the equivalent of a bottle of good whiskey."[27] Another reason for the closure was what McDonald's blamed as the "unique operational complexity" of doing business in an isolated nation with a population of just 300,000.[28] The closure of the fast food company's outlets makes Iceland one of the few European countries, including Albania and Bosnia, without a McDonald's.[29]

Another result of Iceland's financial/economic crash was the "Kreppa boom." In one of the stranger twists, Iceland experienced a baby boom. Kreppa stands for crisis, hence the Kreppa boom. As the *Financial Times'* Andrew Ward observed in August 2009: "Deliveries are up about 3.5 percent so far this year, putting the volcanic island on course to record its most annual births for at least half a century."[30] Although not everyone agrees with the idea of a Kreppa boom, other Icelandic commentators point to the crisis as the cause, arguing that rising unemployment, which shot up to 9 percent has left more time to procreate. At the same time, the collapse of the economy has made many Icelanders turn to relation-ships as a source of comfort. On the popular blog, The Icelandic Weather

Report, Alda Sigmundsdóttir noted: "I think many, many of us have sought solace in love and sex."[31] Baby boom or not, Iceland has one of the highest birth rates in the developed world at 14.3 births per 1,000 people, compared with a European Union average of 9.9.

An important question that Iceland's financial crisis raised was its viability as an independent country. Anne Sibert, a professor and head of the School of Economics, Mathematics, and Statistics at Birkbeck College, London, asked in 2009: "This raised the question—does the recent experience of Iceland suggest that a country can be too small to be a nation state, and what are the costs and benefits of being isolated from the rest of the world?"[32] Certainly many Icelanders must have wondered about this question as their economy, and eventually way of life, became hostage to seemingly harsh and uncaring outside forces that hit the island like a typhoon.

Another pertinent question (as most Icelanders appear to still believe that they should be a nation state) is about making the right decisions vis-à-vis how to develop the economy. Financial services proved to be a bad decision, especially considering the reckless nature of those involved. Following the collapse, the country reverted back to fishing and the energy industry.. Gretar Thor Eythorsson, a professor of political science at Akureyri University, observed in 2010: "We are realizing, after the collapse, that natural resources are the beginning and the end of our economy. Energy and fish are our greatest resources."[33]

In another reflection of the impact of the bad decision over financial services, one of the flashiest of the young Viking entrepreneurs, Jón Ásgeir Jóhannesson, the former billionaire boss of Baugur, ended up accused of fraud by Glitner Bank in May 2010 and had his assets frozen in London (where he was residing), New York, and Reykjavik. The lawsuit against him alleges: "A cabal of businessmen led by convicted white-collar criminal Jon Asgeir Johannesson, engaged in a sweeping conspiracy to wrest control of Iceland's Glitner Bank to fill their pockets and prop up their own failing companies. The individuals siphoned money out of Glitner at the worst possible time for the bank. Having depleted Glitner's cash reserves after April 2007 by engaging in heavy and improper lending to entities that they controlled, the individual defendants left Glitner heavily exposed to the global credit crunch."[34]

## Conclusion

Iceland will go down in history as one of the most spectacular economic and financial collapses. For a country with such a comparatively small population—the entire citizenry would be outnumbered in Manhattan or downtown Tokyo London—Iceland's bank failures symbolize the end of the era of easy money in global capital markets and of Iceland's young Viking entrepreneurs. Along these lines, Iceland's experience in the first decade of the twenty-first century should be a cautionary tale about the dangers of over-confidence and excessive debt for small economies. Add to this the problematic nature of a relatively clannish society where all the major players know each other, the emergence of financial innovation with little or no regulation, rapid riches, and aggressive risk-taking, the stage was set for disaster. When the crisis hit, Iceland lacking any major international supporter, was extremely vulnerable. The country's isolation was starkly underscored by the reluctance of the Nordic countries, barring Norway, to provide any meaningful support, not to mention the outright hostility from the UK and the Netherlands. Even Iceland's old NATO ally, the United States, was unwilling to become engaged in helping the island. The sad reality is that Iceland's troubles are likely to take a considerable amount of time to work through. The financial road back is a long one fraught with difficulties: a lack of investor confidence, pending litigation, and a pervasive societal anger over the collapse. It may prove to be the greatest test in the island's modern history.

## Notes

1. Asgeir Jonsson, *Why Iceland?* (New York: McGraw Hill, 2009), p. 10.
2. Roger Boyes, *Meltdown Iceland: Lessons on the World Financial Crisis from a Small Bankrupt Island*, (New York: Bloomsbury USA, 2009), p. 32.
3. Asgeir Jonsson, *Why Iceland?* (New York: McGraw Hill, 2009), p. 37.
4. Ibid., p. 141.
5. Boyes, *Meltdown Iceland*, p. 46.
6. Jonsson, *Why Iceland*, p. 50.
7. Boyes, *Meltdown Iceland*, p. 59.
8. Ibid., p. 61.
9. Jonsson, *Meltdown Iceland*, p. 44.
10. Joshua Hammer, "Icestorm" *Condé Nast Portfolio*, March 2009, p. 90.
11. Ibid., p. 91.
12. Ibid., pp. 90-91.
13. Abigail Moses and Tasneem Brogger, "Iceland's Biggest Banks Targeted by 'Unscrupulous Speculators'," *Bloomberg*, March 31, 2008. http://www.bloomberg.com/apps/news?pid=newsarchive&sid=aseau2yzmJSU.
14. From Camilla Anderson, "Iceland Gets Help to Recover from Historic Crisis," IMF Survey Magazine Interview, *IMF Survey Online*, December 2, 2008, http://www.imf.org/external/pubs/ft/survey/80/2008/INT111908A.htm.
15. "Icelandic Banks Deliberately Weakened Krona Before Collapse," *IceNews*, March 16, 2010. http://www.icenews.is/index.php/2010/03/16/icelandic-banks-deliberately-weakened-krona-before-collapse/.

16. Quoted from Tony Barber, "Fishing Poses Slippery Catch for Iceland," *Financial Times*, July 9, 2010, p. 4.
17. Andrew Word, "Iceland Watchdog Scents Manipulation," *Financial Times*, August 10, 2009, p. 3.
18. From Camilla Anderson, "Iceland Gets Help to Recover From Historic Crisis," IMF Survey Magazine Interview, *IMF Survey Online*, December 2, 2008, http://www.imf.org/external/pubs/ft/survey/80/2008/INT111908A.htm.
19. Ibid.
20. "Special Prosecutor: Many Cases in Final Stages." *Iceland Review Online*, April 13, 2010. http://icelandreview.com/icelandreview/search/news/default.asp?ew_0_a_id=360651.
21. Willem Buiter and Anne Sibert, "The Collapse of Iceland's Banks: The Predictable End of a Non-Viable Business Model," *Vox*, October 30, 2010.
22. Ibid.
23. Johanna Siguarórdóttis, "Icelanders Are Angry But Will Make Sacrifices," *Financial Times*, August 14, 2009. p. 7.
24. Ibid.
25. Ibid.
26. Andrew Ward, Megan Murphy, and Jim Pickard," Iceland Poised to Seal Pact on Foreign Payback," *Financial Times*, August 17, 2009, p.4. The survey was conducted by the UK law firm, Norton Rose.
27. "McDonald's Pulls Out of Iceland," *BBC News.* October 27, 2009. http://news.bbc.co.uk/2/hi/8327185.stm.
28. Ibid.
29. David Batty, "McDonald's to Quit Iceland as Big Mac Costs Rise," Oct/27/McDonalds-to-quit-Iceland.
30. Andrew Ward, "Banking Meltdown Delivers Baby Boom," *Financial Times*, August 17, 2009, p.4.
31. Ibid.
32. Anne Sibert, "Undersized: Could Greenland Be the Next Iceland?" *Vox*, August 10, 2009, http://www.voxeu.org/index.php?q=node/3857.
33. Barber, "Fishing Poses Slippery Catch for Iceland," *Financial Times*, p. 4.
34. Rowena Mason, "Former Baugur Boss Jon Asgeir Johannesson Accused of $2 billion Fraud," Telegraph.co.uk., May 13, 2010. http://www.telegraph.co.uk/finance/newsbysector/retailandconsumer/7716599/Former-Bauger-boss-Jon-Asgeir-Johannesson-down-to-his-last-million.html.

# 8

# Ireland's Time of Troubles

In 2009 the Irish economy contracted by 7.5 percent, a brutal blow to what had been one of Europe's bright spots. The root cause came from Ireland's financial sector, but other reasons abounded including the impact of external forces on the small country located in the North Atlantic. For the next several years, Ireland was rocked by a time of troubles and its political leaders were forced to make difficult decisions in order to restore financial confidence and return the country to economic growth.

The River Liffey rises in the Wicklow Mountains, meanders for close to 75 miles and funnels through Dublin, where it enters the Irish Sea. It is a central part of Ireland's capital city, crossed and re-crossed by auto and pedestrian bridges. On both sides of the river as it crawls toward Dublin Bay are docks, reflecting the Irish capital's history as a trading port dating back to the Age of Vikings. Cargos of Irish linen and agricultural goods flowed from the docks while incoming ships brought English coal and luxury goods from around the world. In the early twenty-first century the trading ships are long gone, the River Liffey handles little traffic (mainly tourist boats), and the actual port functions have shifted well beyond the city's old center. Commencing in the late 1980s and continuing on in the next two decades, the docklands underwent a profound transformation as aging docks, warehouses, and run-down neighborhoods were transformed into new high-rises, coffee shops, and bridges. Between the Customs House, built in 1791, and the modern $O_2$ Theatre arose the International Financial Services Centre (IFSC), a sprawling clutch of sleek new buildings, concrete, steel and glass, a North Sea base for some of the world's largest financial companies drawn by Ireland's well-educated workforce, smooth-working infrastructure, proximity to other European markets, and tax breaks.

During the 1990s and especially during the period from 2002-2007, the dockland area with its arrangement of George's Quay, City Quay, Sir John Rogerson's Quay, Custom House Quay, and North Wall Quay were part of the epicenter of Ireland's great economic leap forwards. The other related component was a rollicking property boom. The combination of strong economic growth in the 1990s (pushed along by export expansion) and Ireland's assuming the euro as its currency set in place an old-fashioned revolution of rising expectations. Ireland, referred to as the "Celtic Tiger" for its fast-paced growth in the 1990s, saw its standard of living shoot up as jobs flow in and wages increase. The good times had come to Ireland. Despite an economic slow-down, caused in large part by the global downturn in 2001-2002, Ireland embarked upon a fateful second round of turbo growth between 2002 and 2007. Unlike the expansion in the 1990s, the second round was fueled by a property boom in which the banks, developers, and the general public piled on. To a backdrop of strong free market views espoused by the ruling Fianna Fáil government of Taoiseach (prime minister) Bertie Ahern (1997-2008), soft-touch regulatory supervision, and an accommodating international financial system flush with liquidity, Ireland embarked upon a bubble of massive proportions for the size of its economy.

Ireland's bubble economy began to deflate in 2007 when the first sputters of doubt started to hit the property sector. While the property bubble deflated, the disappearance of Bear Stearns in March 2008 clearly signaled that the giant global liquidity party was over and that small open economies like Ireland's would soon face an after-party hangover. By September, Ireland's major banks were in deep trouble and forced to turn to the government for help. As in the US, UK, and other parts of Europe, the government intervened in a massive fashion. The economy soon went into a tailspin. Real GDP for 2008 contracted by 3 percent and by 7.5 percent in 2009. Unemployment moved over 10 percent in 2009 and remained high in 2010. And there was much more bad news to follow in terms of the condition of the country's finances, banks, and standard of living.

By late 2009, the docklands along the Liffey had lost their vigor. Although work was still continuing on the Dublin Convention Centre, a number of building sites sat in the shadow of idle cranes. "For Let" or "For Sale" signs were in ready evidence. The proposed U2 Tower was postponed and it was announced that the Dublin Docklands Development Authority (DDDA) required financial assistance from the government as a result of its earlier purchase of Irish Glass Bottle Site. The DDDA's chairwoman, Professor Niamh Brennan was to understate that the collapse of the property market during 2008 and a plunge of the authority's assets had made 2009 an "exceptionally difficult year."[1] The following year brought little relief.

How did Ireland reach "exceptionally difficult" years in the late 2000s? The nature of Ireland's crisis is both external and domestic. It reflects the challenges small countries face in dealing with international shock waves as well as something in common with larger nations—the ability of greed to overcome common sense in the rush for riches. While some of the behavior of certain individuals can be regarded as "scandalous," the pull of the bubble economy in 2002-2006 was strong and managed to suck in most of Irish society, leaving a handful of naysayers looking like modern Elijahs, set to wander the wilderness. It is the purpose of this chapter to examine Ireland's 2007-2009 crisis as to what caused it, who was responsible, and why the collapse was not entirely complete. This last point is worth further thought, considering the extent of Iceland's collapse and Greece's sovereign debt crisis in 2010, which is remembered by many in pictures of angry demonstrators protesting austerity measures.

## Setting the Stage

Ireland's 2007-2009 crisis did not materialize suddenly; rather, it was the product of several decades of development policies, a shift in the country's ideological moorings, and a self-reinforced sense of correctness (and some would argue smugness) among a relatively close-knit political and economic elites. This combination of factors has created an economy capable of making substantial strides, supported by a high degree of inventiveness, yet still suffering from a number of structural weaknesses. The Celtic Tiger mantle was earned as there was enough ingenuity in transforming the Irish economy from an agricultural to a services structure. The problem was in safeguarding gains and making tough decisions about the next stage.

Ireland gained its independence from the United Kingdom in 1921. Independence was achieved after the failed Easter Uprising in 1916 and a nasty guerrilla war that left a divided island with 26 southern countries opting to form part of a new republic and six northern countries (Northern Ireland) remaining with the United Kingdom. Part of the definition of what the new Irish Republic was came in the form of the economy. Six centuries of English rule had left a legacy of dislike with the political and economic dominance of Ireland's eastern neighbor. However,

Britain was also one of the world's leading economies and the imprint of British commerce and industry was undeniable. Consequently one of the earliest manifestations of Irish nationalism was to be expressed in economic policy.

Emerging from the Irish Civil War (1922-1923), American-born Éamon de Valera became the dominant political figure in the young republic. To put it mildly, the bookish-looking de Valera remains a controversial figure, being given credit for consolidating the new political entity to being vilified as the reason for decades of Irish economic stagnation.[2] He founded one of the country's major political parties, Fianna Fáil in 1926, had a major hand in writing the nation's constitution, and was a strong Catholic conservative. From the 1920s until he stepped down as taoiseach (prime minister) in 1959, de Valera was Ireland's dominant political figure and, as such, he shaped the Irish economy.

De Valera's economic view and the policies that he presided over were driven by nationalistic considerations and a conservative societal view based on the idea of the sturdy Irish yeoman managing his plot of land and finding contentment in the pastoral life. Indeed, de Valera in a March 1943 speech, noted he wanted a self-sufficient Ireland (one not dependent on the UK) composed of "cozy homesteads," populated by men and women who were sufficiently "satisfied with frugal comforts." As Robert Sweeney in his *Banana Republic: The Failure of the Irish State and How to Fix It* noted of de Valera's approach: "The net result of his blatantly unrealistic approach was the stunting of the country's economic growth in its formative years and mass emigration."[3] While such policies shrank the country's population through large-scale emigration and resulted in the loss of many entrepreneurial people, Ireland largely existed as a weak peripheral economy to the rest of Europe, caught between an ongoing brain drain and chronic high unemployment. Although some changes were made under the more enlightened Seán Lemass who followed de Valera in 1959 as taoiseach, major structural changes and dynamic economic growth were still missing through the 1970s and 1980s.

Ireland's economy was increasingly nudged by external forces. In 1973 Ireland joined the European Union (EU), a decision that was, by degrees, to help open the economy. Some reforms were introduced during the 1980s (like the creation of the International Financial Services Centre), but in the 1990s Ireland went into a more dynamic phase. Between 1980 and 1990, real GDP averaged 3.6 percent; it was to more than double by the end of the 1990s, hitting growth rates of 9.8 percent in 1995, 8.1 percent in 1996, 10.8 percent in 1997, and 11.1 percent in 1999.[4] The Irish society that emerged from the 1980s was relatively well educated, increasingly eager for change (membership in the EU clearly forced many Irish to focus on developments elsewhere in Europe as well as the United States), and was still able to offer an inexpensive labor force. In addition, the decision was made in 1994 to reduce the country's corporate tax rate to 12.5 percent, substantially lower than most of Europe at the time. These developments attracted substantial foreign investment, both in terms of capital and actual plants. At the same time, Ireland was to benefit from the expansion in world trade, which was marked by a rapid increase in world market share for Irish exports.

The economic changes introduced in 1994-1997 resulted in putting Ireland on the fast track. As big-name foreign companies moved to the republic, jobs were generated, wages started going up, and the overall standard of living rose. By the end of the decade, the Irish economy was running full throttle. This was reflected by unemployment falling to historic lows. Ireland, a traditional exporter of labor, actually had to turn to immigration (mainly from Poland and the Baltic states) for workers. For the first time, members of the Irish diaspora returned to the homeland, seeking economic opportunities. It was during this period that the Celtic Tiger moniker had its heyday, reflecting a strong pride in what was regarded by many as an economic miracle. A new Ireland was on the march, market-oriented, service- and export-driven, and on a similar wavelength as the dynamic economies of the United States, United Kingdom, Canada, and Australia. Ideas about the free market that had been at play with Reagan and Thatcher in the US and UK respectively clearly had an echo in Ireland, especially within the ranks of Fianna Fáil and the business elite. Considering the strong economic growth and the upswing in the country's standard of living, the free market pitch found a ready acceptance among most opposition parties and the general public. In general, it was hard to argue with prosperity and the country's newfound place in the ranks of some of the world's wealthiest countries. For the first time in modern history, Ireland became a destination for others, not a place where the educated and ambitious often opted to leave in search of better opportunities elsewhere.

## Fateful Decisions

Ireland was well positioned as a small, open economy, strongly tied to the US and UK economies. Although nothing should be taken away from the policy initiatives of the 1990s governments and entrepreneurial nature of the private sector, the country reached a critical fork in the road at the beginning of the twenty-first century. The decisions made in the early part of the decade were to have massive ramifications during 2007-2010. In this there was a convergence of political and socio-economic factors that were to serve up a major financial disaster, leading to the most severe economic downturn since the 1930's. And, as in the United States and United Kingdom (to a lesser extent), housing was to play a disproportionately large role in bringing down the economy. The Celtic Tiger ran well until the bursting of the dot-com bubble in 2000 and the ensuing global economic slowdown following 9/11 in 2001-2002. At this juncture, the Irish economy took a pause—real GDP growth slowed from 9.9 percent in 2000 to 6.0 percent in 2001 and roughly the same in 2002, before slumping even further to 3.6 percent in 2003. What happened to the Celtic Tiger?

The 2001-2003 slow down was caused by a loss of competitiveness, and sensitivity to global conditions. As an EU member and, in particular, a member of the euro currency zone, Ireland had surrendered control over its currency. This meant that the Irish government could not turn to currency appreciation as a mechanism to slow the economy (to curb inflationary pressures) or to currency depreciation to help boost exports and reduce debt. Consequently, the only other option—in the economist's perspective, but not from a politician's view—was to regain competitiveness via wage cuts. Such a policy was not exactly a rallying cry both within government and most of Irish society. Tighter public expenses were another economic policy option—but hardly palatable politically as the Fianna Fáil government of Taoiseach Ahern (who came into office in June 1997 and served until May 2008) had little interest in stirring up labor unrest. Consequently there was a shying away for the politically sensitive issue of eroding competitiveness. The issue became the elephant in the room.

But Ireland was not without options—or so it seemed at the time. The exciting world of housing beckoned. A study from the Dublin-based Economic and Social Research Institute (ESRI) observed:

> Its particular demographic structure meant that Ireland entered the boom period under-endowed with infrastructure in the form of dwellings. The number of adults per dwelling was substantially higher than in the other EU member states (with the exception of Spain). The rapid rise in incomes together with the increased availability of low cost finance as a consequence of EMU membership and the globalization of the financial sector resulted in a boom in the building and construction sector.[5]

Considering that the "home" occupied an important place in Irish society (at least in the national mythos), and higher wages put money in people's pockets, the Irish housing market was ready to take off.

Another important factor in Ireland's property boom was immigration. This came in three varieties—the returning Irish, attracted by their homeland's booming economy; high-salary foreigners employed in the expanding financial sector; and lower-wage paid foreigners, many of them from Poland and the Baltic states, pulled by the promise of jobs, higher wages, and, according to some, better social benefits. No matter what the motivation, this influx of people (many of them to Dublin and other major cities) provided a difficult gauge to fuel for property developers who adopted a "if you build it, they will come" mentality. As Anthony Sweeney observed: "much of the economy had wrapped itself around the construction industry: rather than being a group of separate variables, everything was tied together, which meant it would only need one threat to come loose for the whole to unravel. It was a self-perpetuating fallacy: people were migrating to Ireland because of the construction boom, but the boom was ultimately built on people migrating to Ireland." [6]

Two additional factors played their part—the globalization of the financial sector and a favorable political landscape (which gave way to lighter bank supervision) and an underestimation of risk in housing lending). Ireland's banking system was dominated by two large banks, Bank of Ireland and Allied Irish, but there were other significant financial players in the form of Anglo Irish Bank, Irish Life, EBS, and Irish Nationwide Building Society. (Building societies are roughly equivalent to American savings and loan associations.) The creation of the International Financial Services Center (IFSC), created by an act of the Dial (Ireland's parliament) in 1987 with EU approval, was successful in attracting a considerable amount of offshore financial business, including a strong contingent of foreign banks. As the IFSC's official website states: "More than 430 international operations are approved to trade in the IFSC, while a further 700 managed entities are approved to carry on business under the IFSC programme. The centre is host to half of the world's top 50 banks and to half of the top 20 insurance companies. Merrill Lynch, Sumitomo Bank, ABN Amro, Citibank, AIG, JP Morgan (Chase), Commerzbank, BNP and EMRO are just some of the big-name operations that have been chosen to locate in the area." With those "big-name" operations came a number of foreign experts and those people usually came with large salaries and in need of homes, hence adding additional demand on the local housing market.

The Irish financial services industry was to enjoy a "golden age" in the 2002-2006 period. While manufacturing was to decline, financial services expanded. Although Ireland was to lag behind Luxembourg and Cyprus in terms of financial intermediation as a percent of the private-sector workforce, it accounted for 7 percent of the private sector workforce, which put it slightly ahead of the UK. This further translated into more than 89,000 people employed in financial intermediation in Ireland, with a direct spending of about €6.2 billion on employee remuneration in a year.[7]

For Ireland's housing boom to gain momentum the banks opened up the credit floodgates. The Irish, after all, needed to live the Celtic Tiger lifestyle. Or so they were told. To meet heavy demand, the Irish banks borrowed funds from abroad, while a handful of foreign banks also increased their lending, buoyed by the easy money policies of the period. The combination of these activities was to push up net foreign liabilities of the Irish banking system from a low of 10 percent of GNP in 2003 to over 60 percent of GNP by 2007.[8] As in the United States, loan underwriting was loosened and bank regulation remained inadequate to the task.

Ironically, the International Monetary Fund, in its Article 7 Review of the Irish economy in 2003 fatefully noted: "With external demand slowing, strong credit growth and a prolonged house price boom have, to some extent, sustained domestic demand. Can financial stability and strong macroeconomic be maintained if the global economy remains weak, the euro appreciates further or house prices unwind-perhaps abruptly?"[9]

The IMF's 2003 report on Ireland also had some interesting numbers—real house prices increased over 130 percent since 1993, while credit to households grew in real terms at rates of 15-30 percent each year since 1996.[10] At the time, the risk of a bubble was downplayed by such arguments that the Irish population was young and upwardly mobile in its wages, average household debt to income was low by international standards, and housing supply was growing which would eventually hold prices in check.

The IMF snapshot included commentary on the Irish banks. It noted: "The authorities were concerned about risks to banks from rapid house price and credit growth, but noted that high levels of capitalization and profits provided an adequate cushion to absorb the effects of potential shocks without systemic distress."[11] The Fund report did mention that the Central Bank of Ireland had issued a warning letter to mortgage lenders on the need to maintain "rigorous" lending criteria despite growing competition. In addition, supervisors were conducting "themed" inspections on property loan portfolios of more exposed banks. They were also planning to coordinate a stress-testing exercise more adequately suited to detect risks in loan portfolios and requiring disclosure of lenders' methodology. While all of this sounded pro-active and hands-on from a regulatory/supervisory approach, it did little more than function as a speed bump in a property boom that had much more room to run. Somewhere along the way to the 2007-2009 debacle, Irish bank regulators lost their ability to adequately measure the growing risk of the property market. Instead of the bank regulators functioning as a blinking red light, warning of danger ahead, they became part of a rapidly moving financial/economic/political landscape rushing towards the edge of a precipice.

It was not only the IMF that developed a sense of concern about the property markets. By 2006, it was increasingly observed that the property market was frothy and that the impact of immigration on housing demand was perhaps overstated. In the Goodbody's Stock report of October 2006, *Irish Construction Economics* it was noted that the market was supplying close to 90,000 homes in that year, while its analysis "suggests that demand for homes amounts to an average of 68,000 p.a. over the period 2006-2011."[12]

## The High Life

Ireland's run to riches was not without its lavish side. The purpose of the country's earlier reforms was to change the structure of the economy, open it up to competition, and unshackle the business sector's entrepreneurial spirit. Along the way to remaking Ireland, there was considerable wealth creation. Some of that wealth creation was constructed on strong foundations; some of it was to prove fleeting. There was also a political factor that shall be discussed later in this chapter.

Probably one of the most poignant moments in Ireland's boom was the €1.5 million wedding bash of property developer Seán Dunne. According to one journalists' account, Dunne is "Ireland's best-known developer," with a reputation of "brazen-deal-making and Donald Trump-like lifestyle."[13] And he certainly became a symbol of the excesses of the boom, with an aggressive business style, melding a work-hard, play-hard mentality. In all fairness, Dunne did work hard to acquire his fortune. He was born in the small town of Tullow, outside Dublin. His childhood home lacked electricity or running water. Although he attended a technical college in the 1970s, studying construction economics, he did not stay in Ireland. Like so many others, he left—working as a bartender in New York City and doing a stint on an oil rig in Canada. Real estate work attracted him to London, but Dunne eventually returned to Ireland in 1990, just as the first reforms were gaining traction and with so much more to come. His initial deals were in government-sponsored housing projects, but with the changes in the Irish economy, Dunne soon found a new world of financially-better-off customers, the country's newly moneyed business class and foreigners. Like the Irish economy around him, Dunne's career took off. Probably his biggest deal was the very public purchase of a seven-acre plot in Dublin's classiest neighborhood Ballsbridge. Taking place in July 2005, the total purchase was for €379 million, which included two luxury hotels he planned to tear down and replace with a high-end commercial and residential development. As everyone noted at the time—at €54 million and acre, the purchase was one of the highest amounts ever paid for land in Europe. Sadly for Dunne, his intention to overhaul his plot of land in one of Dublin's most exclusive neighborhoods incurred resistance from the natives, who tied up his plans in court. By the time of the crash, the soaring office tower cut in the shape of a diamond and surrounding community of expensive houses and shops remained a dream of a fleeting golden age that was yet to be consummated.

While Dunne's property adventures were newsworthy in the Irish press, his second marriage to Gayle Killilea, described as "a former gossip columnist 20 years his junior," was downright scintillating. With shades of Dennis Kozlowski's 2000 birthday bash for his wife held in Sardinia for $2 million and Stephen A. Schwarzman's (the Blackstone Group founder) $3 million birthday, Dunne's wedding at a seventeenth-century villa on the Italian Riviera and two-week wedding cruise on the yacht *Christina O*, with 44 guests was viewed by many in Ireland "as a conspicuous and garish expression of the man and his business."[14] The *Christina O* was formerly owned by none other than Aristotle Onassis.

It is hardly fair to single out Dunne. As one of Ireland's rag-to-riches story and high-profile activities, he is notable in the public eye. Yet Ireland's boom briefly gave it the world's third highest count per capita of billionaires, behind only Kuwait and Switzerland.

One reflection of Ireland's lavish lifestyle was a short-lived boom in helicopter sales. As a social column in, *The First Post*, gushed in early 2008: "When the crowds gathered at the Galway Races last July, race-goers could barely hear themselves speak for the noise of helicopters overhead. This year, there will be more, as a leather-seated twin-engine Agusta 109 becomes *the* must-have among Ireland's oligarchs."[15] The same column went on to flutter that "such is the buoyant mood among the country's moneyed elite that three out of every five helicopters sold by Sloane Helicopters are bought by rich Irish entrepreneurs, making it the top market in Europe."

Ireland's boom also did raise the national standard of living. For all the glamour of the lavish life, there were improvements in social services, healthcare, and education. One reflection of this was how Ireland rose from the lower levels of GDP per capita among OECD country ranks in the late 1980s to number four in 2008. According to OECD data, Ireland's estimated GDP per capita stood at $47,800, which placed it behind Luxembourg, Norway, and the United States and ahead of Switzerland, Canada, and the United Kingdom.[16] Considering that the property markets were booming, the wealthy were partying, and the national level of wealth appeared on the rise, Ireland appeared to be on the road to a new level of economic development, leaving behind a past of high structural unemployment, emigration, and limited business prospects. The next turn in the road, however, was to clarify the country's vulnerabilities, both domestically and externally.

## Countdown to the Crash

The Irish bubble reached its peak in 2006, but there was a certain amount of impetus in 2007 as the writing on the wall became clearer to a growing number of people. Probably the classic silly expression in 2006 was that of Taoiseach Ahern, who astutely observed: "The boom is getting boomier." At that juncture Ireland had become a construction economy, with one in eight state employees directly employed in that sector. Although the IMF, OECD, and *The Economist* magazine all sounded warnings about the property boom going bust, there remained plenty of naysayers. For his part, Seán Dunne lashed out at the "economists" who had "mistakenly forecast the end of the housing and property boom in Ireland" for the last six years.[17] The property developer went on to call the economists a deluded bunch of "hyenas," those "harbingers of doom and gloom." Rounding things out, Dunne finished: "The hyenas have stopped laughing … each and every one of them was wrong."

Despite Dunne's snarling reaction to warnings over property markets, that sector was starting to cool by the second half of 2006. Part of the "jolt" to the housing market came from Progressive Democrat leader Michael McDowell, who proposed dramatic reductions in stamp duty for house buyers.[18] McDowell was seeking to launch an early election campaign and wanted an issue. His suggestion that the Irish government was willing to forgo stamp duty returns from land and property of €3 billion implied that at least part of the government (albeit a junior coalition partner) felt the good times were to continue. It also functioned as a brake on housing. As journalist Shane Ross observed: "The suggestions by the leader of the junior party in the governing coalition that stamp duty cuts may be in the offing did not cause property prices to fall immediately, but the volume of transactions virtually froze as buyers held back in anticipation of the change."[19] Yet it did not appear to be a major factor in the May 24, 2007 general elections in which the incumbent Fianna Fáil government won re-election. The ruling party saw its seats fall by four; its opposition, Fine Gael actually gained 20 seats. Fianna Fáil, with 78 seats, then formed a coalition government with its long-time partner, the Progressive Democrats (down two seats), and new allies, the Greens. The timing of the election was at least partially driven by a brewing corruption scandal around Taoiseach Ahern, which raised issues over his fitness to stand. Despite Ahern's damaging appearances at the Mahon Tribunal (investigating his past personal finances), the taoiseach was able to form the new government and hand it over to his chosen successor, Brian Cowen, formerly the finance minister.

Despite Taoiseach Ahern's re-election and prediction of a soft landing, one of the more forthright "hyenas," economist Morgan Kelly (from University College Dublin or UCD), published a report in the summer with ESRI that speculated that housing prices in Ireland could fall between 40 to 60 percent over a period of 8 to 9 years. As Professor Kelly stated: "The unusually large size of the Irish house building industry suggest that any significant house price fall that does occur could impose a difficult adjustment on the economy."[20] Although Kelly was dismissed by a number of financial firm economists and property developers as a scaremonger, he had accurately pointed out a looming problem. Indeed, dark clouds were growing over Irish housing as the nonbank mortgage sector in the US was rapidly cooling to a backdrop of failing companies. This was brought home in April 2007 when New Century Financial in the United States failed, making it one of early large sub-prime mortgage lenders to signal that the global era of loose money was quickly coming to an end. This was followed in June by troubles at two of Bear Stearns' hedge funds, the heart of the global financial system. And next door to Ireland came the news in September 2007 that the UK's ninth largest bank and major mortgage lender, Northern Rock, was in deep trouble, complete with a run on the bank and Bank of England intervention.

Although Irish regulators started tracking the downward trends in international markets in mid-2007, the awareness of the size and scope of the problem facing their own banks vis-à-vis property-related lending was not acknowledged. Indeed, on August 31, 2007, Patrick Neary, the head financial regulator, stated: "The domestic economy remains sound and there is no cause for alarm."[21]

But the alarm bells were going off. In Ireland the international storm had one of its first casualties in the International Securities and Trading Corporation (ISTC) in late 2007. ISTC invested in banks and was headed by Tiarnan O'Mahony who had worked at Anglo Irish Bank. He was also the chairman of the Irish Pensions Board, which meant his role as a government appointee was to oversee the performance and regulation of pension funds and to recommend ways of preparing people for their retirements. Although ISTC was expected to be a relatively safe investor, it was disclosed in August 2007 that it had exposure to US sub-prime mortgage loans. Confidence and investor money soon fled, leaving the company to fail with a loss of €820 million.

The global jitters continued through year-end 2007 and into 2008. March was the end of Bear Stearns, which was echoed in Ireland by downward pressure on bank and building society stock share prices. Indeed there was growing scrutiny of what was on bank balance sheets, in particular, Allied Irish, Bank of Ireland, and Anglo Irish, all with considerable exposure in the UK. And the UK, where banks had loaded up on sub-prime and mortgage-backed securities, was becoming a substantial risk on its own. Then came the problems at Fannie Mae and Freddie Mac, which were increasingly hit by rising mortgage defaults. In early September, the US government stepped in, assuming control of the two mortgage lenders. This was followed by a rescue of AIG and then on September 15, 2008 the failure of Lehman Brothers. To a backdrop of declining earnings, defensive statements by top management at the banks, and last-minute maneuvers for mergers (with Anglo Irish seeking some type of marriage), the Irish financial system came to the edge of a precipice.

The weakest link in the chain proved to be Ireland's third largest bank, Anglo Irish Bank. Although Allied Irish and Bank of Ireland had mismanaged their property market exposure at home and in the UK, Anglo Irish was to become the poster child of bank mismanagement. As Patrick Honohan (future head of the Central Bank of Ireland) and Philip Lane noted: "Traditionally conservative institutions, the two big banks' lending decisions appear to have been destabilized in the mid-2000s by the reckless expansion of the third one, Anglo Irish Bank. The latter bank was allowed to grow at an average real rate of 36% per annum, bringing its market share from 3% to 18% of Irish-controlled banks in 10 years."[22] But Anglo Irish's expansion under CEO Sean FitzPatrick came with significant problems, including self-lending to top management, poor underwriting, and a certain degree of opaqueness, helped along by light-handed regulation. These problems were magnified by an unwillingness of the bank's senior management to recognize the depth of problems facing their institution.

Even the rating agencies fell afoul of the bank's opaqueness. In its December 2006 review of Anglo Irish, Moody's lauded it for "Good credit quality supported by rigorous lending approach" and observed: "Moody's expects that forward business momentum in the UK and US will together counterbalance the anticipated deceleration in growth opportunities in Ireland."[23] In 2007, Anglo Irish drifted further into trouble as the property market gradually cooled. By 2008, the bank was heading toward the brink, a development marked by the frantic efforts of its CEO FitzPatrick to find a merger partner. By early September, as the global financial system was also heading toward the precipice, Anglo Irish was in dire shape.

To a backdrop of Anglo Irish's troubles, problems at Irish building societies, the image of people waiting in line earlier at Northern Rock in the UK (and briefly at that bank's office in Dublin), and the global meltdown, the government in late September found itself forced to act. No doubt, this dire situation was reinforced by a letter sent on September 22 from Michael Walsh, chairman of Irish Nationwide, one of the country's largest building societies, to David Doyle, the secretary-general in the Department of Finance. In it Walsh clearly stated that Irish Nationwide was on the edge of collapse, which would create chaos for 180,000 depositors of the building society, cause a distressed sale of its entire loan book, and probably suck other banks down.[24] As Honohan and Lane observed: "At the end of September 2008, apparently faced with the inability of Anglo Irish Bank to rollover its debt and fearing a contagious reaction onto the other banks, the government announced a blanket guarantee of liabilities of the main Irish-controlled banks."[25] The Celtic Tiger had hit the wall.

## Casting Blame

As in any national crisis there is a reflexive action to cast blame. Indeed, one of the important exercises for any society is to conduct a postmortem of how did we get here? Public anger was focused on the country's bankers, regulators, property developers, and government. And there was plenty to be angry about. After all, the combination of a massive global economic crash and the bursting of the property bubble and ensuing near-collapse of the country's major banks spelled upcoming hardship for the country. This was immediately a point of public worry given what had happened earlier with Bank North. Although Finance Minister Brian Lenihan acted to prevent a collapse, the Fianna Fáil government was clearly regarded as one of the accountable parties. This was, in fact, an aspect to Ireland's crisis that pointed back to the almost incestuous coziness between the ruling party, government, the property developers and the banks. It is also pointed back to the state of Irish politics.

While Ireland is regarded as a well-functioning democracy, it is also a relatively small society and the set of relationships between members of the Dáil (Ireland's parliament) and their constituents is close. In fact, it has been argued that there is a certain sense of clientelism at work in the Irish Republic that pushes parliamentarians (like politicians elsewhere) to bring home the spoils (for the constituents and key allies in the economic sector). It is this last area, relations between politicians and the business elite that became the focus of public ire in the crisis in September-October 2008 and its economically bruising aftermath.

At the beginning of his book, *The Bankers: How the Banks Brought Ireland to Its Knees,* Ross, described on the jacket as a "journalist, independent senator, and long-time champion of citizens against misbehaving corporations," writes about the "bankers' last supper," held on November 26, 2008. To a background of a banking crisis "at fever pitch" and the nation's finances "in peril," a party was held to mark the retirement of the chairman of the Financial Regulator, Brian Patterson. In essence, the Irish financial elite, implied Ross, got together for a last booze-up as the ship was sinking. Among those in attendance were Patrick Neary, Patterson's chief executive at the Financial Regulator, Jim Farrell, Patterson's successor, Eugene Sheehy, the head of AIB, Richie Boucher, then head of the Bank of Ireland's Irish retail division, Denis Casey, head of Irish

Life, Fergus Murphy, the chief executive of the EBS, and Pat Farrell, the president of the Irish Banking Federation (who was also the host). Ross was to sarcastically note: "Here was the Irish banking aristocracy in action, wining and dining their regulators in undisturbed luxury just as a local volcano was erupting before their eyes."[26]

Ross has plenty more to say about Ireland's bankers, calling them "rogues" and "buccaneers," emphasizing that "while the smaller scandals and the smaller banks have come and gone, the activities of the larger ones suggest that banking skullduggery is endemic." Ross clearly has an axe to grind and his book was popular with an Irish public staggering beneath the weight of the banking crisis. The lavish lifestyle of many of the well-to-do bankers reflected a certain in-your-face behavior (much as US and UK investment bankers have been accused), but the banking establishment per se cannot be fingered for endemic skullduggery. Sadly the property bubble was not the result of a small cabal of bankers lurking in the shadows, pulling strings to which the rest of society moved (no matter how attractive such a conspiracy may appear). Instead, the bankers were responsible for bad business decisions, inadequate risk management, and old fashioned greed.

The combination of questionable ethnics and poor decision making rapidly became identified with Sean FitzPatrick, the CEO of Anglo Irish Bank. Born in 1948, FitzPatrick was the son of a farmer. His mother was a former civil servant. Small in stature, he was to emerge as one of the movers and shakers in the modern Irish banking scene, pushed along by considerable drive and vision of taking what was a modestly-sized bank into one of his country's most significant.[27] FitzPatrick managed his way through Presentation College, where he showed some proficiency with rugby and demonstrated a highly competitive streak. From Presentation College, FitzPatrick went on to University College, Dublin. After his graduation, the world of accountancy beckoned where FitzPatrick met Charlie McCreevy, later to become minister of finance. FitzPatrick eventually landed a job in 1976 at Irish Bank of Commerce, a small financial institution, which was soon bought by City of Dublin Bank. Within two years, City of Dublin bought yet another bank, Anglo Irish Bank. And FitzPatrick was along for the ride, initially being the financial controller, but moving up to become the CEO for the Anglo Irish part of operations. He developed a reputation for being hard-boiled, and ruthless, a little out of sorts with the more traditional Bank of Ireland and AIB crowd. Yet he was successful in transforming what was a small institution into the country's number three bank, with a particular focus on business loans.

By the late 1990s and early 2000s, Anglo Irish had gained builders and developers as its largest customers.

Anglo Irish's major expansion occurred just as the property boom got launched. This meant that compensation went up; the good times had arrived. At the same time, FitzPatrick's network of connections extended throughout the business world. One of the more controversial actions was FitzPatrick's board membership of the Dublin Docklands Development Authority. Brought to the DDDA by his friend and chairman, Las Bradshaw, FitzPatrick assumed his seat in 1998 and stayed for nine years. In turn, Bradshaw was to join the Anglo Irish board in 2004. What raised eyebrows was that DDDA business was being funded by FitzPatrick's bank, raising certain ethical issues.

What was to be titillating to the public was the whiff of scandal that percolated upwards into the media headlines in 2008 as the financial crisis enfolded. Indeed, as Anglo Irish was open to government intervention post-September, some questionable finances were revealed. By January 2009, the problems were so extensive at Anglo Irish that the government was forced to nationalize it. This was reflected by the announcement that the bank posted the largest loss in Irish corporate history— €4.1 billion in the six months to the end of March 2009. It also emerged that eight senior serving managers at the bank owed amounts ranging from €835,000 to €7.1 million at the end of September.[28] *The Irish Times* keyed in on Fitz-Patrick: "The bank's former chairman, Seán FitzPatrick, is understood to owe a substantially larger sum. He at one stage was involved in a ploy to hide loans of up to €122 million from shareholders."[29] Such allegations were accompanied by a well-publicized visit to the bank's headquarters in October 2009 by the Gardai (national police) to remove electronic material. It also came out that FitzPatrick had hidden loans of around €87 million from the authorities by stashing them in Irish Nationwide, using the money for property investments and film-finance deals.[30]

While FitzPatrick and Anglo Irish were heading into deeper trouble, the turmoil they caused rippled through the Irish political system. The Fianna Fáil government was secure in its majority in the Dáil, but the situation was hardly ideal. Cowen's position as the head of the government was relatively new and he stepped in for the scandal-ridden Ahern. Additionally, the financial nature of the crisis did not reflect well on the new taoiseach, considering he had been finance minister in the late days of the property bubble. If nothing else the crisis demonstrated the incestuous nature between the politicians and business. That intricate set of relationships was best captured by the "Galway tent."

Galway, Ireland is the location of important horse races each July. As Paschal Taggart, property investors and former chairman of Bord na gCon, the semi-state greyhound racing organization, observed of Fianna Fáil's tent: "I never saw any business done in the tent. It was real end-of-term stuff for everyone. It was the end of July, the Dáil was in recess, the school exams were over and it was the beginning of the builders' holidays. It was fun, fun, fun with a few glasses of wine drunk, meaning that everyone was in the best of form."[31]

The Fianna Fáil Galway tent was created by Taoiseach Albert Reynolds in 1994 and it became one of regular functions that Taoiseach Ahern excelled. While fund-raising was the primary stated purpose, the Galway tent was a place to meet and greet, make contacts, and renew old relationships. The bankers and developers clearly had their place at the tent. Indeed, Seán Dunne met his second wife at the tent. And Dunne was close to Ahern, something not missed by anyone in attendance. Equally welcome at the Fianna Fáil tent were Michael and Tom Bailey, two long-time Fianna Fáil supporters and developers. Despite having gotten into trouble with the authorities over tax issues, having been accused of making false allegations, and having to settle on tax evasion with the government, the Baileys were still welcome at the tent.

Like all good things, the Galway Tent came to an end. The tent came to symbolize the party of the movers and shakers, who presided over Irish fortunes from 1994 to 2008. It captured the swagger of an economic and political elite that had taken their country down a road of considerable promise. However, the road had hit some very large bumps, throwing Ireland's comfortable set of relationships off kilter. Cowen inherited a deepening storm; he was astute enough to understand that it was time to kill the tent and what it came to represent. As Ross noted: "Cower believed that the image of builders and politicians scratching each other's backs, at a time when the excesses of property developers had brought about a national crisis, was doing damage to the party."[32]

## Dealing with the Aftermath

The events of 2007-2008 were a shock to Ireland as the events underscored the island economy's vulnerability to larger forces. A later written IMF report was to note that the Irish economy was then in a state of "near free fall." That situation was defined by an output contraction by about 10 percent (between 2008-09), unemployment rose from 4.5 percent in 2007 to around 13 percent in March 2010, a shift from balanced public finances in the 2003-07 period to a fiscal deficit of 14.5 percent of GDP in 2009 and an increase in public debt from 25 percent of GDP in 2006 to 64 percent in 2009.[33] The rising tide of red ink in public finances was the result of the collapse of taxes from 2007 from a peak of €47.2 billion to €33 billion in 2009.[34]

Ireland's crisis, like those in Iceland and eastern Europe, was the issue of a small economy facing the headwinds of a global storm. Journalist Matt Cooper observed: "External forces seemingly had taken control of Ireland's economic destiny and, by extension, its social stability."[35] Needless to say, this situation was unnerving as it indicated that contagion from large economies to smaller ones, especially those with higher leveraged property markets, could push a nation over the edge, into the abyss of national chaos. Although the results from the crisis were brutal, Ireland did not go over the edge.

Unlike Iceland, Ireland benefited from two key factors. First and foremost, Ireland's leadership was able to act. Despite the grave situation facing him, Taoiseach Cowen, only five months into the job, had served as finance minister and had a core group of people around him who did not panic. Cowen was long in the shadow of Ahern, but in September 2008 he was his own man. Although Cowen could be blamed for not having done more as finance minister in averting the crisis, he did understand the significance of events facing him and the country. The bottom line was that Allied Irish, Bank of Ireland, and Anglo Irish were too big to fail. Cowen's decision to guarantee all the deposits and liabilities of the banks was taken in the early hours of September 30, 2008 and it brought a halt in the slide over the edge. But moving back to a "normal situation" was going to take far longer and will be accomplished only at substantial cost to the Irish people.

Second, Ireland benefited from its membership in the European Union, something that provided it a stable currency at the height of the crisis. Although the point should not be overstated, EU membership also carried with it, rightfully or wrongfully, the idea that Ireland would be supported, probably in the worst case by other EU countries if defaults loomed. Support from the EU was critical as it clearly underscored that other forces could be put in motion to help stabilize the situation. Whether or not this was accurate if Ireland heading into a default mode is up to debate; however the perception is initially what mattered. The example of European support, no matter how reluctant, for Greece in 2009-2010, demonstrates the degree to which the EU was willing to go to prevent sovereign defaults among its member states.

The Cowen government also introduced the National Asset Management Agency (NAMA) in April 2009. By that time it was painfully evident that the crisis was not just a passing storm, but a longer-term structural adjustment in the Irish economy. To get the banks back to some degree of functioning, it was believed necessary to clean up the bank balance sheets, hence NAMA was created to function as an asset management company dealing with €70-80 billion of assets transferred from the banks. Highly controversial, the NAMA bill was published in July 2009. The transfer of assets started in early 2010 and was expected to be done later that same year.

It should also be noted that the bailing out of the banks doubled Ireland's national debt and pushed the fiscal deficit over 10 percent of GDP in 2009. Probably one of the most bruising elements of the crisis, but something regarded by the Cowen government as necessary was the passage of an austerity budget for 2010. As journalist Quentin Fottrell observed: "Ireland delivered what many economists billed as the most painful budget in a generation, making €4 billion ($6 billion) in spending cuts to curb the country's soaring debt."[36] Among the cuts in the budget were €760 million from social-welfare programs, €1 billion from public-service payrolls. The last led to trade union unrest in the lead-up to the budget in December.

The austere budget was certainly debated in Ireland and understandably there was a degree of resentment over what many perceived as a bailout of the wealthy. There was also some recognition that the trade unions had benefited from the bubble as well during the Ahern years in terms of higher salaries. Indeed, there was some umbrage at the trade unions becoming militant over austerity. As one opinion piece in the *Irish Independent* by Martina Devlin stated: "In refusing to swallow their medicine, these people are casting a cold eye on Fianna Fáil, the senior partner in Government, a party which opened doors for property developers with a glut of tax reliefs, and winked as banks over-lent until developers went belly-up and bankers needed a bailout."[37] The flavor of public opinion was further reflected by the same opinion piece: "Yet they are expected to pay for others' mistakes—even as property developers continue to cruise town in their Bentleys and no banker looks close to swapping his bespoke suits for prison issue clothes."

To address some of angry public sentiment, the 2010 budget reduced ministerial pay by 15 percent, which included a voluntary 10 percent pay cut earlier in the year by Ireland's senior ministers, whose €225,000 annual salaries exceed those of their European colleagues. At the same time, the prime minister's salary was cut by 20 percent. Equally important, the budget left the country's 12.5 percent corporate tax rate intact, something that has been critical in making Ireland attractive to multinational corporations. It was also something that other European countries, such as Germany and France, would have liked to have seen go up. Part of the reason for Ireland's aggressive cuts in the budget was no doubt meant to contain any dependence on the EU, which could have sought to impose their less business friendly and higher taxes on Ireland.

One of the other actions taken by the Cowen government was to bring in Dr. Patrick Honohan, a respected academic, to head the central bank. This was important as Honohan had been critical of weak bank supervision and his appointment restored some degree of confidence in at least one part of the Irish government.

Honohan also had a reputation for honesty and was not tainted by the earlier gold rush. At the same time, his appointment meant that the old established set at the heart of business-finance-and-government would receive greater scrutiny. In December 2009, the central bank head proposed to the Dáil for a major public investigation into the financial crisis. While this clearly appealed to the opposition parties, Labour and Fine Gael, it also quickly gained the support from some parts of the financial industry, including the Corporate Governance Association of Ireland (CGAI) and the IBOA trade union. Indeed, the CGAI's chairman Jerry Kelly stated that such an investigation would help people understand exactly what went wrong and what lessons could be learned from the crisis.[38]

The government's response to their central bank head's proposal was cool. The taoiseach stated: "From my point of view, the resources of the State are currently involved in ensuring banking stability and that we can deal with economic and financial issues that arise. I am sure that there will be economic historians and economists who will continue to talk about the failure of the regulatory system in this and other countries regarding the challenge faced by us. However, I would have to carefully consider such an inquiry before giving any commitment."[39]

The post-crisis environment that Ireland found itself in 2010 was one that was both difficult and held some hope of recovery. On one hand the banking system was largely stabilized (at considerable cost to the public), the government's bad bank was created to offload the bad loans from the banks, manufacturing and exports were performing in a stronger fashion and held some hope for further gains, and there was a return, albeit weakly, to economic growth. On the other hand, there was a cost—a real GDP contraction of 7 percent in 2009 made inroads into the country's standard of living, the government's aggressive measures to regain policy credibility and competitiveness resulted in lower wages for state workers, higher taxes (with an eye to trimming large fiscal deficits), and ongoing high unemployment. Moreover, significant challenges remained, including the need to wean the banking sector from public support. According to the International Monetary Fund's 2010 report on Ireland: "Rather than aiming to time the market for an upturn in property prices, the goal should be to reduce the large overhang of property in state hands, restart market transactions and, thus help normalize the property market."[40]

Ireland also faces the ongoing risk of contagion from other countries' sovereign problems—a possible default in Greece, Spain, or Portugal could evaporate liquidity in international capital markets at a time when Ireland could need to raise funds to meet fiscal shortfalls or help recapitalize its banks. Indeed, the bank losses left a substantial hole in Ireland's finances, especially when taking into account the government's intention to maintain sovereign guarantees in the face of what some have estimated as €72 billion of bank outstanding debt coming due in 2010. This led to some nervous moments and calls for the banks' creditors (bondholders) to assume some of the cost (via debt-to-equity swaps, something that cannot be entirely ruled out in the upcoming years).

Ireland's economic/financial crisis gained international attention, but was eclipsed by Greece's problems in 2010. Ireland was a point of concern to the EU; Greece threatened, as we shall see in the next chapter, to bring the EU house down. Ireland implemented tough austerity measures with minor social unrest; Greece was convulsed by rioting anarchists, communists, and old-age pensioners, some of whom looked suspiciously middle-aged). Although Ireland's numbers were and are daunting, Greece's looked and remain almost impossible.

What made the difference between Ireland and Greece was partially economic and partially socio-political. On the economic side, Ireland early on indicated that it is willing and able to pay its debts (though this is going to be challenging), backed by low long-term interest rates, moderate long-term growth rates, a reasonably low starting point for net debt and a capacity (both political and economic) to bear fiscal pain. As the National University of Ireland, Galway's Professor of Economics John McHale observed in May 2010: "Greece's problem is that it looks fundamentally insolvent. It has been locked into high interest rates on much of its large debt, has poor growth prospects, and has not convinced markets it can [accept] the necessary pain. Ireland is better positioned on each dimension."[41]

There is another important dimension—societal expectations. Two points are worth considering—the Irish benefited from one economic boom and structural transformation (and Greece's economic restructuring has proven much more superficial) and there is a greater trust in the country's political and social institutions than in Greece. Although the Irish complain about the corruption in their country's political and business classes, there remains some degree of trust (some might cynically argue fatalism) in the ability of the government to right the ship. In Greece, one is more reminded of Edward Banfield's *The Moral Basis of a Backward Society* (1958) in which people have a difficulty in working beyond family lines due to a deep mistrust of larger organizations, such as government. Most Irish probably have a greater faith in their institutions that exist outside of their families, though there is obviously a critical eye to patterns of corruption in government. Nonetheless, the somewhat greater trust in government (with a track record of helping push one of the more remarkable economic transformations in the twentieth century) appears to be a factor in why Ireland avoided the social turmoil that hit Greece in the financial chaos that marked 2009-2010.

## Conclusion

Ireland's financial sector helped land the country in one of its most painful economic crises. While the banks played a critical role in bringing the economic boom to a second phase in 2002-2007, they had a lot of help from the ruling political party, Fianna Fáil, the regulators, and the property developers. There was also a degree of collusion with the country's trade unions, especially in the public sector in the form of big wage increases during the Ahern years. Last, but hardly least, the Irish public was part of the process as it re-elected Fianna Fáil twice, giving it three consecutive turns in the office. If the Fianna Fáil message of a market economy was so bad and the examples of in-your-face wealth so unbearable, the voters could have voted the rascals out. Moreover, Ireland's press is hardly meek in bringing forth corruption scandals, all of which meant that the dirty underbelly of Irish society was readily evident. At the end of the day Ireland was a small country that enjoyed a rapid transformation in its economy during the 1900s and took a wrong turn in the early 2000s. Despite considerable achievements, the economic transformation eventually pushed the country down the wrong road and raised serious doubt as to the future direction. It left Ireland little doubt about the vicissitudes of external factors, which meshed with local bad business decisions. A total collapse was averted by difficult decisions on the part of the government and by a high degree of societal cohesiveness, and the perceived value of EU membership. The 2007-2011 period will no doubt be long remembered as one of the country's worst crises, a testament to bad decisions and greed gone awry. The post-crisis period can be expected to be lengthy and challenging as Ireland struggles to regain its footing in a radically different global economic landscape.

## Notes

1.  Laura Slattery, "Docklands Body Will Need Aid Over Glass Bottle Site," *Irish Times*, November 27, 2009, http://www.irishtimes.com/newspaper/finance/2009/1127/1224259546360_pf.html.
2.  For differing accounts of Éamon de Valera see Tim Pat Coogan, *De Valera: Long Fellow, Long Shadow* (London: Arrow, 1993) or Diarmaid Ferriter, *Judging Dev: A Reassessment of Eamon de Valera* (Dublin: Royal Irish Academy, 2007).
3.  Robert Sweeney, *Banana Republic: The Failure of the Irish State and How to Fix It* (Dublin: Gill & Macmillan, 2009), p. 9.
4.  Organization for Economic Cooperation and Development (OECD), *OECD Economic Outlook Volume 2004/2 No. 76*, (Paris: OECD: December 2004), p. 167.
5.  Adele Bergin, Thomas Conefrey, John FitzGerald, and Ide Kearney, "Recovery Scenarios for Ireland," The Economic and Social Research Institute (Dublin), Research Series, No. 7, May 2009, p. 4.
6.  Sweeney, *Banana Republic,* pp. 21-22.
7.  Data courteously supplied by the Irish Banking Federation in November 2009.
8.  Adele Bergin, Thomas Conefrey, John FitzGerald, and Ide Kearney, "Recovery Scenarios for Ireland," The Economic and Social Research Institute (Dublin), Research Series, No. 7, May 2009, p. 5.
9.  International Monetary Fund, *Ireland Staff Report for the 2003 Article IV Consultation*, Washington DC, July 9, 2003, p. 9.
10. Ibid., p. 15.
11. Ibid., p. 16.
12. *Irish Construction Economics*, Goodbody's Stockbrokers (Dublin), October 2006, p. 42.
13. This description came from London Thomas Jr., "The Irish Economy's Rise Was Steep, and the Fall Was Fast," *The New York Times*, January 4, 2009.
14. Ibid. It should be noted that Kozlowski's party for his wife was charged to his company, Tyco, and was lovingly videotaped. What was most memorable was that it featured an ice sculpture of Michelangelo's David spewing vodka from his penis and a birthday cake in the shape of a woman's breasts with sparklers mounted on top. Adding to the fun, Kowlowski flew in Jimmy Buffett and his group for entertainment at the cost of $250,000. Needless to say this was all in very bad taste and only helped sink the executive when other issues, such as tax evasion, were brought against him.
15. Flight of the O'Ligarchs," *The First Post*, February 7, 2008, http://www.thefirstpost.co.uk/15875, news-comment, news-politics, flight-of-the-oligarchs?/
16. Christopher Khoury and Ian T. Brown, "Among OECD Nations, U.S. Lags in Personal Health Care," http://www.gallup.com/poll/117205/americans-not-feeling-health-benefits-high-spending.a...
17. Quoted from Proinsias O'Mahony, "Best to Ignore the Cheerleaders for the Property Sector," *The Southern Star* (Co. Cork), January 31, 2009.

18. Shane Ross, *The Bankers: How the Banks Brought Ireland to Its Knees* (Dublin: Penguin, Ireland, 2009). p. 169.
19. Ibid., p. 170.
20. Morgan Kelly, "On the Likely Extent of Falls in Irish House Prices," *Quarterly Economic Commentary*, (ISRI), Summer 2007, p. 42.
21. Emmet Oliver, "Smug Arrogance to Grim Reality—How It All Came Tumbling Down" *The Independent* (Dublin), July 17, 2010.
22. Patrick Honohan and Philip Lane, "Ireland in Crisis," *Vox* (London), February 28, 2009. http://www.voxeu.org/index.php?q=node/3162.
23. Fidelma Mannion, Edward Vincent and Antonio Caraballo, Anglo-Irish Bank Corporation, Plc Analysis, Moody's Investors Service, December 2006.
24. Oliver, "Smug Arrogance."
25. Honahan and Lane, "Ireland in Crisis," *Vox.*
26. Shane Ross, *The Bankers: How the Banks Brought Ireland to Its Knees* (Dublin: Penguin Ireland, 2009), p. 5.
27. Ross described FitzPatrick as "a little man with a little bank that became a rather big bank." He notes that FitzPatrick was very much like Charlie Haughey: "Both were small in stature. Both were self-made. Both cut corners. Both had strong, pushy mothers. And both became super-rich from humble beginnings." Ross, *The Bankers*, p. 34.
28. Colm Keena, "Drumm Meets New Anglo Irish Chief Executive to Discuss Personal Loans," *The Irish Times*, October 8, 2009. http://www.irishtimes.com/newspaper/finance/2009/1008/1224256167383_pf.html.
29. Ibid.
30. Andrew Lynch, "Seanie's Free Flights Perk Another Snub to Hard-Hit Workers," *Heraldie*, September 30, 2009, http://www.herald.ie/option/seanies-free-flights-perk-another-snub-to-hardhit-workers-1.
31. Ross, *The Bankers*, p. 117.
32. Ibid.
33. International Monetary Fund, IMF Executive Board Concludes 2010 Article IV Consultation with Ireland," International Monetary Fund (Washington, D.C.), Public Information Notice No. 10/86, July 14, 2010.
34. Daniel McConnell, "National Debt Set to Double to euro 150 bn, Latest Figures reveal," *Sunday Independent* (Dublin), January 17, 2010.
35. Matt Cooper, *Who Really Runs Ireland?: The Story of the Elite Who Led Ireland From Bust to Boom...And Back Again* (Dublin: Penguin Ireland, 2009), p. xii.
36. Quinten Fottrell, "Ireland Cuts Budget in Bid to Tame Debt," *The Wall Street Journal*, December 10, 2009.
37. Martina Devlin, "Unions Need to Wake Up and Realise That We Are Insolvent," *Irish Independent* (Dublin), November 14, 2009. p. 14.
38. Fionnan Sheahan and Thomas Molloy, "Cowen Denies Blocking Finance Probe," *Independent*, December 17, 2009, http://www.independent.ie/business/irish/cowen-denies-blocking-finance-probe-1978689.
39. Quoted from Michael O'Regan, "Cowen Cautious About Holding Inquiry on Causes of Banking Crisis," *Irish Times*, December 19, 2009.
40. Quoted from Louisa Fahy and Joe Brennan, "Ireland Stabilizing After 'Near Free Fall,' IMF Says," *Bloomberg*, July 14, 2010.
41. John McHale, "State's Solvency Faces Rigorous Test on International Markets," *Irish Times*, May 29, 2010, http://www.irishtimes.com/newspaper/opinion/2010/0529/1224271389834_pf.html.

# 9

# Acropolis Now

The cover of a May 2010 issue of *The Economist* graphically captured the Greek sovereign debt crisis. Large bold letters headlined the story, "Acropolis Now: Europe's Debt Crisis Spins Out of Control." Indeed, on May 6-7, in response to worries over Greece's ability to repay its upcoming debt obligations, the Bloomberg financial news service reported that global stock markets from Tokyo to New York lost some $1.7 trillion in value. *The Economist* cover emphasized the dramatic nature of the situation. Above the Acropolis and a setting tropical sun flew a fleet of rescue helicopters marked IMF and EU. At the foreground, with a dour look on her face was German Chancellor Angela Merkel, dressed in jungle camouflage. Observers versed in cinematic history could hardly miss the parody of the famous film *Apocalypse Now*, itself a Vietnam War reinvention of Joseph Conrad's novella *Heart of Darkness*.

For global financial markets in early May, Greece represented the horror of a world poised to plunge into the darkness of sovereign default, civil unrest, and economic depression all launched by the collapse of a small country with large debt problems. Greece, accounting for only 2.2 percent of the EU's population and 2.0 percent of its annual GDP, was apparently threatening the survival of the entire European economic superpower. As *The Economist* aptly noted: "It will strike some as mystifying that a small, peripheral economy should suddenly threaten the world's biggest economic area."[1] But threaten it did. In Lisbon, Madrid, and Rome, bond prices plunged. There was talk of European defaults and a sovereign debt contagion spreading to Britain, Japan, and even the United States.

The Greek case is an excellent example of a small country's economic problems highlighting problems in larger economies and threatening to spread financial troubles. The viability of some of Greece's larger European neighbors, confronting similarly over-leveraged balance sheets and bloated public sectors, were called into question by Greece's downfall. As a result, Greece has been referred to as the "canary in the coalmine" of the European Union. Greece's problems were not only an immediate threat to the economic sustainability of the EU's economy, but a blow against the viability of the euro as a common currency, the European economic model, and the European project itself.

The core ideas behind the advance of the European Union in the second half of the twentieth century—the creation of a peaceful European identity, based on trade, commerce and the rule of law, supported by an extensive, government-funded social safety-net paid for by relatively high taxes, public spending, and when needed, public borrowing—came under attack. In 2009 and 2010, Greece's problems, while partially its own making, represented larger instabilities throughout Europe and the world. The threat of Greek default was real, as was the fear that Greece's problems would spread throughout the sovereign debt market.

A unified Europe was designed to remove political instability and military rivalry through economic integration and mutual dependence. With the exception of the small wars in the Balkans during the 1990s, this experiment led to the development of one of the most affluent and peaceful parts of the global community. The EU became the club to join, with its membership expanding to 27 countries in 2007. Four other states remain official candidate countries. New additions include a number of nations formerly under communist control. In the early twenty-first century, the EU faced a number of challenges. The aging demographics of many members, including its largest states, (Germany, France, Italy, and Spain) became more pronounced. The government sector provided the most dynamic jobs growth. Prosperity was increasingly financed by debt through access to cheap money. This cycle allowed many European governments to put off difficult adjustments in re-focusing spending, reigning in social programs and pensions, and increasing the retirement age. In an era of low global interest rates, European governments and consumers went on a borrowing spree, making parts of European sovereign debt a highly leveraged play.

Greece's place in what became the great deleveraging of the 2010s was its emergence as the weakest link in the European chain. As part of Europe's grand experiment of peaceful economic development, the rest of the EU largely turned a blind eye to idiosyncratic elements of the Greek economy. Greece exhibiting a society-wide aversion to paying taxes, official corruption, opaque accounting practices, and a willingness to have others pay for Greece's revenue shortfalls through EU funding or borrowing from European banks (who were happy to have the business) and northern European pension funds purchasing Greek bonds (with slightly better rates of return than German or French debt). The fact that Greek yields were only slightly higher meant that Greece could borrow at historically low rates—near parity with developed economies like Germany and France. In short, no market discipline was imposed on Greece. The killer for Greece was the belief that it could continuously rollover its debts. When global liquidity dried up and growth stopped, the dance came to an end and Greece's addiction to cheap money took center stage.

### Historical Instability

Greece is a country of a little over 11 million people, located at the end of the Balkan Peninsula. Sandwiched between the Ionian Sea to the west and the Aegean to the east, Greece achieved independence from the Ottoman Empire in 1830. Covered in mountains, modern Greece also has more than 2,000 islands, of which only some 200 are inhabited. The economy has always been relatively fragile, based on a combination of agriculture (tobacco, olives, and wine), tourism, and shipping. This led to a fair amount of emigration and to the occasional debt default. Indeed, since Greece gained independence in 1830, it has defaulted or rescheduled its debt five times. Economists Carmen Reinhart and Kenneth Rogoff go even further, describing Greece as existing in a "perpetual state of default," having spent 50.6 percent of the years since independence in default or rescheduling—one of the highest rates in Europe.[2]

German occupation during the Second World War was followed by a harsh civil war between monarchists and communists. Three decades of political instability, including a period of military dictatorship followed. In the summer of 1974, the military *junta* ruling the country collapsed and democracy was restored under the Third Republic. A few years later, on January 1, 1981, Greece joined the European Union, bringing a peripheral and traditionally weak economy into the broader European experiment. Greece's EU membership was significant because it pumped considerable capital into the country. This massive financial shot in the arm also helped transform what was a relatively low per capita income in Europe into a nation with one of the higher standards of livings in Southern Europe.

Greece's entry into the EU, however, did not resolve the country's broader economic challenges. Greek economic growth continued in fits and starts, driven by private and public consumption for the better part of the last thirty years. Greece grew because Greeks spent more and because of the inflow of European funds. Insufficient investment, however, went into long-term projects or improvements in infrastructure. The model was not peaceful. Greece faced its share of recessions, significant deficits, and austerity measures. Currency devaluation was used on more than one occasion to help stimulate growth through competitive devaluation. In 2001, the Greek economy introduced a major change by joining the common European currency, the euro. In 2004, Athens hosted the summer Olympics. Both events pointed to an enhanced creditworthiness and a view that the days of sovereign defaults were firmly in the past. Joining the euro gave Greece access to cheaper credit than it had ever enjoyed previously, the "borrow and spend cycle" of the past accelerated. The deficit grew larger and larger, spending habits were intensified. An illusion took hold that money was cheap and that growth would continue forever. A relaxed revenue collection system and a deep national mistrust of the government's ability to use tax revenues efficiently lead to widespread tax evasion.

Greece's past economic policies shared important similarities with their current troubles. Many of the characteristics of Greek finance that jolted the world in 2009-2010 can be traced back to the early 1980s. The 1980s was a period of major change in Greece. In 1981, as the country joined the EU, Andreas Papandreou, the leader of Greece's socialist party, PASOK (the Pan-Hellenic Socialist Movement) came to office with an ambitious program of state spending and intervention into the economy.

PASOK's ideology was an essential ingredient in the increased state involvement in the economy during the 1980s. The party sought to remake the Greek political landscape. Opponents were pensioned off and replaced by supporters in the civil service, the universities, and the central bank. PASOK's ideology had a distinctively Third World tone to it. Political scientist Panayote E. Dimitras, in a 1985 *Foreign Policy* article noted:

> From the outset, PASOK assumed a posture and espoused an ideological line closely resembling those of African and Asian liberation movements. In fact, PASOK's declared aim was the 'national liberation' of Greece from foreign political and economic domination. In international politics, PASOK opposed both military blocs [NATO and the Warsaw Pact] and what is called 'the logic of Yalta and Potsdam'. That opposition, however, was not evenhanded. Like many Third World movements, PASOK's criticism of the Soviet Union was rare and relatively gentle, while criticism of the United States was unrelenting and violent.[3]

PASOK regarded capitalism with disdain and linked it to the United States, which had supported the military dictatorship. In a speech delivered in 1984, Prime Minister Papandreou stated:

> A leveling consumerist model has invaded our country and ... threatens to transform us into a cultural colony. The main vehicle of that invasion is the mass media. They have created the well-known culture: the culture of exhibition and of hedonism, based on acceptance and not on critical processes. It is a pompous, parasitic, faked, and tasteless, standardized subculture created with the least common denominator as a criterion ... It threatens our physiognomy, our specificity, our heritage, our very existence ... Our traditional popular culture, with its fighting resistance character is ... our aggressive confrontation to the imported capitalist model.[4]

The rise of PASOK and its anti-capitalist rhetoric coincided with a crisis for the Greek economy. Greece's economic growth had slowed from an already modest 2.0 percent growth in 1980 to -0.2 percent in 1981, a trend related to the international recession and higher oil prices. As in many countries, a path of austerity was unappealing. Moreover, it did not fit PASOK's desire for new social spending and income redistribution. Despite the economic slowdown, there was still wealth in the private sector and substantial external borrowing. The PASOK government's plan was to tax wealthy Greeks and to tap international markets in order to stimulate domestic demand. At the same time a greater role was placed on the "socialization" of certain activities through participation of local authorities, workers' representatives and public interest groups. As one observer noted: "Anti-capitalistic, the new government perceived the state as being able to mobilize the resources and possess the political will needed to break through the bottlenecks, bend the inflexibilities, and force the pace of growth. The reform of Greece's political economy would be top-down and imposed."[5]

Although PASOK did not create Greece's economic difficulties, its policies created numerous vulnerabilities. Its anti-capitalist mentality and policies led to capital flight, a further sag in private sector activity and a steep decline in foreign direct investment. FDI in the Greek economy fell from a high of $672 million in 1980 to $436 million in 1982 and remained at only $439 million in 1983.

Greece was also hurt by its entrance in to the European Union, which as economist Nicholis Gianaris noted, "caught protected sleepy Greek firms unprepared for the imported European products that flooded the home markets." This new wave of imports even outsold Greek food products, causing the country's food trade surpluses to turn into deficits. Greek reforms, including a 15.5 percent devaluation of the drachma at the beginning of 1983 and invocation of a clause in the accession agreement to restrict imports from the EU to 1980 levels, did little to halt the deterioration in the external accounts.

The Greek economy failed to resume substantial growth despite the government's efforts: real GDP shrank 1.1 percent in 1983. This led the government to rely more heavily on increased foreign borrowing to stimulate domestic growth. These efforts were in part rewarded in 1984 and 1985 as the growth rate picked up to 2.0 percent and 2.5 percent respectively.[6] Economic growth was regarded as a priority because of elections held in February 1985.

With the right still struggling to rebuild its shattered reputation, PASOK won re-election, but the economic crisis did not abate. By the end of 1985, the budget deficit had reached a then historic high of 9 percent. At the same time, the country's debt came under intense focus. Three major problems confronted PASOK, all related to debt management. The country's short-term debt had risen to $4.5 billion; the debt service ratio had shot upwards from 11 percent of GDP in 1981 to 25 percent of GDP in 1985 when the current account deficit hit a record of $3.3 billion. Additionally, the net public sector debt had reached a hefty 80 percent of gross national product, one of the highest ratios for an OECD country. Although this was not yet a full-blown crisis, it indicated that the government's policies had increased Greece's dependency on imported capital, most of which ironically came from West European and US commercial banks.

Greece's deteriorating economy pushed the PASOK government into accepting an austerity program in October 1985. Like other countries in southeast Europe, Greece could only turn to the IMF or the EEC. Ideologically, the PASOK government regarded the IMF with suspicion, especially as it emphasized structural adjustment programmers that liberalized trade, reduced state spending and subsidies and promoted the development of private sector. The IMF also favored direct foreign investment; PASOK looked upon this with suspicion, especially if it came from the United States. The EEC provided an alternative path out of the debt crisis that other southern European countries lacked.

The October 1985 Stabilization Program was a comprehensive two-year package that included fiscal and economic measures as well as a six-year, $1.75 billion loan from the EEC for current account balance of payments assistance. There were clear targets attached to the loan which included a reduced public sector borrowing requirement; a reduction of the external deficit from 10 percent of GNP to 3 percent; and a fall in inflation from 25 percent at the end of 1985 to 10 percent by the end of 1987. The program's tools included price and wage controls, monetary restrictions, curbs on tax evasion and public expenditure growth, a 15 percent devaluation of the drachma and higher prices for public services.

The initial reaction to the austerity program was manifested by street demonstrations and a wave of strikes. Hard-line PASOK supporters felt betrayed and there were a number of defections from the ruling party. At the same time, support from labor unions diminished. The Stabilization Program, which ended in 1987, did have some successes and helped reduce the likelihood of Greek debt rescheduling. The current account deficit was reduced from 1985's $3.3 billion to $1.3 billion in 1987. The budget deficit, which reached a high of 9 percent of GDP in 1985, was brought down to 6.5 percent in 1987 (despite being a record 1.16 trillion drachmas). Inflation was also reduced from a high of 22.5 percent in 1985 to 16.3 percent in 1987.

Papandreou's change in direction from expansion to restraint helped stabilize the country. This also meant that PASOK pragmatically retreated from its antagonistic approach to the private sector. An OECD report commented: "the government appears to have shown greater recognition of the key role of the private sector has to play in moving the economy back to a sustainable path of rapid growth, thereby serving to improve the business climate."[7] This was reflected by a greater inflow of direct investment which rebounded sharply from $471 million in 1986 to $683 million 1987.

By the end of 1988, Greece had weathered the financial storm without a rescheduling of its external debt. The combination of austerity and EEC assistance, including the disbursement of the second half of the EEC $1.75 billion loan in early 1987 has guaranteed that. The EEC loan allowed the government to repay foreign debt early and build up its international reserves, which stood at $2.7 billion at the end of 1987. Greece's creditworthiness improved, which gave it access to $1.5 billion of new loans from commercial banks in 1987 and about the same in 1988. Greece's total external debt stood at $24.5 billion in 1988. Although the size of the debt grew moderately, the economy expanded by 4.3 percent in 1988 and the improvement of most sectors, enhanced the country's debt service capacity. It appeared that Greece was on its way out of the debt problem.

Although the PASOK government was eventually replaced, Greece in the 1990s did undertake some reforms earmarked to take it into the EMU. Inflation was brought down, protective economic barriers were dismantled, wage constraints were attempted, and there was some degree of fiscal consolidation. By 2000, Greece was on track to adopt the euro. By 2006, Greece was a well-established member of the EU and the euro zone with a working parliamentary system that rotated the country's two political parties, the left-of-center Pan-PASOK and the right-of-center New Democracy (ND), in and out of office. Both parties, dominated by political families, were well connected to the country's business elite. For people across Europe, Greece became a place to enjoy fun in the sun, a combination of beaches, picturesque islands, bustling tavernas, and ancient ruins. At the same time, Greek companies, including banks, extended business networks throughout the region. Although there was much talk of official corruption, high debt, and a highly fragmented pension system, no alarm bells were going off. There were few indications that Greece would become the catalyst for a global market crisis in 2010.

The Moody's Investors Service annual report of January 2006 reflected a cautious, yet hopeful view on Greece. It flagged high debt, pension problems, and a sizeable current account deficit as challenges. At the same time, the report concluded that "private consumption should remain an engine of growth over the medium term, providing fiscal revenues through value-added tax (VAT)."[8] The rating agency report also noted that the budget deficit, which had ballooned to 6.6 percent in 2004 due to unexpected costs related to the Olympics, was being brought under control. Greece, in fact, worked with Eurostat, the official keeper of European Community statistics, to verify that the deficit was effectively well over the 3 percent of GDP threshold agreed under the EU's Maastricht treaty. Greece was not alone in flouting the 3 percent rule, but its economy was more fragile than its larger partners. Eurostat's involvement was meant to provide Greece with better official statistics and to remove any opaqueness in Greek financial matters. Moody's expected the fiscal deficit to fall to 4.3 percent of GDP for year-end 2005.

Another important point in the Moody's annual report concerned tax revenues. The rating agency aptly reported: "There is scope for an increase in tax revenues through limiting tax evasion. A planned 7.1% increase in revenues based on highest VAT income and efforts to limit tax fraud by companies and the self-employed. In addition, current expenditures could be decreased through improved efficiency in the public sector."[9]

Along the last lines, Moody's observed the largest category of budget expenditure was personnel outlays (wage bill). Ever optimistic, Moody's (as well as many other Greek observers) emphasized that the "new culture" of fiscal transparency could finally start to reduce debt ratios, and that the country benefited from its "buoyant democratic process" and the changing geopolitical situation in the Balkans. The latter was to boost the Greek economy via increasing tourism and a reduction of military expenditures. At the same time, Greek companies invested in growth opportunities in Eastern Europe, the Balkans, and Turkey, marketing itself as a gateway to Europe for these developing economies.

Signs of trouble were there, and came to light during the premiership of Kostas Karamanlis beginning in 2004. Karamanlis, the leader of the New Democracy party and nephew of its founder, became the country's youngest prime minister in 2004 following more than a decade of socialist rule. Re-elected in 2007, Karamanlis found that his popularity was undermined by a series of scandals. The most damaging was a land deal with an Orthodox monastery on Mt. Athos that cost the government more than €100 million and forced two of the prime minister's closest aides to resign. Sadly, this type of official corruption was not an isolated event.

While Moody's, other rating agencies, and Eurostat observed many of the challenges facing Greece, they and many investors missed (perhaps willingly) the deep-rooted structural and societal nature of the country's problems. In a sense, EU membership provided excellent camouflage for a small country with a weak economy and a change-resistant society addicted to foreign capital that allowed it to live beyond its means. Greece came to represent a Faustian bargain between European aspirations for a superior socio-economic model, based on a kinder and gentler form of capitalism, without the rough and tumble aspects of its Anglo-American incarnation. The global economic shocks of 2007-8 made Greece's position unsustainable.

At first, the breaking economic crisis did little to change the spending habits of the Greek government. The budget office, with apparent disregard for the global situation, projected an increase in government revenues for 2009 and signed off on a 17.2 percent increase in government spending. This massive increase in spending included an 11.5 increase in pensions and benefits for civil servants, an 28.1 percent increase in insurance, government healthcare programs, and social security, and a 21.5 percent increase in "various" other operating expenses. The irresponsible spending combined with a decrease of 4.7 percent in government revenues to create a 122.6 percent increase in the budget deficit between 2008 and 2009, from €9.96 billion to €22.18 billion.[10] The Greek government was testing its financial limits.

Greek economic growth had been hard hit by the global recession and the fiscal situation had deteriorated rapidly. Public sector debt was about to reach 100 percent of GDP, with €53 billion in debt coming due in 2010. Many Greeks were unhappy with their scandal-plagued government, which many perceived as inefficient, corrupt, and with a bias towards the wealthy upper class. A spate of small-scale bombings in 2009 thought to be conducted by anarchists did little to improve public sentiment. Indeed, Karamanlis stated in calling the election: "The consequences of the economic crisis are visible; we have two difficult, crucial years ahead of us."[11] The Greek prime minister was to have no idea how prophetic his words were to be.

The vote on October 4, 2009 allowed a very angry Greek electorate to oust the New Democracy government only two years into its second term. With a voter turnout of a little over 70 percent, PASOK captured around 44 percent of the vote, trouncing New Democracy by ten percentage points. The new ruling party won a solid majority of 160 seats out of 300. The victory of PASOK under the tall and articulate George Papandreou promised a break with the past; circumstances demanded that he deliver dramatic changes. Nevertheless, during the last months of 2009, international markets, while worried about Greece's large €53 billion looming debt repayments for 2010, were willing to give the new government time to put its house in order.

### The Crux of the Problem

The problem for Greece, the European Union, and ultimately for the world as a whole, was that the financial landscape had changed and could no longer sustain past arrangements. Following the easy money period, the first round in global deleveraging occurred in late 2007-2008 and was focused on American sub-prime excesses, Iceland's highly leveraged banks, and Ireland's housing bubble. Part of averting a global depression on the scale of the 1930s was a coordinated response of the G-20 countries to pump a huge amount of liquidity into national economies. This was done in the United States, China, and a number of large European counties. Critical to all of this was that the leading emerging market economies, Brazil, India, and China, maintained growth and were fiscally sound. For small countries everywhere this was a positive development.

The problem that struck Greece was growing doubt over the viability of a global recovery coupled with revelations about the extent of the country's financial mismanagement. Global economic policy makers averted a depression, but as 2009 headed into its final months, investor doubts over how governments were going to repay the surge in borrowing in large economies, like the United States and the United Kingdom, began to erode confidence. Despite the robust behavior of global debt and equity markets in 2009, it was increasingly evident that the events of 2007-2008 were not an ordinary cyclical recession; this was going to be a protracted period of painful structural adjustment and much of it would take place in the "industrial" countries of the OECD.

Greece was one of the weak links in the European Union's chain. While newer EU members, such as Latvia, Hungary, and Lithuania, were still developing economies and were able to receive assistance from the IMF, Greece—a mature economy and member of the euro zone—was different. While a source of national pride and currency stability, Greece's membership in the EU and, in particular the currency union also had a downside. While membership brought a huge flow of convergence payments from Brussels into Greece to help pull up the standard of living close to the EU mean, not all of the money was used wisely and some of it disappeared into the pockets of corrupt officials. Greece also lost the ability to devalue its currency—a valuable strategy in past crises. At the same time, many of the problems facing the Greek economy, such as making it more efficient and competitive as well as finding new industries were left for another day. Indeed, it can be argued that much of what could have happened via the European Union, in particular, a more fulsome economic modernization and integration, did not take root. This left Greece with an aggressive deficit in economic terms and a heavy dependence on external financing.

## Countdown to the Meltdown

The Papandreou government initially perceived the economic situation as bad. However, the size and scope of the problem was astonishing to many of the incoming government. The new finance minister, George Papaconstantinou, wrote on November 30, 2009:

> The fiscal situation is dramatic, with a public deficit estimated at 12.7% of GDP this year and debt above 110% of GDP. On top of this, Greek statistics and Greek policies now suffer a complete lack of credibility on account of the fact that, before losing the elections, the previous government was reporting a fiscal deficit only as half as high as we know to be the case. Further, these problems are compounded by a persistent current-account deficit, itself the result of an economic development model that has clearly run its course.[12]

While the new finance minister covered the litany of problems confronting the new administration, the credibility factor emerged as the largest and for good reason.

The PASOK government passed an austerity budget in late December for 2010, which cut public spending by 10 percent and vowed to crack down on tax evasion. Despite Prime Minister Papandreou's claim to reduce the deficit to 9.1 percent of GDP in 2010, Greece's credibility was seriously eroded due to the unreliability of official statistics, a track record of corruption, and a failure to tackle longstanding structural problems, usually by employing only one-off measures. Along these lines, the budget was quickly criticized by both the EU and the rating agencies for being weak on permanent reforms, such as trimming the public sector wage bill. Market sentiment, critical for any new ventures to see Greek bonds, was looking for something beyond words and promises.

The Greek position was hurt by the ongoing questions over the fiscal deficit numbers. The outgoing New Democracy government had placed it at 6-7 percent of GDP, well above 2008's level of 5.6 percent.. The first official tally of the PASOK government was 12.5 percent of GDP, a rude shock announced in late October 2009. At the same time, it was revealed that Greece's public debt was probably 111.5 percent of GDP at year-end 2010, up from 99.2 percent in 2008. This led short sellers to start betting against Greece's sovereign bonds. As Greek credit spreads widened (increasing the cost of debt refinancing) it raised questions about the ability of Athens to finance its debt of €53 billion coming due in 2010. This was a particularly acute issue considering the low level of foreign exchange reserves, which were well under the amount of debt coming due. From their highs of $18.9 billion in 1999, Greek foreign exchange reserves were $5.5 billion ten years later.

As Greece sailed into 2010, the financial seas had become far choppier. In a rare televised address to the country in February, Prime Minister Papandreou touched on how the country's debt had ballooned to €300 billion, with potentially negative effects for the euro zone. The Greek leader stated: "The time has come to take brave decisions here in Greece just as other countries in Europe have also taken. We all have a debt and duty towards our homeland to work together at this difficult time to protect our economy."[13]

But there was much more to Greece's problems and how it became the center of a global sovereign debt crisis. The Greeks developed a society in which there was a strong current of mistrust of government related to official corruption. There was a sense of entitlement over access to outside capital flows to pay for a lifestyle beyond the means of many Greeks and an increasingly deteriorating economic competitiveness. Tax evasion was a major problem, particularly among high earners, and the very large public sector weighed down government balance sheets. The corruption issue was one of Greece's greatest concerns, but as the economic crisis intensified, the stories and statistics started to tumble out into the international media.

A study conducted by Transparency International gave some scope of the problem as it indicated that Greek citizens paid an average of €1,355 ($1,800) in bribes in 2009 for public services ranging from speeding up the issue of driver's licenses and construction permits, to getting admitted into public hospitals or manipulating tax returns.[14] This culture of "the envelope," according to the same study, also encompassed bribes paid for private sector services such as lawyers, doctors, or banks that were even higher. The international corruption watchdog calculated that Greek households paid a total of €787 million in bribes in 2009—€462 million to public employees and €325 million to the private sector. All this, in a country with a total GDP of €238 billion. What was even more damaging about the study was that it did not encompass corruption occurring within the government, but was focused only on the small-scale daily occurrences. It is important to underscore that while such evidence of corruption was disheartening and damaging to Greek credibility, such activities were understood to be going on a long time.

Why had Europeans ignored Greek corruption and indirectly supported it by providing generous financial aid? While the EU membership was a cornucopia of financial benefits for Greece, Greece was a blessing for many northern European bankers, pension fund managers, and insurance companies. For the bankers, dominated by French and German institutions (and to a lesser extent UK banks), Greece's ongoing need for a debt issuance, necessary to pay off short term debts coming due, was a steady stream of business in terms of fees and trading. The problem with this situation was that European banks became intricately involved in keeping the Greek house of cards standing. That involvement meant a substantial exposure to Greece. At the end of 2009, banks headquartered in the euro zone had lent $206 billion to Greece (more than half the value of the country's entire GDP), with German and French banks having the largest exposure.[15]

## The Crisis—From Greece to the EU

As Greece shifted into crisis mode in January 2010, driven by revelations of larger-than-expected fiscal deficits, international investors became extremely reluctant to lend any more money to Athens. The question now arose as to whether the Papandreou administration would have the money to meet its debt obligations. Despite rumblings from the EU about some type of support, investor backing for Greece wilted. In early 2010, Greece had been able to issue bonds, which were heavily oversubscribed. On March 29, it came to market with a new €5 billion bond issue, but subscriptions were less than expected. On March 30, Athens failed for the first time to raise a targeted allocation when if offered a fresh tranche of an existing, but illiquid, 20-year bond; against a target of €1 billion, the government was only able to raise €390 million, damagingly short of expectations.[16] *The Economist* was quick to comment that: "for many observers this was a clear signal that Greece will need a bail-out soon."[17]

The Papandreou government's austerity programs still did not convince the markets. By April, there was growing trepidation about the Greek banks' ability to withstand the storm regardless of a government €28 billion bank support program. Although the government was talking tough, April was marked by a civil servant strike, which closed hospitals and shut the 2,500-year-old Acropolis (Greece's top tourist attraction) to visitors. As much of this was televised to the rest of the world, investors continued to question the ability of Prime Minister Papandreou to deliver austerity and structural reforms in the face of such vehement public opposition. It also did not help that this civil unrest occurred at a time when the Greek government was meeting with EU and IMF officials to negotiate loan conditions. Jacques Cailloux, chief economist at the Royal Bank of Scotland Group PLC observed on April 22: "Papandreou is caught between a rock and a hard place. The market has zero confidence in what the Greeks are saying, and any further austerity measures pushed for by the IMF could be the ones that break the camel's back if they are deemed unfair by the population. He doesn't have any option though."[18] Compounding the problem was the announcement by the EU of a support program that was vague, reflecting difficulties in how the respective EU member governments were going to raise capital as well as who would bear the heaviest burden. Additionally, rumors circulated in markets that wealthy Greeks were pulling their money out of the country.

The dilemma that emerged by April 2010 was that the Greek problem—the threatened default of an EU member—had graduated to a euro zone problem, pulling down the euro's value, casting doubt over the other southern European countries, and raising questions as to the future of the EU. From an average of $1.34 in April, the euro declined to an average of $1.25 in May before touching bottom at an average of $1.22 in June. Moreover, the longer the crisis continued, the more terrifying it became. There was an increasingly deep-seated fear that if Greece were to default, the crisis would spread into Portugal, Spain, and possibly Italy. On a superficial basis, Portugal shares a number of similarities with Greece: it is a small country of 10 million with a large fiscal deficit (9.4 percent of GDP in 2009), and a substantial (though far more manageable) debt burden (80 percent of GDP). Worse, a full-blown sovereign crisis might not be confined the Southern Europe since many countries—including some large economies—confronted large current account deficits and weak growth prospects. What started as a fire in a small country ran the risk of becoming an inferno, spreading to the EU and beyond, a situation left open by the euro zone bank exposure. Euro zone banks accounted for almost two-thirds (62 percent) of all internationally active banks' exposures to the residents of the euro area for Greece, Ireland, Portugal, and Spain. According to the Bank for International Settlements, these banks had an exposure of $727 billion in Spain, $402 billion to Ireland, $244 billion to Portugal and $206 billion in Greece.[19] To break down the exposure further, the largest amount was taken on by French and German banks—at year-end 2009, they had combined exposures of about $958 billion ($493 billion and $465 billion, respectively) to the residents of these countries.

Rounding out this dismal picture, UK banks had substantial exposures to Ireland ($230 billion), which made them the largest lenders out of Europe.[20] Exposure to Spain was $140 billion, mainly to the non-bank private sector ($79 billion), and Portugal was $100 billion. The exposure of European banks to Greece and other troubled Southern European countries in 2010 was a slow-moving crisis that was borne out in international markets by volatility, an evaporation of credit, and investor angst.

The argument that emerged in early 2010 and played out in the spring was this: if a country like Greece unraveled, it would eventually be forced to pull out of the euro, which in turn, could set off a process of other euro zone countries coming under severe pressure (i.e., unable to go to markets to raise new debt to repay the old debt) for a number of the same reasons. In a worst-case scenario, Europe would be split into countries strong enough to maintain the currency link and those unable to do so. For many investors and policymakers there was a real concern that an unraveling of the euro currency zone would destroy confidence in the global economic recovery and cause a double-dip recession, placing the global economy on a track similar to the 1930s. Furthermore, the countervailing pressures to raise new capital in order to foster economic growth while at the same time reducing deficits to keep borrowing rates down, was threatened by the prospect of anemic growth among euro zone countries. Implementing austerity measures would confront countries with low growth and an increasing cost of debt-servicing—an unsustainable debt cycle.

For all of Europe's talk of its high standard of living, its ability to turn swords into ploughshares, and financial muscle, Greece became an unlikely test to the durability of the experiment of Jean Monnet, its visionary founding father. Greece's struggles were a major setback to the European experiment. In some circles, it was feared that it would have far-reaching political ramifications, diminishing the power of the European Union at a time when it hoped to rival the United States, an emerging China, and a resurgent Russia.

At the same time, the crisis highlighted the fact that the same national divides and byzantine bureaucracy undermining the EU's efforts to be a major political player were obstacles to implementing a rescue package for the Greeks. In spite of European groaning over the power of "Eurocrats" in Brussels, the crisis demonstrated the reality that in times of emergency, there was no clear chain of command, no clear leadership, and few mechanisms to implement relief quickly. As in foreign affairs, the question on everyone's lips became "who is in charge?"

Germany was certainly better placed than most to deal with the crisis. Europe's largest economy, it also boasted one of its healthier balance sheets and a greater capacity to provide financial assistance than any of its EU partners. German resistance to bailing out the Greeks intensified through the first part of 2010, greatly complicating the EU's support efforts. Indeed, German voters punished Chancellor Angela Merkel's ruling coalition in state elections in May because of her hazy agreement on some manner of German support. As the German magazine *Der Spiegel* observed: "Politicians in Germany are reluctant to rescue Greece, partly because such a move would be deeply unpopular after Germans have undergone reforms in recent years to keep their budget deficit under control."[21] Many Germans were questioning why their austerity and fiscal responsibility should be compromised to rescue the Greeks from decades of financial mismanagement and corruption. In the end, the realization in Berlin was that if Greece was not rescued, the entire European Union would be under pressure. Other countries, Ireland, Portugal, and, most importantly, Spain would also come under enormous pressure risking a series of sovereign defaults.

As the major economic power in the EU, German support was critical. Without Germany, any rescue effort was doomed to fail. It was this confluence of economic, political and financial forces that pushed the EU down the road to creating a massive bail-out mechanism for Greece—and any other member countries that were to follow it down the road in to financing problems.

### Dealing with Armageddon

The EU opted for a shock and awe approach to Greece designed to stop the rot before it reached any further. A €750 billion program took shape, supplementing an earlier €110 billion Greek rescue package. The total European safety net was eventually €850 billion (roughly $1 trillion). The key components of the program were:

1.  €60 billion stabilization fund from the EU Commission;
2.  €440 billion in loan guarantees from euro member countries (this facility has a three-year shelf life and will sell debt and use that cash to buy the bonds of euro-area countries in need;
3.  €250 billion from the IMF.

It was also announced the European Central Bank (ECB) would buy government securities and private securities on the secondary market. The ECB further announced a six-month refinancing operation with full allotment in May at a rate linked to the main refinancing rate of 1 percent. Across the Atlantic, the Federal Reserve indicated that it was re-opening dollar-swap lines with the ECB, the Bank of Japan, the Bank of England, the Bank of Canada, and the Swiss National Bank.

This massive program brought stability in the market's attitude toward Greece, but the road ahead remained difficult. Reforms that had been announced earlier had failed to secure investor confidence in the government's efforts due to well-televised displays of public disorder that rocked Athens throughout the spring. As the rest of Europe watched, the Greek public went on a rampage of strikes, protests, and riots. Transportation networks ground to a halt. Airports were closed. Protesters clashed with police, set off bombs, and torched automobiles.

In one high-profile case, a petrol bomb was thrown at a bank killing three people. Bank employees staged a strike in retaliation.

Greek credibility had not been helped by another revision, in late April 2010, of economic data that showed a fiscal deficit was in fact around 13.6 percent of GDP, not the earlier 12.7 percent revision. (In November 2010, the 2009 fiscal deficit was revised upward again to 15.4 percent.) This was followed by Moody's cutting its ratings on Greek sovereign debt from A2 to A3, stating, there was "a significant risk that debt may only stabilize at a higher and more costly level that previously estimated." Standard and Poor's went further, reducing Greek bonds to non-investment grade (BB+) on April 27.

The critical issue facing Greece was how to regain credibility. The core issue was captured by *The Financial Times'* Ralph Atkins and Kerin Hope (May 6, 2010): "Now it is Greece's moment to decide its fate: can it become a functioning state, capable of living within its means, or will it remain a malfunctioning country?"[22] Greece needed to reinvent itself. The old system of weak political institutions plagued by corruption, excessive patronage, mistrust of the state and lack of responsibility by both elites and citizenry had to change if investors' perceptions were to change. Prime Minister Papandreou understood this and showed fortitude in the face of widespread public agitation over the necessary programs. As he stated in May 2010: "We can to show a Greece that is changing, that is being reborn. There has to be a new collective Greek conscience."[23] To his words were added those of Finance Minister Papaconstantinou that Greece "is a member of the euro zone, will always be a member of the euro zone, will always remain a member of the European Union."[24] Fortunately for Greece, Papandreou's words were supported by hundreds of billions of euros in credit from Germany and the rest of Europe.

Despite the rhetoric and hard-nosed structural adjustment program of the Greek government and the EU support program, significant doubts about Greece's ability to avoid a sovereign default remained. Indeed, a number of prominent economists argued that the EU rescue program was only postponing the inevitable—the harshness of cutting so much out of the budget would leave Greek society in such a state that the government's political will would erode and, with that, EU/IMF targets would be missed, resulting in another terminal crisis of confidence, which would end in default.[25] Dramatic reductions in government spending would prevent the growth of Greece's economy and would, in some views, continue the contraction since the Greek government would need substantial growth to find the necessary funds to repay the European and IMF loans.

In spite of the austerity measures, the bailout provisions, the emergency funds, and the government assurances, the possibility of a Greek default cannot be discounted. Although it is not inevitable, the reforms required by Greece to bring its fiscal deficit and public debt and regain a degree of competitiveness are daunting. The annual World Bank "Doing Business" survey for 2010 provides some idea of the challenge facing Greece. Under the World Bank assessment, 183 countries were surveyed. Greece ranked 109 in terms of "ease of doing business." As a piece in *The Wall Street Journal* acidly observed: "At 109 Greece ranks below such models of transparency and disclosure as Egypt (106), Zambia (90), Rwanda (67), and Kazakhstan (63). A country has to work hard to do this poorly."[26] The other dismal showings included ranking 140 in terms of starting a business, 147 in employing workers, 107 in registering property, and 154 in protecting investors. All in all, Greece ranked far behind the other 26 members of the European Union as well as other OECD economies. The conclusion of *The Wall Street Journal* was: "The Doing Business survey reveals an economy that's hostile to free enterprise and private property, primed for corruption, lacking in labor and capital mobility, stifled by powerful trade unions, and unlikely to grow without deep-rooted changes."[27]

Beyond the business environment issue, Greece also faces the daunting task of fiscal consolidation, which promises to cut spending and tax cuts equal to 14 percent of the country's €237 billion GDP in a bid to bring Greece's deficit within the EU limit of 3 percent. Such steep cuts will in all likelihood prolong the country's recession and pushed up unemployment to a 10-year high of 11.7 percent in the first quarter of 2010. All of this leaves Greece in a state of disarray. A June 17, 2010 poll of 2,100 Greeks showed 52.6 percent believed that the country would default on its debt, while seven in ten Greeks believe the economy was headed in the wrong direction.[28]

The Papandreou government is offering deep-seated changes to the Greek economy and in 2010 appeared committed to transforming the old model. One example of the newfound vigor over structural reform was in the passage of the tough 3-year austerity program agreed with its euro zone partners and the IMF, the legislation was passed by 172 votes to 121 in the 300-member chamber. There were three abstentions by PASOK deputies, who were promptly expelled from the ruling party. While the Communists and most members of New Democracy opposed the austerity bill, the far-right LAOS Party backed PASOK, as did Dora

Bakoyannis, New Democracy's former foreign minister, who entertains ideas of launching her own centrist political party.

The Papandreou government's reform program has an aggressive agenda. It includes not only fiscal restructuring, but overhauling how the country conducts business. This encompasses privatization, making the tourist sector more competitive (including looking to non-traditional markets like Asia), and pursuing green technology in terms of reducing dependence on oil, gas, and coal. Moreover, labor market reforms are required.

The austerity measures combine new taxes and substantial spending cuts. The VAT is being raised from 19 to 21 percent with the aim of bringing in an additional €1.3 billion. One-off taxes on corporations and vacation homes are valued at €1 billion and €200 million respectively. Taxes on earnings of more than €100,000 will increase. A supplemental tax on luxury goods (yachts, and cars worth more than €35,000) is expected to bring in an additional €100 million. Taxes on cigarettes (€300 million), gasoline (€450 million), and electricity (€250 million) are all being raised. Even Greece's public sector is subject to the belt-tightening. Holiday bonuses are being reduced by 30 percent for a €740 million savings. Overtime hours are being restricted. Pensions are to be frozen and pension subsidies are set to be reduced by €150 million. Bonuses and pay reductions for public sector employees are being cut by 7 percent, saving another €360 million. Public sector health benefits are being cut by as much as 10 percent.

Another important element of the Greek government's program was privatization. In early June, it announced long-delayed plans meant to help the fiscal situation and push along the creation of a new economy. One of the major items in the program was to privatize 49 percent of the operations division of the unprofitable state-owned railways company, the Hellenic Railways Organization (OSE). This would be a major step forward, considering that the company has over €10 billion in debt and loses €1 billion a year. Other items to be sold included state holdings in several casinos, a 39 percent stake in the Greek post office, and stakes in state-owned services, including the waterworks companies of Greece's two major cities, Athens and Thessaloniki. The privatization program also falls under the three-year austerity program and will include a restructuring of the country's natural-gas monopoly to prepare it for privatization.

The real challenge for Greece over the next few years is one of political will. Greeks are being asked for a steep cut in spending, a reduction in their entitlements, and to embrace foreign capital (something which has been traditionally regarded with suspicion). Benefits will probably be felt only by the next generation. Although the capital can be Chinese, Libyan, or Russian, Greece has to work better to capture foreign investment and keep it. Prime Minister Papandreou and many of the younger technocrats he has brought into government appear to understand this. The prime minister stated in June 2010: "I know that markets aren't convinced. I know that, I've lived through this crisis. They're not going to be convinced by political programs. But they will be convinced if we do have results."[29]

Parts of Greek society, however, remain opposed. Greece is one of the few countries in the EU to still have a Communist Party (KKE) with parliamentary representation. The KKE remains vehemently anti-capitalist and openly Marxist-Leninist. It is also strongly opposed to PASOK's economic restructuring, something that it will no doubt express via its close ties to some of the country's largest public sector trade unions. Indeed, the KKE, which was a prime force in the April-May 2010 anti-austerity riots, wants Greece to quit the EU and default on its external debt, but at the same time, maintain early retirement and public and private sectors wages and pensions.

It would be inaccurate to represent KKE, which holds only 21 seats in the Greek Parliament, as a dominant force in Greece. Nonetheless, it is a strident voice of opposition and plays to public sentiments about the unfairness and the harsh bite of austerity measures to the working class. KKE has attacked the PASOK government as traitors to the left for its alliance with the external forces of the EU and IMF. KKE also plays to Greek sentiment of being a small country victim of larger, impersonal and calculating powers.

Greece should consider the recent experience of other small European economies. During the 1990s, Finland and Norway experienced profound financial/economic crises, while in the past few years Iceland and Ireland tumbled into their own dire set of problems. Certainly in the cases of Finland and Ireland, very difficult decisions were made to rectify the situation, including a willingness to restructure the economies, which meant tough approaches on competitiveness and social issues. In Finland, high unemployment was an outcome—in the short term—but set the stage for stronger long-term growth. In both cases, restructuring of the banking sector was undertaken, though in Greece the banks have not been the problem. In Iceland and Ireland, banking crises precipitated a sovereign crisis as the government was forced to increase borrowing to bail the banks out. In Greece, the domestic banks, natural holders of Greek paper, were faced with exposure to a scary government balance sheet.

PASOK's challenge is to build societal consensus and maintain a steady stream of reforms that develop a sense of momentum. The risk, as it was in Finland and as it is in Ireland, is debtor/reform fatigue. This was something that emerged during the 1980s, with a number of heavily indebted Latin American economies that experienced a "lost decade." Confronted with a long road through austerity and reform measures, Greek society runs the risk of having its attitude transform from recognition that changes are necessary to defiance. The next elections must be held by 2012. Can Papandreou maintain reforms, hit targets, reshape the Greek economy, and stave off a default on external debt through this period? The tasks, as many have stated will be Herculean in size and scope, with a tremendous amount of pressure being exerted on the government from within and without.

There is another important element to Greece's debt problems—the political will from the rest of the EU. The massive rescue package put together for the Greeks was also a covert rescue of European banks. The consequence of this is that the EU's fortunes are even more closely aligned with Greece's, hence Brussels and the leading EU members must maintain pressure on Athens to maintain its discipline. This also means that the EU has—for the foreseeable future—opted not to allow a sovereign member default. A default, which is still possible, would be messy and painful and run the risk of contagion. Furthermore, the rescue package, aimed to help forestall debt problems with Portugal and Spain, also requires painful structural changes (and accompanying popular resistance) throughout the EU on such items as pensions, retirement ages, working hours, and social benefits. In the *Financial Times* Martin Wolf correctly observed: "The attempted rescue of Greece is just the beginning of the story. Much more still needs to be done, in responding to the immediate crisis and in reforming the eurozone itself, in the not too distant future."[30] Considering the round of fiscal retrenchment that followed in 2010 in Germany, the UK, Italy, Spain, Portugal, and Hungary, the message was received by some governments, but the verdict of overall EU reform remained a question mark.

## Conclusion

Greece's crash is noteworthy because of the impact such a small country had on the larger European economy. Greece's sovereign crisis cast a shadow over the US, as highlighted by a May 2010 *Wall Street Journal* headline, "Greece Fuels Fears of Contagion in U.S.," which began with the following sentence: "Investors and policy makers are starting to worry that the economic crisis in Greece could cross the Atlantic and undermine the U.S. economic recovery, in the same way that U.S. housing woes in 2008 battered Europe."[31]

The lessons from Greece are many. First and foremost, the accumulation of massive debt is never a good thing. It is a situation that is aggravated by a lack of transparency and disclosure. Related to this is that borrowing money is not a substitute for actual economic reform. Easy access to money and continued global economic growth functioned as an ongoing disincentive to tackle difficult and painful reforms. The sad outcome is that those difficult and painful reforms now are being implemented but in a harsher and shorter period of time with no guarantee of success. Greece is ultimately left as a small and narrow-based economy being pushed very hard by external forces—some of which it has come to depend upon.

Another factor is that Greece as a small economy benefited from EU membership. Although harsh words were exchanged between the Greeks and other Europeans, notably the Germans, the EU stepped up to help Greece avoid a sovereign default. As Ireland also benefited from EU membership, so did Greece. The sharp contrast to this is obviously Iceland, which found itself alone at a heightened time of the crisis. For Greece, however, EU membership came with an imposition of harsh reforms, something that Ireland self-imposed. Although Ireland's approach is equally painful, there is a desire to work through the pain to restore credibility. In Greece, the willingness and ability to implement the EU/IMF program remains an issue. Opposition to the government and social unrest continues. Whether Greece defaults in the end or not, the road back to stability for the Greek economy will be long and painful. Other countries confronting similar debt issues would do well to beware of the example borne by the Greeks.

## Notes

1. "Acropolis Now," *The Economist*, May 1, 2010, p. 11.
2. Matthew Dalton, "Default and Greece: History's Judgment," *The Wall Street Journal*, April 26, 2010. http://blog.wsj.com/brussels/2010/04/26/default-and-greece-historys-judgement/.
3. Panayoti E. Dimitras, "Greece: A New Danger," *Foreign Policy*, (Spring 1985), p. 54.

4.  Quoted from Scott B. MacDonald, "Southern Europe," in Scott B. MacDonald, Margie Lindsay and David L. Crum, editors, *The Global Debt Crisis: Forecasting for the Future* (London: Pinter Publishers, 1990), p. 152.
5.  MacDonald, Linsay and Crum, *The Global Debt Crisis*, p. 153.
6.  Economist Intelligence Unit. EIU.com
7.  Organization for Economic Cooperation and Development, Greece Economic Survey 1986/1987 (Paris Organization for Economic Cooperation and Development, July 1987).
8.  Sara Bertin-Leveca, Kockerbeck Alexander, and Vincent Truglia, Greece (Analysis), *Moody's Investors Service*, January 2006, p. 2.
9.  Ibid., p. 3.
10. Greek Budget 2010: http://www.mof-glk.gr/proypologismos/2010/books/proyp/index.html.
11. Quoted from "Greek PM Calls Snap Election in Response to Economic Turmoil," *Deutsche Welle*, September 2, 2009. http://www.dw-world.de/dw/article/0,,4620611,00.html.
12. George Papaconstantinou, "The 'Greek Problem,'" *The Wall Street Journal*, November 30, 2009. http://online.wsj.com/article/SB100014240527487039394045745658316127 1014.html.
13. Helena Smith, "Greece's Papandreou Makes TV Appeal for Unity Over Financial Crisis," *Guardian.Co.UK*, February 2, 2010.
14. "Greek Corruption Booming, Says Transparency International," *Der Spiegel Online*, February 3, 2010, http://www.spiegel.de/international/europe/0.1518.681184.00.html.
15. Bank for International Settlements, *BIS Quarterly Review: International Banking and Financial Market Developments* (June 2010), p. 19.
16. "Greece's Deepening Debt Crisis," *The Economist*, April 10, 2010, p. 73.
17. Ibid., p.74.
18. Quoted from Maria Petrakis, "Papandreou Faces Bond Rout as Budget Worsens, Workers Strike," *Bloomberg*, April 22, 2010.
19. Bank for International Settlements, *BIS Quarterly Review*, June 2010, p. 19.
20. Ibid., p. 21.
21. "Greek Corruption Booming, Says Transparency International," *Der Spiegel Online*.
22. Ralph Atkins and Kerin Hope, "A Herculean Task," *Financial Times*, May 6, 2010, p. 9.
23. Ibid., p. xx.
24. Quoted from Geoffrey T. Smith and Adam Cohen, "Greece Expects Bailout Package by Early May," *The Wall Street Journal*, April 26, 2010, p. A12.
25. Arvind Subramanion, "Greek Deal Lets Banks Profit From an 'Immoral Hazard,'" *Financial Times*, May 7, 2010. p. 9.
26. "The Greek Economy Explained," *The Wall Street Journal*, May 7, 2010, p. A16.
27. Ibid., p. xx.
28. Maria Petrakis and Tom Keene, "Papandreou Says Cuts to Overcome Investor Skepticism," *Bloomberg*, June 21, 2010.
29. Ibid.
30. Martin Wolf, "A Bail-out for Greece Is Just the Beginning," *Financial Times*, May 5, 2010, p. 9.
31. Bob Davis and Mark Gongloff, "Greece Fuels Fears of Contagion in U.S," *The Wall Street Journal*, May 6, 2010, p. A10.

# 10

# Conclusion

*"Power without responsibility—the prerogative of the harlot throughout the ages."*
—Rudyard Kipling

Switzerland, an Alpine country of 7.6 million people, has been highly successful in generating one of the highest per capita incomes in the world based on a very workable and open economy. To many people around the world, Switzerland's success is a reflection of hard work, innovation, and thrift. Yet Switzerland's path to prosperity was not always one of peace and purpose. Much of the country's earlier history was marked by war and conflict, which produced a stream of in-demand Swiss mercenaries. Over time the Swiss settled down, adopted neutrality in the choppy European affairs around their mountain fastness and developed a highly efficient modern economy, increasingly driven by financial services. Although the country's major banks have at times struggled with the vicissitudes of international markets, the country has largely avoided any major crashes. Even in the 2008-2009 financial panic, which hit its major banks hard, the Swiss economy was not sunk and national currency, the Swiss franc, functioned as a refuge currency.

Why has Switzerland been successful in riding the waves of international finance compared to other countries, such as Iceland and Ireland? Anyone venturing into the Swiss National Museum in Zurich is given part of the answer. On the second floor, tucked away behind several rooms is the Swiss wall of bragging. On the wall is a dramatic digital comparison of Switzerland vis-à-vis Germany, France, and Italy chronicling records of national strikes, inflation, and GDP growth, dating back to the turn of the century. Considering that the tables compare back through the 1920s and 1930s, a period when Switzerland was observed as a safe harbor, the Alpine country looks remarkably better than its neighbors, with its graphs reassuringly flat, while the others gyrate apparently wildly. The not so subtle message is that the Swiss were prudent with their national development (i.e., went into financial services), harmonious in their social affairs (not a lot of strikes or labor-management strife), and avoided getting entangled in Europe's highly destructive conflicts. Indeed, the last was a tremendous comparative advantage for the Swiss as it reinforced its safe harbor for smart money status. Although one can argue the pros and cons of Switzerland's role as a financial safe harbor (and offshore financial center where it is often proclaimed the wealthy evade taxes and nasty dictators stash their money), the small Alpine country has been highly successful in embracing finance as a means of national development while avoiding a major crash. This certainly raises the issue of why some small countries are successful in steering into finance (either through the development of offshore banking and/or becoming major borrowers) and others have massive problems.

Switzerland's experience indicates that a small (or smallish) country can be highly successful in embracing financial services and open markets. Singapore and Hong Kong also fit that mode as do a handful of Caribbean states and dependencies, such as The Bahamas, Aruba, Bermuda, and the Cayman Islands. Certainly, for many of the successful small countries, a critical element is the recognition that international integration is very dynamic and difficult to avoid, considering linkages along the lines of currency, trade, movement of people, investment and technology. In many regards, most policymakers in small economies focus on issues of management. Economic policymakers repeatedly find themselves challenged by technological and financial innovations and how to manage risk in the context of a globalized economy. None of this is easy. Getting it right has massive upside; getting it wrong can result in a national crisis. It must also be considered that financial experimentation can create a situation in which there is an acceleration of risk, something painfully evident in the diverse cases examined in this book. But for all of the crashes of small countries, there are some successes. Indeed, a number of countries have embraced finance as a means to power national development and have not suffered spectacular crashes. This leaves an open-ended question: why did Austria and Iceland crash while and Luxembourg and Bermuda prosper?

## Luxembourg and Bermuda

*Luxembourg*

The Grand Duchy of Luxembourg has a history of being a survivor. Tracing its existence in one form or another to A.D. 963, Luxembourg was built up around what the historian James Newcomer called "one small promontory of some 150 acres surrounded by three valleys, the route of two watercourses."[1] The modern nation sits with France to the south, Germany to the east, and Belgium to the west. Modern Luxembourg's economy through much of the nineteenth century was dominated by agriculture, supplemented by some commerce from the various towns. When the grand duchy formally achieved full independence in 1867, the result of a great power conference, the Congress of London, the economy began to shift away from agriculture to iron and steel. Blessed with substantial iron deposits and a member of the German Zollverein (customs union), Luxembourg developed a world-class steel industry, benefiting from the rapid industrialization and access to its larger and more powerful German neighbor.

Luxembourg's steel industry was the dominant force in the country's economy through the 1970s. At that point, challenges multiplied from new competitors close to cheap inputs in developing nations, new technologies, and labor-management issues. Indeed, this combination of factors resulted in worldwide oversupply. The 1970s and 1980s were also a period marked by two oil shocks, which resonated heavily in Luxembourg. All of this left the steel industry, labor unions, and government in a quandary. Much of Luxembourg's prosperity was tied to steel, yet global conditions had shifted against Luxembourg. Measures were taken in the mid- and late 1970s to restructure and modernize the steel industry as well as provide some degree of social support. Significantly, this was a consensus-driven process, including labor, management and government. The result was the consolidation of the industry into ARBED (Acieries Reunie de Burbach-Eich-Differdange), a financial restructuring of what had become a debt-laden sector, and synergy of agreements with the Belgian steel industry. Accordingly, the Luxembourg government played a key role in this restructuring, largely through the Societe Nationale de Credit et d'Investissement (National Credit and Investment Company), which eventually became a major shareholder in ARBED.[2]

To a backdrop of a troubled steel industry, the government with the input from the private sector, made a fateful decision to further promote the development of the country's financial sector.[3] Luxembourg's banking system was already more significant vis-à-vis its GDP than many other European countries due to a high level of bank secrecy, higher taxes in other countries and geographical location, which was enhanced by an efficient transportation infrastructure. For Belgians, French, and Germans visiting the bank in Luxembourg could be a day trip, giving rise to the "Belgian dentist" stereotype in Luxembourg. It should also be noted that in contrast to France, Germany, and the United Kingdom, Luxembourg has enjoyed labor peace and political stability since the end of World War II in a fashion comparable to Switzerland.

Luxembourg benefited from other factors in making an attractive offshore financial center. This included a well-educated workforce, the decision of the European Union (EU) to locate the European Investment Bank in the grand duchy, and most people in Luxembourg favored economic integration with the rest of Europe vis-à-vis the EU. By 1984, Luxembourg was well on its way to becoming a more significant player in global offshore finance. As Newcomer noted: "Belgian nationals are easing their home tax burdens by Luxembourg deposits. Swiss banks are escaping withholding taxes on anonymous accounts by placing them in Luxembourg. The Arabs consider Luxembourg to be a safer place for their money than Germany...."[4]

The path to becoming a major offshore financial center was not without challenges. Considering the high level of bank secrecy initially offered by Luxembourg, hot money was attracted to the country, including some that came from criminal activities. Two of the most bruising scandals were Banco Ambrosiano in 1982 and the Bank for Commerce and Credit International (BCCI) in the late 1980s. Banco Ambrosiano was an Italian bank with strong links to the Vatican, which ended up in a messy money laundering scandal, complete with a trail of bodies. In Luxembourg, the bank's subsidiary, Banco Ambrosiano Holdings, SA, caught up in the scandal, defaulted on its debt, leaving a bad memory. BCCI was a major international bank established by Pakistani banker Agha Hasan Abedi, with operations in 78 countries, including Luxembourg where it was registered. The bank was heavily involved in international money laundering and was thought to have been established with the intent to avoid being under the auspices of one strong banking regulatory authority. Several investigations into the bank revealed high levels of criminality and the bank was finally closed in 1991 in Luxembourg. Although these scandals were embarrassing, their damage to the Luxembourg economy was minimal and helped push the country to tighten its regulation and international cooperation.

From 1986 to 1992 financial services as a contribution to the economy expanded by 26.5 percent and by 15.6 percent in 1996-1996.[5] The pace picked up again from 1996 to 2000 at 26.1 percent. In 2005, there were around 220 offshore banks, with their balance sheets having in excess of €600 billion, which made Luxembourg Europe's second largest banking player after the United Kingdom (London).

By the early twenty-first century the financial sector in Luxembourg was well established as the major economic driver, directly generating around 25 percent of its added value, employing some 12 percent of the total workforce, and accounting for 40 percent of tax receipts. One government publication noted: "The sector is therefore crucial to Luxembourg's external trade balance; it accounted for 77.6% of the surplus of the service balance of trade in 2001. In other words, exports of financial items compensate for the deficits generated by other items, and in particular the commercial and revenues balances."[6]

Although the Luxembourg economy was buffeted by the global economic downturn in 2008-2009, with its real GDP growth (at 0.0 percent and -3.4 percent respectively) and unemployment rising close to six percent over the period, there was no crash. There were no panics at the banks, though the government of Luxembourg did help in two interventions alongside the Dutch and Belgian governments (in the cases of Dexia and Fortis, multinational banks that got into trouble with too much leverage). Indeed, Luxembourg continued to stay focused on financial services as the main driver of the economy. Economic growth resumed in 2010, albeit at a slow pace, partially a reflection of the anemic Euro-zone recovery. By 2011, Luxembourg remained one of the most affluent countries in the world, a small economy making its way among the giants.

What has made Luxembourg successful as a small country with an economy dominated by financial services? A combination of factors stands out—a willingness to embrace the financial sector, but with a focus on foreign depositors, followed by an offering of other more valued-added financial services—asset management, financial and tax planning, leasing and insurance. At the same time, the central bank was given a high degree of autonomy and is viewed with a degree of international respect. Equally significant, the development of local financial institutions and investment was pursued along a relatively conservative approach. While

Luxembourg developed its own banks, they did not evolve along the lines of Iceland's Kaupthing and Glitner, but have proven to be more prudent in their business growth. Perhaps Luxembourg's longstanding existence as a small country surrounded by larger countries instilled in its inhabitants a strong sense of conservatism, a sense of caution about overextending national activities beyond the country resource base. Last, but hardly least, was the fateful decision by Luxembourg to be an active force in Europe's economic integration under the EU flag. While this has represented challenges along the way (especially vis-à-vis the issue of bank secrecy and tax evasion), generally the EU experience has allowed Luxembourg to play a significant role in the fate of Europe, well beyond its size.

*Bermuda*

Another example of a small country that is heavily involved in finance is Bermuda, a self-governing British Overseas Territory that was first settled in 1609 by shipwrecked English colonists heading for Virginia. The United Kingdom appoints a governor and deputy governor to the island and London maintains control over defense, external affairs, and internal security, with all other laws coming under the authority of the Government of Bermuda, headed by the elected premier. With a population of 66,163, this small entity, about one-third the size of Washington, D.C., off the coast of the United States, emerged as a major offshore financial center in the mid-twentieth century. It also has one of the highest per capita incomes in the world.

Although some of Bermuda's promotional materials stress geographical location as the key factor in having a competitive advantage (as it is for luxury tourism) in international business, there is much more to this island. Indeed, one Bermudian publication observed: "A strong infrastructure, sensible regulations and a friendly tax regime. These are just some of the ingredients that make Bermuda the domicile of choice."[7] It is also important to stress other key factors—a well-educated population, political stability, close links to the United States and United Kingdom, and some long-range thinking about what type of business should drive national development. Like many small economies, Bermuda faced the dilemma of how to differentiate itself from the rest of the world beyond fun-in-the-sun tourism. The island's leadership also was aware that the days of Bermuda's geo-military significance as an Atlantic base for the UK and US were diminishing. After careful consideration, the decision of making Bermuda into an offshore "domicile of choice" for the global insurance industry was made, with a particular linkage to American and British multinational insurance firms. The combination of tax breaks, location, and infrastructure helped push along the concept, but once the first insurance operations were attracted, more were to follow. Moreover, the push into insurance had an important knock-on effect in the rest of the economy. As one report noted: "The growth in the captive insurance concept in the 1960s and 1970s led to the development of support services in the accounting, legal and administrative fields. By the 1980s, almost any big name in business either had a presence or an alliance in Bermuda either to take advantage of being a direct player or to better service clients with Bermuda-based interests."[8]

Bermuda's standing in the global insurance industry took another step forward following the September 11, 2001 attacks, which saw a number of reinsurance companies relocate to the island. Bermuda's reinsurers weathered a violent hurricane season in 2005 and the island economy survived much of the global financial crisis in the 2007-09 period without considerable dislocation.

Bermuda's success has not always been easy. The island's political stability has occasionally been punctured by racial issues defined by a black majority seeking political and economic empowerment from a white minority. This should not be taken out of context, or portrayed as a nasty, prolonged struggle between elements of Bermuda's population, as was the case in other colonial situations. However, tensions did lead to the assassination of the British governor, Sir Richard Sharples, and his aide-de-camp, Captain Hugh Sayers, and race riots in 1977 (following the hangings of the two men convicted of that action). The high cost of living on the island also leaves some degree of friction between the better-offs and lesser-offs. One reflection that the "race issue" remains a factor was evident in the publishing of a book by Quito Swan (a Bermudian) in 2010 entitled, *Black Power in Bermuda—The Struggle for Decolonization*. The book sold out in two weeks.[9]

Another factor is that Bermuda, as a small island with a high international profile, has sometimes been "smeared" as a tax haven by American politicians critical of large corporations getting tax breaks from an offshore center. Because of this, Bermuda has been pro-active in dealing with worldwide regulatory, legal, and fiscal changes. This has helped reinforce a reputation for a relatively corruption-free and pleasant place to do business. The island-state's central bank, the Bermuda Monetary Authority (BMA) is the integrated (i.e., covering all financial sectors) regulator of the financial services sector and has a good reputation internationally.

Why has not the Bermudian economy crashed like Iceland's and Greece's? Although Bermuda has been hit by the ups and downs of the global economy and seen periods of substandard growth, the dominance of the financial sector has not resulted in catastrophic consequences. This is largely because of the nature of financial sector involvement—insurance that is domiciled in Bermuda but by companies that are not likely to look to the state for a bailout or some type of rescue. If they have major problems they go bankrupt. Indeed, much of the risk inherent in those economies working in Bermuda is more tightly connected to larger economies, such as the United States or United Kingdom. At the same time, a closing down of the insurance industry in Bermuda would hurt the local economy, considering the important role of that sector. Yet Bermuda has worked hard to maintain a vigilant eye to any threats to the treaties with the United States and other developed countries that guarantee the sector's livelihood.

Bermuda is a small state that is pro-active in long-range planning and international diplomacy (as it has representatives) to maintain a competitive advantage. These attributes are supported by a political culture that is generally not prone to corruption and supportive of democracy and political stability. The financial authorities have also been given a degree of relative autonomy from the political process, a factor that has bolstered an overall good reputation in business circles. Bermuda's success in the global financial sector, albeit in insurance, has been the result of a conservative and well-thought out approach, seeking to take advantage of location, history and the development of human capital. This approach could be a reflection of the island-state's acute awareness of its slender base of natural resources.

## Lessons Learned

For small states the global economy can be an unfriendly sea in which the waves caused by larger actors can become threatening. This is the case for financial contagion just as much as the march of armies, something that Luxembourg experienced during the two world wars and the Franco-Prussian War. Considering the trials and tribulations of many small countries in dealing with financial and economic challenges, especially in the twentieth century, there are some lessons worth noting.

First and foremost, small countries need to give adequate time, resources and thought as to how they want to develop their financial sectors. That is critical if a particular government makes the decision to embrace financial services as an engine of growth or incur large debt loads to develop sectors of the economy or to upgrade infrastructure. Without the right allocation of resources, including regulatory actors empowered and willing to act, the decision to go the route of offshore finance or aggressively liberalize the financial sector can attract the wrong participants. The problems that can follow include money laundering, other forms of financial fraud and out-of-control financial speculation. None of those are positives for economic development as they cause distortions and crashes.

Another important and interrelated concern pertains to the role of the central bank. In small economies the independence of the central bank is exceedingly important. As small countries can be highly interconnected places with everyone knowing everyone else, the selection of a neutral referee is significant and difficult. This means a strict adherence to independent policy formulation, something that is also a challenge.

Related to the first two lessons is the adoption of a "too big to fail" policy for banks. In most economies banks are significant players, functioning as the major financial intermediaries. This situation translates into the central importance of a key or group of key actors that would have a highly disruptive impact if failures were to occur. At the same time, banks can grow too big to save—i.e., their role looms disproportionately over the economic landscape. This was clearly an issue for Iceland where the top three banks expanded well beyond the size of the country's GDP. Consequently when the banks got into trouble via speculation and too rapid expansion, the liabilities were well beyond the ability of the country to absorb and the government was forced to seek outside help, a painful experience from which Iceland is still seeking to recover.

Directly related to having a too big to fail policy is the proper regulation of non-bank financial institutions, such as private equity firms, hedge funds, and conglomerates. Active at times in financial services or owners of banks these firms can have a massive impact on the direction of the economy. This was the case in Iceland, where private holding companies held ownership in the major banks, but were ultimately unstable as the economy began to implode, contributing to the agony of the Icelandic crash.

Small countries must give considerable attention to the issue of interlocking directorates, groups of powerful people who can constitute an alternative pole of political/economic power. Simply stated, there is one question that many countries must contend with —do people sitting on multiple boards and inhabiting the same social haunts constitute a power bloc? While this is a concern for even large countries, in a small country the influence of a strategically placed group of people can result in economic distortions, some of which can be oligarchic in nature. Part of the outrage over Wall Street in the United States in 2008-2010 was the sentiment that the financial fat cats held a disproportionate amount of influence, especially in Washington. A similar sentiment was in evidence in Iceland, Ireland, and Greece over the same period. Some of the more conspiratorial aspects of interlocking directorates are probably overstated (i.e., they can form shadow governments), but one way of contending with such an issue is to foster a culture of transparency and disclosure or to limit the number of boards that individuals are allowed to sit on.

Beyond these policy lessons, we would add the need for general prudent economic policies. This pertains to such issues as fiscal policies, the management of public sector debt and monetary policies. One last point is the matching of economic challenges with the expertise at hand. That includes the accumulation of large amounts of debt and it raises the question—if a country lacks the necessary structural frameworks and experience to develop a new financial sector, let alone supervise it, why track in that direction? Indeed, the adoption of financial services raises some serious questions even for larger countries like the United States and United Kingdom. The historian Joyce Appleby observed on the rise of financial capitalism in the United States, with an eye to the disastrous financial collapse of 2008-2009: "More damaging to the nation in the long run, physicists, mathematicians, and computer experts were drawn away from their original work to join the high-earning financial wizards. At least 40 percent of Ivy League graduates went into finance in the early years of the twenty-first century. With multi-million dollar annual incomes commonplace, Wall Street formed a tight little winners' circle where all the incentives were thrown on the take-more-risk side and positive disincentives discouraged caution and even candor."[10] If a large economy like the United States is overcome by greed and a devil-may-care attitude about risk, it is that much more dangerous for smaller countries with fewer resources and smaller talent pools. In some cases, the role of financial services in a nation's development must be moderated.

The last issue pertains to international integration. In many regards, the integration issue is a thorny one—small countries appear damned if they seek integration into a larger regional economic bloc as with Greece or not as with Iceland. But the discussion is not so simple as integration (good) and non-integration (bad). It could be argued that Ireland and Portugal have both used integration in a more effective way than Greece did. And all three have been hurt by their inability to devalue their currencies to regain a competitive advantage. At the same time, Luxembourg, another EU member, maintained a comparatively successful track record during the same period of stress in international financial markets. At the end of the day, individual country actors driven by the dynamics of internal politics and economic needs loom large as to how countries make prudent or imprudent decisions. External factors also play a significant role, but as demonstrated by the lessons learned there are policy options that can reduce risks and manage the process of development.

## Conclusion

It is hoped that people learn from their mistakes, but the historical record over several centuries for small countries indicates otherwise. Too much debt, inept and corrupt economic management, bad luck, hubris, and the impact of larger and more powerful economic actors represent problems and challenges that contribute to the list of crashes that have marked the economies discussed in this book. And recovery can be a multi-year experience even in the economies where the authorities get things right. But not every case of small-country economics has been a disaster, which indicates that there exists a certain balance of planning, conservatism, a responsible leadership elite, awareness of the need to manage international integration and market economics. It is the achievement of this balance that makes a difference between a Luxembourg, Singapore, and Bermuda on one side of the ledger and an Iceland, Greece, and Dominican Republic (in the nineteenth century) on the other. Ultimately the issue of size does play an important role in whether nations crash and how they exit from such a traumatic event. No doubt future historians will continue to have plenty of material to work from considering the ability of men and women to find their way into financial folly, lured by the siren call of easy money.

# Notes

1.  James Newcomer, *The Grand Duchy of Luxembourg: The Evolution of Nation-hood 963 A.D. to 1983* (New York: University Press of America, 1984), p. 21. In his later Luxembourg edition (1995), the same author gave his historical scope: "Amid the Western European nations, generous in extent and population, stands the Grand Duchy of Luxembourg, upright, proud, and independent. It lived in infancy of nine hundred years. Its adolescence endured a hundred. It came of age with the celebration of its thousandth birthday something like three decades ago. Its culture, economy and government define a physiognomy, give it a stature that ranges it self-confidently alongside nations ten times, a hundred times, five hundred times its size." From James Newcomer, *The Grand Duchy of Luxembourg: The Evolution of Nationwide* (Luxembourg: Editions Emile Borschette/Librairie Le Bon Livre, 1995), p. 15. For other histories of Luxembourg see Jean-Marie Kreins, *Histoire du Luxembourg* (Paris: Presses Universitaires de France, 1996) and Glibert Trausch, et al, *Histoire du Luxembourg: Le destin europeen d'un "petit pays"* (Toulouse, France: Editions Privat, 2003).
2.  Statec Luxembourg, *Economic and Social Portrait of Luxembourg* (Luxembourg: Central Service for Statistics and Economic Studies, March 2003), p. 15.
3.  Trausch, et al., *Histoire du Luxembourg*, p. 263.
4.  Newcomer, *The Grand Duchy of Luxembourg*, p. 289.
5.  Statec Luxembourg, *Economic and Social Portrait of Luxembourg*, p. 22.
6.  Ibid., p. 117.
7.  Nicolette J. Reiss, "Bermuda, The Business Domicile of Choice", *Destination Bermuda*, (Hamilton) 2010/2011, p. 48.
8.  Ibid., p. 51.
9.  Ruth O'Kelly-Lynch, "Inside 'Black Power in Bermuda'", *The Royal Gazette*, (Bermuda), August 2, 2010.
10. Joyce Appleby, *The Relentless Revolution: A History of Capitalism* (New York: W.W. Norton & Company, 2010), p. 406.

# Bibliography

## Works Consulted for Chapters 1 and 2

### Online Sources

*The Bank of Scotland, (www.bankforfscotland.co.uk/info/history/history-info.html)*
*The International Monetary Fund (www.Imf.org)*
"The Rise and Fall of Albania's Pyramid Schemes," *Finance and Development*, March 2000, http://www.imf.org/external/pubs/ft/andd/2000/03/jarvis.htm.
VOX
Anne Sibert, "Undersized: Could Greenland Be the New Iceland? Should It Be?; *VOX*, August 10, 2009, http://www.voxeu.org/index.php?q=node/3857.
*The World Bank (www.worldbank.org)*
Easterly, William and Aart Kray, "Small States, Small Problems?" Policy Research Paper 2139, 1999.

### Secondary Sources

Cameron, Alan, *Bank of Scotland, 1695-1995: A Very Singular Institution* (Edinburgh: Mainstream Publishing Company, 1995).
Davies, K.G., *The Royal Africa Company*, (London: Longmans, Green, 1957).
Epstein, M., *The English Levant Company: Its Foundation and Its History to 1640*, (New York: Franklin, 1969).
Jalan, B., Ed, *Problems and Policies in Small Economies*, (New York: St. Martin's Press, 1982).
Kindleberger, Charles P., *Manias, Panics, and Crashes: A History of Financial Crises,* (New York: John Wiley & Sons, Inc. 1978, 1996).
Linklater, Eric, *The Survival of Scotland*, (Garden City: Doubleday & Company, Inc. 1968).
Posner, Richard A, *A Failure of Capitalism: The Crisis of '08 and the Descent Into Depression*, (Cambridge: Harvard University Press, 2009).
Prebble, John, *Darien: The Scottish Dream of Empire*, (London: Birlinn Ltd, 2000).
Pryde, George S., *Scotland from 1603 to Present Day,* (London: Thomas Nelson and Sons, Lt., 1969).
Reinhart, Carmen M. and Kenneth Rogoff, *This Time Is Different: Eight Centuries of Financial Folly*, (Princeton: Princeton University Press, 2009).
Richardson, Bonham C., *The Caribbean in the Wider World, 1492-1992*, (New York: Cambridge University Press, 1992).
Rose, Craig, *England in the 1690s: Revolution, Religion and War*, (London: Blackwell Publishers, 1999).

Scott, W.R., *The Constitution and Finance of English, Scottish and Irish Joint-Stock Companies to 1720*, Vol. ii (Cambridge: Cambridge University Press, 1912).

Shaw, John Stuart, *The Political History of Eighteenth-Century Scotland*, (New York: Palgrave Macmillan, 1999).

Sinclair, David, *The Pound: A Biography*, (London: Century, 2000).

Steel, Tom, *Scotland's Story*, (London: Fontana/Collins, 1989).

Willion, T.S., *The Early History of the Russian Company, 1553-1603*, (Manchester: University of Manchester Press, 1956).

Wood, Alfred C., *A History of the Levant Company*, (Oxford: Oxford University Press, 1935).

Woodward Jr., Ralph Lee, *Central America: A Nation Divided* (New York: Oxford University Press, 1976).

## Journal Articles

Bingham, Hiram, "The Early History of the Scots Darien Company," *The Scottish Historical Review*, Vol. III (1996).

Farrugla, Charles, "The Special Working Environment of Senior Administrators in Small States," *World Development* 21, 1993; 417-457.

## Magazines and Periodicals

*The Financial Times*
*The Wall Street Journal*

# Works Consulted for Chapter 3

## Online Sources

*USAID*
"The Dominican Republic: An Economic Snapshot," December 2005 (Washington, D.C.)
http://www.usaid.gov/our-work/cross-cutting -programs/wid/pubs/Dominican Republic_Economic_Snapshot_Dec 2005.pdf.
*The International Monetary Fund (www.imf.org)*
Jamaica: Staff Report for the 1999 Article IV Consultation, January 2000, IMF Country Report NO 0/8 (Washington, D.C.)

## Secondary Sources

Atkins, G. Pope and Larman Curtis Wilson, *The Dominican Republic and the United States: From Imperialism to Transnationalism*, (Athens: University of Georgia Press, 1998).

Dye, Alan B., *Cuban Sugar in the Age of Mass Production: Technology and the Economics of the Sugar Central, 1899-1929*, (Palo Alto, CA.: Stanford University Press, 1998).

Edson, Hubert, *Sugar: From Scarcity to Surplus*, (New York: Chemical Publishing Co., Inc., 1958).

Grogan, Kevin, "Cuba's Dance of the Millions: Examining the Causes and Consequences of Violent Price Fluctuations in the Sugar Market Between 1919 and 1920," University of Florida, 2004.

Heinl, Robert Debs, Nancy Gordon Heinl, and Michael Heinl, *Written in Blood: The story of the Haitian People, 1492-1995*, (New York: University Press of America, Inc., 1996).

Hoetink, H., *The Dominican Republic 1850-1900: Notes for a Historical Sociology*, (Baltimore: The Johns Hopkins University Press, 1982).

Hopwood, Derek, *Egypt: Politics and Society 1945-1984*, (Boston: Unwin Hyman, 1985).

Jenks, Lealand H., *Our Cuban Colony: A Study in Sugar*, (New York: Vanguard Press, 1928).

Knight, Melvin M., *The Americans in Santo Domingo*, (New York: Vanguard Press, 1928).

Logan, R.W., *Haiti and the Dominican Republic*, (New York: Oxford University Press, 1968).

Morris, Edmund, *Theodore Rex*, (New York: Random House, 2001).

Parker, William Belmont, *Cubans of To-Day*, (New York: G.P. Putnam's Sons, 1919).

Plummer, Brenda Gayle, *Haiti and the United States The Psychological Moment* (Athens: The University of Georgia Press, 1992).

Pons, Frank Moya, *The Dominican Republic: A National History*, (Princeton, N.J.: First Markus Weiner Publishers, 1998)

Rotberg, Robert, *Haiti: The Politics of Squalor*, (Boston: Houghton Mifflin, 1971).

Thomas, Hugh, *Cuba: The Pursuit of Freedom*, (New York: Da Capo Press, 1998).

Veeser, Cyrus, *A World Safe for Capitalism: Dollar Diplomacy and America's Rise to Global Power*, (New York: Columbia University Press, 2002).

Wallinch, Henry Christopher, *Monetary Problems of an Export Economy: The Cuban Experience 1914-1917*, (Boston: Harvard University Press, 1950).

**Journal Articles**

Speck, Mary "Prosperity, Progress and Wealth: Cuban Enterprise during the Early Republic, 1902-1927, *Cuban Studies*," Volume 36, 2005, pp. 50-86.

**Magazines and Newspapers**

*The Financial Times*, "Ministers Urged to Cancel Haiti Debt," January 26, 2010 (Harvey Morris, Benedict Mander, and Robin Kwong).

*The New York Times*, "San Domingo Is Willing: Agrees to the Scheme of Her American Debt Holders," February 11, 1893.

# Works Consulted for Chapter 4

**Online Sources**

*The Times*

**Secondary Sources**

Ahamed, Liqquat, *Lords of Finance: The Bankers Who Broke the World*, (London: Penguin Books, 2009).

Beller, Steve, *A Concise History of Austria*, (Cambridge: Cambridge University Press, 2009).

DeLong, J. Bradford, "Slouching toward Utopia? The Economic History of the Twentieth Century," February 1997.

Eichengreen, Barry, *Golden Fetters: The Gold Standard and the Great Depression, 1919-1939*, (New York: Oxford University Press, 1992).

Elon, Amos, *Founder: A Man and His Time*, (New York: Penguin, 1997).

Ferguson, Niall, *The House of Rothschild (Vol. 1): Money's Prophets: 1798-1848*, (New York: Viking Press, 1988).

_____, *The House of Rothschild (Vol. 2): The World's Banker. 1849-1999*, (London: Penguin Books 1998).

Jelavish, Barbara, *Modern Austria: Empire and Republic, 1815-1986*, (Cambridge: University of Cambridge Press, 1987).

Kindleberger, Charles P., *The World in Depression, 1929-1939*, (University of California Press, 1986).

Morton, Frederic, *The Rothschilds, a Family Portrait*, (New York: Atheneum Publishers, 1962).

Moss, David, "Danatbank," (Cambridge: Harvard Business School, 2009).

Okey, Robin, *The Habsburg Monarchy c. 1765-1918, From Enlightenment to Eclipse*, (New York: Palgrave Macmillan, 2001).

Schubert, Aurel, *The Credit-Anstalt Crisis of 1931*, (New York: Cambridge University Press, 1991).

Stadler, Karl R., *Austria*, (New York: Praeger Publishers, 1971).

### Journal Articles

Ferguson, Thomas and Peter Temin, "Made in Germany: The German Currency Crisis of July 1931," *Research in Economic History* 21 (2003).

Sokal, Max, "Austrian Banks," *Annals of the American Academy of Political and Social Science*, Vol. 98, Supplement: Present Day Social and Industrial Conditions in Austria (Nov., 1921).

### Magazines and Periodicals

*Time Magazine*, "Austria: Three-Room President," December 17, 1928.

*Time Magazine*, "Austria: Black Week," June 8, 1930.

# Works Consulted for Chapter 5

### Online Sources

*The Economist:* Economist Intelligence Unit (EIU), Country Data for Finland.

### Secondary Sources

Kirby, David, *A Concise History of Finland* (New York: Cambridge University Press, 2008).

Goodhart, Charles Albert, *The Central Bank and the Financial System*, (London: MIT Press, 1995).

### Journal Articles

Drees, Burkhard and Ceyla Pazarbaşioğlu, *The Nordic Banking Crises: Pitfalls in Financial Liberation?* International Monetary Fund, (Washington, D.C.), Occasional Paper # 161, (April 1998).

Halme, Liisa and Rahoitustar Kastus, Financial Supervision Authority, "The 1990s Banking Crisis in Finland: Main Causes and Consequences, Lessons for the Future."

Hamalainen, Pekka Kalevi, "The Finnish Solution," *The Wilson Quarterly* (1976-), Vol. 10, No. 4 (Autumn, 1986), pp. 59-75.

Honkapohja Seppo and Erkki Koskela, "The Economic Crisis of the 1990s in Finland," Keskusteluaiheita – Discussion Papers, The Research Institute of the Finnish Economy (Helsinki, 9/8/1999).

Järvenpää, Pauli O., "Finland: An Image of Continuity in Turbulent Europe," *Annals of the American Academy of Political and Social Science*, Vol. 512, (Nov., 1990), pp. 125-139.

## Magazines and Periodicals

*The New York Times*

Professor Osmo Suovaniemi, M.D., Ph.D., President + CEO of Biohit Plc., "Being an Investor in Finland", www.biohit.com/upload/dia/literature/BeingInvestorInFinland.pdf.2005.

Stefan Ingves, Director, Monetary and Exchange Affairs Department, Seminar on Financial Crisis, Kredittilsynet, The Banking, Insurance and Securities Commission of Norway, Oslo, September 11, 2002, "The Nordic Banking Crisis from an International Perspective." p. 2.

Staffan Marklund and Anders Nordlund, "Economic Problems, Welfare Convergence and Political Instability", in Mikko Kautto, Chapter 2. Matti Heikkilï, Bjorn Huinden, Staff on Marklund and Niels Ploug, eds., *Nordic Social Policy: Changing Welfare States* (London: Routledge, 1999), p. 43.

Kenneth Newton, "Political Support Social Capital, Civil Society, and Political and Economic Performance," UC Irvine: Center for the Study of Democracy, August 22, 2006.

# Works Consulted for Chapter 6

## Online Sources

*The International Monetary Fund (www.imf.org)*

Carvajal, Ana, Hunter Monroe, Catherine Pattillo, and Brion Wynter, "Ponzi Schemes in the Caribbean," *IMF Working Paper,* (2009).

Jarvis, Christopher, "The Rise and Fall of Albania's Pyramid Schemes," *Finance & Development,* (March 2000), Vol. 37, No. 1.

International Monetary Policy, "IMF Approves Emergency Post Conflict Assistance for Albania", Press Release 95151, November 7, 1997 (Washington, D.C).

International Narcotics and Law Enforcement Affairs, *1998 International Narcotics Control Strategy Report*, (Washington, D.C.: US Department of State, 1998)

*Radio Free Europe (www.rferl.org)*

Sterling, Bruce, "Life as an Albanian Ponzi Scheme Model", Radio Free Europe/Radio Liberty, Prague, Czech Republic, Vol. 4, No. 42, 6 June 2000.

*The World Bank (www.worldbank.org)*

Elbirt, C., "Albania under the Shadows of the Pyramid Schemes", *Transition*, (World Bank: October 1997).

## Secondary Sources

Bezemer, Dirk J. ed. *On Eagle's Wings: The Albanian Economy in Transition,* (New York: Nova Science Publisher, Inc., 2009).

Deliso, Christopher, *The Coming Balkan Caliphate: The Threat of Radical Islam to Europe and the West,* (Westport, CT.: Praeger International, 2007).

Fijnaut, Cyrille and Letizia Paoli, eds., *Organized Crime in Europe: Concepts, Patterns, and Control Policies in the European Union and Beyond* (Dordrecht: Springer, 2004).

Pettifer, James and Miranda Vickers, *The Albanian Question: Reshaping the Balkans,* (London: I.B. Tauris & Co. Ltd., 2007).

Smith Jr., Edward and Edwin Pechous, "Crisis Management and Conflict Resolution in the Late 20th Century Europe: Albania – A Case Study." Institute for Defense Analyses, Alexandria, Virginia.

Vickers, Miranda, and James Pettifer, *Albania: From Anarchy to a Balkan Identity,* (New York: New York University Press, 2000).

## Journal Articles

Bezemer, Dirk, "Post-Socialist Financial Fragility: The Case of Albania", *Cambridge Journal of Economics* 25: 1-23 (2001).

## Magazines and Periodicals

*The Financial Times*
*The Times*
*The Victoria Advocate*

# Works Consulted for Chapter 7

## Online Sources

*BBC News (www.bbc.co.uk)*
*Bloomberg*
Moses, Abigail and Tasneem Brogger, "Iceland's Biggest Banks Targeted by 'Unscrupulous Speculators,'" March 31, 2008
http://www.bloomberg.com/apps/news?pid=newsarchive&sid=aseau2yzmJSU.
*Ice News*
"Icelandic Banks Deliberately Weakened Krona Before Collapse", IceNews, March 16, 2010. http://www.icenews.is/index.php/2010/03/16/icelandic-banks-deliberately-weakened-krona-before-collapse/.
Iceland Review
Special Prosecutor: Many Cases in Final Stages." Iceland Review Online, April 13, 2010. http://icelandreview.com/icelandreview/search/news/default.asp?ew_0_a_id=360651.
The International Monetary Fund (www.Imf.org)
Anderson, Camilla, "Iceland Gets Help to Recover from Historic Crisis," IMF Survey Magazine Interview, IMF Survey Online, December 2, 2008, http://www.imf.org/external/pubs/ft/survey/80/2008/INT111908A.htm.

## Secondary Sources

Boyes, Roger, *Meltdown Iceland: Lessons on the World Financial Crisis from a Small Bankrupt Island*, (New York: Bloomsbury, 2009).
Jonsson, Asgeir, *Why Iceland?* (New York: McGraw Hill, 2009).

## Journal Articles

Buiter, Willem and Anne Sibert, "The Collapse of Iceland's Banks: The Predictable End of a Non-Viable Business Model," *Vox*, October 30, 2010.
Sibert, Anee, "Undersized: Could Greenland Be the Next Iceland?" *VOX*, August 10, 2009, http://www.voxeu.org/index.php?q=node/3857.

## Magazines and Periodicals

Hammer, Joshua, "Icestorm," *Condé Nast Portfolio*, March 2009.
*The Financial Times*

# Works Consulted for Chapter 8

## Online Sources

*Bloomberg*
*The First Post (www.thefirstpost.co.uk)*
*The Gallup Organization (www.gallup.com)*
*The International Monetary Fund (www.imf.org)*
*VOX*
Honohan, Patrick and Philip Lane, "Ireland in Crisis," *Vox*, (London), February 28, 2009. http://www.voxeu.org/index.php?q=node/3162.

## Secondary Sources

Coogan, Tim Pat, *De Valera: Long Fellow, Long Shadow*, (London: Arrow, 1993).
Cooper, Matt, *Who Really Runs Ireland?: The Story of the Elite Who Led Ireland From Bust to Boom...And Back Again*, (Dublin: Penguin Ireland, 2009).
Ferriter, Diarmaid, *Judging Dev: A Reassessment of Eamon de Valera*, (Dublin: Royal Irish Academy, 2007).
Ross, Shane, *The Bankers: How the Banks Brought Ireland to Its Knees*, (Dublin: Penguin, Ireland, 2009).
Sweeney, Robert, *Banana Republic: The Failure of the Irish State and How to Fix It*, (Dublin: Grill and Macmillan, 2009).

## Journal Articles

Bergin, Adele, Thomas Conefrey, John FitzGerald, and Ide Kearney, "Recovery Scenarios for Ireland," The Economic and Social Research Institute (Dublin), *Research Series, No.7*, May 2009.

## Magazines and Periodicals

*The Herald (www.herald.ie)*
*The Independent (Ireland)*
*The Irish Times*

Organization for Economic Cooperation and Development (OECD), *OECD Economic Outlook Volume 2004/2 No. 76*, (Paris:OECD: December 2004).
*The New York Times*
*The Southern Star*
*The Wall Street Journal*

# Works Consulted for Chapter 9

## Online Sources

*The Bank for International Settlements (BIS)*
*The Economist Intelligence Unit*
*Moody's Investors Service*
*Organization for Economic Development and Cooperation (www.oecd.org)*
*Greek Budget 2010: http://www.mof-glk.gr/proypologismos/2010/books/proyp/index. html*

## Secondary Sources

MacDonald, Scott B., "Southern Europe," in *The Global Debt Crisis: Forecasting the Future*, eds., Scott B. MacDonald, Margie Lindsay and David L. Crum, (London: Pinter Publishers, 1990).

## Journal Articles

Dimitras, Panayoti E., "Greece: A New Danger," *Foreign Policy*, (Spring 1985).

## Magazines and Periodicals

Deutsche Welle
The Economist
The Financial Times
The Guardian
Der Spiegel
*Vanity Fair*, "Beware of Greeks Bearing Bonds," Michael Lewis, (October 1, 2010).
The Wall Street Journal

# Index

# DATE DUE